書目（外一種）

5

東亞圖書館 編

喬曉勤 主編

國家圖書館出版社

第五册目録

2

The University of Toronto Chinese Library

. . . .

Accession No. 2456   Index No. 075-d d g g

Title 東林十八高賢傳 Tung Lin shih Pa Kao Hsien Chuan

Classification B 117

Subject

References

Author 東林寺 Tung Lin Szŭ

Edition 毘耶室梓行
Printing in Pi Ya shih Tzu Hsin.

Index

Bound in 一冊 1 tsé

Remarks 竹紙 Bamboo paper

1

The University of Toronto Chinese Library

. . . .

Accession No. 2457   Index No. 085-igkc

Title 渤海國志 Po Hai Kuo Chih

Classification B227

Subject

References

Author 清唐晏纂 Compiled by: Ch'ing, T'ang Yen

Edition 求恕齋刊 Chiu Shu Chai block-printing edt?

Index

Bound in 四卷一冊 4 chüan, 1 tsê

Remarks 竹紙 Bamboo paper

2

Accession No. 2458   Index No. 067-y f b i

Title 文章軌範 Wen Chang Kuei Fan

Classification D73

Subject

References

Author 宋 謝枋得選 Selected by: Sung, Hsieh Fang Tei

Edition 桐蔭書屋校刊本 Tung Yin Shu Wu collated edition

Index 硃批 Commentarie w red   綿建紙 Mien-lien paper

Bound in 七卷二册 7 chüan, 2 tsé

Remarks

The University of Toronto Chinese Library

. . . .

Accession No. 2459   Index No. 086-l f i f

Title 燕京歲時記 Yen Ching Sui Shih Chi

627 77   450

Classification

Subject C 308

References

Author 清富察敦崇禮臣代編
edited by Ching, Fu Ch'a Tun Ch'ung Li Chen

Edition 京都文德齋刻本
Ching Tu Wen Te Chai Block-printing edition

Index

Bound in 一冊 1 tsê

Remarks 光緒丙午年刻
Dated Kuang Hsü Ping Wu period
綿連紙 Mien-lien paper

4

The University of Toronto Chinese Library

. . . .

Accession No. 2460   Index No. 077-又了子f

Title 止園通書 Chih Yüan T'ung Shu

Classification C 338

Subject

References

Author 尹昌衡著 Yin Chang Hêng

Edition 上海中華書局代印 Printed by Shanghai
"Chung Hua" Book Company
民國八年初版
First edition published in the 8th year

Index of The Republic

Bound in 2 Chüan, 1 Tsé

Remarks

The University of Toronto Chinese Library

. . . .

Accession No. 2461   Index No. 075-ℓℓ a 0

Title 東坡尺牘 Tung P'o chih Tu

420 507

Classification D 4₃

Subject

References

Author 宋蘇軾撰 *Written by* Sung, Su Shih

Edition 廣益書局石印
Kuang I Book Company Lithographic edition

Index

Bound in 二册 2 tie

Remarks 民國元年印 Printed in the 1st year of the Republic
油光紙 Oil paper

Accession No. 2463   Index No. 002-chmm

Title 中國戲劇之組織 Chung Kuo Hsi Chü Chih
                                          Tsu Chih

Classification 108 113 C368

Subject

References

Author 齊如山著 Chi Ju Shan

Edition 北華印刷局印
Printed by Pei Hua Pring Press

Index

Bound in 一冊 1 tsé

Remarks 民國十七年印 The 17th year of The Republic
平粉連纸 powder-like cotton paper

7

The University of Toronto Chinese Library

· ·

Accession No. 2464   Index No. 149 - f k l k

Title 詩夢鐘聲錄 Shih Meng Chung Sheng Lu

Classification D >3 446

Subject

References

Author 清榮廷虞臣等集錄
        Ching, Jung T'ing, Yü Chen and others collected & copied

Edition 家藏版 ~~Home edition~~ Private ~~family~~ edition
         光緒年刻 Dated Kuang-Hsü period
         白毛辺纸 無套
         White mao-pien paper, no t'ao

Index

Bound in 一冊 1 tsé

Remarks

Accession No. 2465   Index No. 067-zm fb

Title 文學研究法 Wen Hsüeh Yen Chiu Fa

Classification C 218

Subject

References

Author 姚孟振編
edited by Yao Meng Chen
Edition 東城印字館鉛印
"Tung Cheng Yin Tzü Kuan" type-setting edition

Index

Bound in 一冊 1 tsé

Remarks 油光紙 Oil paper

The University of Toronto Chinese Library

. . . .

Accession No. 2466   Index No. 001=b d f z

Title 三農椿言 San Wei Ke Yen

428 600°

Classification C 13

Subject

References

Author 清計文卿輯 Compiled by:
Ching Chi Wen Ching

Edition 寄觀閣藏版
Blocks preserved in "Chi Kuan Ko"

Index

Bound in 一卷一册 1 chüan, 1 tsé

Remarks 光緒丁酉年刻 Dated "Kuang Hsü" Ting Yu period
東昌紙 Tung Chang paper

The University of Toronto Chinese Library

....

Accession No. 2467   Index No. 030-e b c d

Title 味古齋所見集 Wei Ku Chai Shuo Chien Chi

   599 259   471

Classification D 43

Subject

References

Author

Edition 紫色版 printed in purple

Index

Bound in 一冊 1 tsé

Remarks

The University of Toronto Chinese Library
....

Accession No. 2468   Index No. 149-hghz

Title 論語管見 Lun Yü Kuan Chien

Classification A 134

Subject

References

Author 日本龜谷軒著
Japanese, Kuei Ku Sheng Hsüan

Edition 日本吉川半七刊印
Japan, Chi Chüan Pan Chi block-print

Index

Bound in 一冊 1 tse

Remarks 明治十年印 Dated - The 10th year of Ming Ch'ih
白紙 white paper

The University of Toronto Chinese Library
. . . .

Accession No. 2469   Index No. 085-h k k z

Title 清嘉慶二年時憲書 Ch'ing Chia Ch'ing ER Nien
                                    shih Hsin Shu

Classification B 157

Subject

References

Author 清欽天監編 edited by:
       ↑Ch'ing, Ch'in T'ien Chien
Edition 官版 Official-printed edition

Index

Bound in 一册 1 ts'e

Remarks 白竹紙 white bamboo paper

The University of Toronto Chinese Library

....

Accession No. 2472   Index No. 040-ghdg

Title 容菴弟子記 Jung An Ti 書 Tzu Chi

Classification B 222

Subject

References

Author 民國袁世凱傳記沈祖憲等編纂
The Republic, Yuan Shih Han's biography, Compiled by Shen
Edition 鉛印本 Type-setting edition   Tsu Hsien

Index

Bound in 一冊 1 tsl

Remarks 洋紙 imported paper

The University of Toronto Chinese Library

· ·

Accession No. 2473   Index No. 184-f e d

Title 養真集 Yang Chen Chi

Classification D 33

Subject

References

Author 養真子著 Yang Chen Tzü

Edition 鉛印本
        Type-setting edition

Index

Bound in 上下二卷 一冊
         2 Chüan, 1 Tsé
Remarks 洋紙 Imported paper

. . . .

Accession No. 2474   Index No. 030-dgdh

Title 呂語集粹 *Lü Yü Chi Tsui*

Classification C 338

Subject

References

Author 清尹會一輯 Compiled by: *Ch'ing, Yin Hui I*

Edition 家藏版 ~~Home edition~~
Private ~~family~~ edition

Index

Bound in 四卷一冊 *4 chüan, 1 tsé*

Remarks 連史紙 *Lien-shih paper*

The University of Toronto Chinese Library

. . . .

Accession No. 2475   Index No. 039-gldc

Title 孫徵君年譜 Sun Chêng Chün Nien Pu'

Classification B107

Subject

References

Author 清魏蓮陸合編次
Chêng Wei Lien Lu Hê edited in order

Edition 光緒丁亥年刻 Dated "Kuang-Hsü" Ting Hai Period

粉紙
Powder paper

Index

Bound in 2 Tsê

Remarks

The University of Toronto Chinese Library

. . . .

Accession No. 2476   Index No. 037-3 m b a

Title 大學古本質言 Ta Hsueh Ku Pen Chih Yen

Classification C 13

Subject

References

Author 清劉沅著 Ch'ing, Liu yüan

Edition 鉛印本 Type-setting edition
北京道德學社印
Printed by "Peiping Tao Tê Hsueh Shê"

Index 有光紙 A kind of imported paper

Bound in 一冊 1 tsé

Remarks

The University of Toronto Chinese Library

. . . .

Accession No. 2477   Index No. 035-g3a

Title 夏小正 Hsia Hsiao Cheng

Classification C 308

Subject

References

Author 清王筠集傳 Ch'ing, Wang Yün & collected
Commentaries

Edition 賀惠等校刊本
檢 Hui and others collated edition

綿連紙 mien-lien paper

Index

Bound in 一册 1 tsé

Remarks

The University of Toronto Chinese Library

· ·

Accession No. 2478   Index No. 012—bh亭f

Title 六朝文絜 Liu Chao Wên Chieh

Classification 万63

Subject

References

Author 清許槤輯 Compiled by: Ching, Hsü Lien

Edition 家藏版 Private ~~print~~ family edition

Index

Bound in 四卷一冊 4 Chüan 1 Tsé

Remarks 光緒年刻 Dated "Kuang-Hsü" period
          綿連紙 Mien-Lien Paper

20

The University of Toronto Chinese Library

. . . .

Accession No. 2479   Index No. 096-3Gjc

Title 玉海瑣記 Yü Hai So Chi

Classification C308

Subject

References

Author

Edition 浙江書局版
Published by "Chekiang Book Company"

Index

Bound in 上下二冊
          2 Jᵈⁱ'e
Remarks 竹紙 Bamboo paper

The University of Toronto Chinese Library

. . . .

Accession No. 2480   Index No. 149—αfh

Title   詩餘錄 Fang Yü Lu

Classification C 338

Subject

References

Author   王國維署

Edition   Wang Kuo Wei

Index

Bound in   1 Tsé

Remarks

The University of Toronto Chinese Library

. . . .

Accession No. 2481   Index No. 042-319

Title 小兒語 Hsiao Erh Yü

Classification C 308

Subject

References

Author 明 呂得勝 Ming, Lü Te Sheng.

Edition 翻明萬曆版 Selected + printed from Ming, Wan Lio
                    edition.

Index

Bound in   1 tsê

Remarks 白紙 White paper.

The University of Toronto Chinese Library

· ·

Accession No. 2482   Index No. 042-3fg

Title 小兒語 Hsiao Erh Yü

Classification C 308

Subject

References

Author 漁隱閒翁撰 *Written by* Yü Yin Hsien Wêng

Edition 寶琴齋刊 Pao Chin Chai block printing edition
道光十年刻 The 10th year of "Tao-Kuang"

Index

Bound in 1 Tsé

Remarks 白綿紙 Po-Mien paper

The University of Toronto Chinese Library

．．．．．．．．．．．．．．．．．．．

Accession No. 2484   Index No. 039-zbef

Title 子平真詮 T'zu Ping Chen Chüan

Classification C 13

Subject

References

Author 清沈孝瞻著 Ch'ing, Shang Hsiao Chan

Edition 報暉草堂刊版 Pao Fei Tsao Tang engraved
                                              blocks

Index

Bound in 一冊 1 ts'e

Remarks 光緒年刻 Dated Kuang-Hsü period
        綿連紙 Mien-lien paper

• . . . .

Accession No. 2485   Index No. 067-z l j 米 e

Title 文選類篇 Wen Hsüan Lei Chün

Classification D 73

Subject

References

Author 慈銘. 何松 Tzu chi, Ho Sung,

Edition 光緒年 Printing in Kuang Hsü period.
         迷杜常搐惺齋

Index

Bound in 14 Chüan, 1 Tsé

Remarks

The University of Toronto Chinese Library
....

Accession No. 2486   Index No. 133-hv3K

Title 臺灣生熟番紀事 Tai Wan sheng shou Fan chi Shih

Classification β 222

Subject

References

Author 清 黃逢昶稿 Ch'ing, Huang Feng Ch'ang

Edition 家藏版 袖珍本
Private family printed edition   pocket edition

Index

Bound in 一册 1 tśe

Remarks 光緒十一年刻 The 11th year of "Kuang-Hsü"
綿連紙 Mien-lien paper

The University of Toronto Chinese Library

....

Accession No. 2488   Index No. 019-Ymi

Title 勸學篇 Ch'üan Hsüeh Pien

Classification C 308

Subject

References

Author 清 張之洞 撰 ^Written by Ch'ing, Chang Chih Tung

Edition 兩湖書院刊
大字本
large character edition

Index

Bound in 一冊 1 ts'e

Remarks 光緒戊戌年刊 block engraving in Kuang Hsü "Wu-Hsü"
綿連紙 Mien-Lien paper

28

The University of Toronto Chinese Library
....

Accession No. 2489   Index No. 140-dzhL

Title 芸香館遺詩 Yün Hsiang Kuan Yi-shih

Classification D 33

Subject

References

Author 清女史那遜蘭保蓮友撰
Written by Chung, Nii Shih Na sun Lan Pao Lien Yii,

Edition 家藏版   白棉紙無套
~~Home edition~~   White cotton paper.
private family ~~printed~~ edition

Index

Bound in 二卷一冊 2 chüan, 1 tsé

Remarks

Accession No. 2490   Index No. 140—NfCC

Title 藏書記要 Tsang shu chi yao

Classification B 222

Subject

References

Author 孫從記 take notes by Sun Ts'ung

Edition 潘氏錄刊本 Pan shih copied from block-print edition

Index

Bound in 一册 1 tsè

Remarks 嘉慶年刻 Block engraving in "Chia-Ching" period
皮紙 Mulberry bark paper

The University of Toronto Chinese Library

. . . .

Accession No. 2491   Index No. 156-9 dibt

Title 趙忠節公遺墨 Chao Chung Chieh Kung Yi Mo

Classification D 33

Subject

References

Author 趙景賢著 Chao Ching Hsien

Edition 家藏版 Private-printed family edition

Index

Bound in 一册 1 tsê

Remarks 光緒八年刻 block engraving in the 8th year of
白紙 white paper   Kuang Hsü.

31

The University of Toronto Chinese Library

....

Accession No. 2492   Index No. 037—a b i m

Title 太上感應編 T'ai shang Kan Ying Pien

Classification C 731

Subject

References

Author 清惠棟箋註 Annotated by Ching, Hui Tung Chien
羅椒先生引經

Edition 家藏版 family
Private-printed edition

Index

Bound in 一冊 1 tsé

Remarks 乾隆年刻 Block engraving in Chien-Lung period
綿連紙 Mien-Lien paper
夾板 Wooden folder

32

Accession No. 2493   Index No. 114-dcag

Title 禹貢本義 Yü Kung Pen Yi

Classification A 134

Subject

References

Author 清楊守敬撰 Written by Ch'ing, Yang Shou Ching

Edition 刊於鄂城菊灣 Block engraving in Ao Cheng, Chü Wan,

Index

Bound in 一冊 1 tsè

Remarks 光緒丙午年刊 Dated— Kwang Hsü "Ping-Wu" 洋紙 Imported paper

The University of Toronto Chinese Library

....

Accession No. 2494   Index No. 075—VhfL

Title 蟫華閣遺集 Yü Hua Ko Yi Chi

Classification D 33

Subject

References

Author 清 盛昱撰 Written by Ching, Sheng Yü

Edition 家藏版   夾硬紙夾板

~~Home edition~~   , wooden folder

Private-printed edition (family)

Index

Bound in 四卷一冊 4 chüan, 1 tsê

Remarks

34

The University of Toronto Chinese Library

. . . .

Accession No. 2495   Index No. 001- b q h e

Title 三經誼詁 San Ching I Ku

Classification A 137

Subject

References

Author 馬其永旦學 Ma chi ch'ang.

Edition 民國年印 ~~Published~~ Printing in "Ming Kuo"

子粉連紙 Powder-like cotton paper

Index

Bound in 3 Chüan . 1 Tsé

Remarks

35

The University of Toronto Chinese Library

. . . .

Accession No. 2496   Index No. 012—bh 新干

Title 六朝文絜 *Liu Chao Wên Chieh*

Classification 万 63

Subject

References

Author 清許梿評選 *Commented & Selected by Ching, Hsü Hsiao P'ing*

Edition 家藏版 *Private family-printed edition*
袖珍本 *Pocket edition*

Index

Bound in 四卷一冊 *4 Chüan, 1 Ts'e*

Remarks 光緒丁丑年刊 *Block engraving in Kuang-Hsü "Ting Chou" Period.*
綿連紙 *Mien-Lien paper*

36

The University of Toronto Chinese Library

Accession No. 2497   Index No. 060—hhdh
Title 御製朋黨論 Yü chih P'eng Tang Lun

Classification A 124

Subject

References

Author 清雍正帝撰
Written by Ch'ing, Yung Cheng (Emperor)
Edition 殿版 Palace edition.

Index

Bound in 二冊 2 tsé
Remarks 滿文一冊 開化紙 Paper made in Kai Hua

漢文一冊 毛邊紙 ~~bam~~ bamboo paper

夾版 wooden folder

The University of Toronto Chinese Library

· ·

Accession No. 2498   Index No. 118-苓了了

Title 篆文老子 Chuan Wên Lao Tzǔ

Classification C 731

Subject

References

Author 田伏侯寫 Copied by T'ien Fu Chi Hou

Edition 家藏版 Private-Printed family edition

Index

Bound in 一冊 1 Tsê

Remarks 單宣紙
a kind of cotton paper made in "Hsüan Chêng"

The University of Toronto Chinese Library

....

Accession No. 2500   Index No. 031-bKhi

Title 四聲精辨 Szu sheng ching pien

Classification A 166

Subject

References

Author not given

Edition 袖珍本 Pocket edition

Index

Bound in 五卷五冊 5 chüan, 5 tsé

Remarks 白紙 White paper

The University of Toronto Chinese Library

· ·

Accession No. 2501   Index No. 010-dgph

Title 先哲叢說 Hsien Che Ts'ung T'an

Classification C₁₃

Subject

References

Author 日本谷壯太郎輯 *Compiled by* Japan, Ku Chuang Tai Lang

Edition 江島喜兵衛版袖珍
Chiang Tao Hsi P'ing Wei Pan Pocket edition

Index

Bound in 四卷四冊 4 Chüan 4 Ts'é

Remarks 明治十七年印 Printed in the 17th year of "Ming-Chih"
白紙 White paper

The University of Toronto Chinese Library

· ·

Accession No. 2502　　　　Index No. 007-bg j f

Title 五經類典囊括 Wu Ching Lei Tien Nang Kuo

Classification A 137

Subject

References

Author 同文書局主人編輯 Edited & Complete Compiled by the master of Tung Wen Book Co.

Edition 同文書局石印袖珍本 Tung Wen Book Co. Lithographic ed., Pocket ed.

Index

Bound in 六十四卷六冊 64 Chüan 6 Tsê

Remarks 光緒十年石印 Lithographic ed. in the 10th year 連史紙 "Lien Shih" paper of "Kuang Hsü"

The University of Toronto Chinese Library

....

Accession No. 2503   Index No. 031-6 f 6 d
                                                    6 g
Title 四書典林 Szu Shu Tien Lin
       四書古人典林 Szu Shu Ku gen Tien Lin
Classification C 6

Subject

References

Author 清江永原編 Edited by Ching, Chiang Yung Yuan
Edition 同文書局石印 Jung Wen Book Company Litho-
                              graphic edition

Index

Bound in 十八卷 古人典 林世卷 芝四冊 袖珍本精印
          18 Chüan   pocket-edition
Remarks 光緒年印 Printed in "Kuang Hsü" Period Fine-printed
         綿連紙 Mien-Lien paper

....

Accession No. 2504   Index No. 180 — Yün d c m

Title 韵字鑑 Yün Tzu Chien

Classification A 166

Subject

References

Author

Edition 披雲軒刊 *Block engraved by*
Pei Yün Hsüan *Block Printing edition.*
道光年 Tao-Kuang Period.

Index

Bound in 2 卷 4 册, 2 chüan. 4 Ts'e

Remarks

43

The University of Toronto Chinese Library

. . . .

Accession No. 2505   Index No. 007-bgкy

Title 五經圖彙 Wu Ching Tu Hui

Classification A137

Subject

References

Author 日本松本愚山著書編纂
Edited & Compiled by Japanese, Sung Peng Yü Shan.

Edition 明治十六年 The 16th year of "Ming Chih"

Index

Bound in 3 Chüan 1 Tse

Remarks

. . . .

Accession No. 2506   Index No. 024-aa c f

Title 千百年眼 Ch'ien Po Nien Yen

Classification C 308

Subject

References

Author 明張扑仲纂。 *Compiled by* Ming, Chang Han Chung

Edition 銅版, 四明王氏刊于日本 ~~~~
copper plate. block-engraved by Szu Ming Wang Shih.

Index

Bound in 十二卷 二四 12 Chuan 2 Ts'e

Remarks 光緒年刻 block-engraving in Kuang-Hsü period.
連史紙 "Lien shih" paper
駱繼漢藏 Preserved by Lao Chi Han

The University of Toronto Chinese Library

. . . .

Accession No. 2507   Index No. 040-ƒⱼᴄ𝓰

Title   宦鄉要則 Huan Hsiang Yao Tse

Classification B32

Subject

References

Author 清張鑑瀛著 Ching, Chang Chien Ying

Edition 經書閣石印 Cheng Hsiang Ko Lithographic edition

Index

Bound in 七卷四冊 7 Chüan 4 Tsè

Remarks 光緒己亥年印 Printing in Kuang Hsü "chi-Hai"
        淨毛太紙 Imported "Mao Tai" paper

46

The University of Toronto Chinese Library
....

Accession No. 2508   Index No. 031-b f f d

Title 四書典林 Szu Shu Tien Lin

Classification C/3

Subject

References

Author 清江永撰 *Written by* Ch'ing, Chiang ~~Yung~~ Yung.

Edition 鴻寶齋石印 Hung Pao Chai Lithographic ed.

Index

Bound in 三十卷 附四書,古人典林十二卷 計四冊

Remarks 光緒年印 Dated: Kuang-Hsü period
白綿紙 "Po-Mien" paper

The University of Toronto Chinese Library

. . . .

Accession No. 2509   Index No. 010-b h e b

Title 元朝秘史 (270) Yüan Cháo Mi Shih

Classification B 41

Subject

References

Author Not stated

Edition 道光廿七年秋靈石楊氏刊本
Dated Tao-Kwang 27/1847

Index

Bound in 15 Chüan 2 Tśe

Remarks

The University of Toronto Chinese Library

.·:.··················

Accession No. 2510   Index No. 067-ᵧfᵧᶜ

Title 文料大成 Wen Liao Ta Ch'eng

Classification B 52

Subject

References

Author 清冷香子編 *edited by* Ch'ing, Leng Hsiang Tzu

Edition 名德堂版 Ming Te Tang Blocks.

Index

Bound in 四十卷 十四冊 40 Chüan 14 Ts'e

Remarks 光緒年刻 ℗ Blocks engraved in "Kuang Hsü" Period
毛太紙 Mao-Tai paper

Accession No. 2511   Index No. 149 - f b i f

Title 詩句題解 Shih Chü T'i Chieh

Classification A 31

Subject

References

Author Collected by Shen Chi Chuang

Edition 慎記莊石印
Shen Chi Chuang Lithographic edition

Index

Bound in 四卷 四冊 4 Chuan 4 Tsê

Remarks 光緒年刻 Block-engraved in "Kuang Hsü" period
粉紙
Powder paper

The University of Toronto Chinese Library
. . . .

Accession No. 2512   Index No. 149-f b i f

Title 詩句題解 Shih Chü Tí Chieh

Classification A 31

Subject

References

Author Collected by Shen Chi Chuang

Edition 慎記莊石印
Shen Chi Chuang Lithographic edition

Index

Bound in 4 Chüan 4 Tse

Remarks 光緒年刻 Block engraved in "Kuang Hsü Period"
粉紙 powder paper

. . . .

Accession No. 2513   Index No. 167-n b f z

Title 鑄史駢言 Chu Shih Pien Yen

Classification C 328

Subject

References

Author 清孫玉田編 edited by Cheang, Sun Yü T'ien

Edition

Index

Bound in 十二卷四冊 20 Chuan 4 Tsè

Remarks 光緒二年刻 Blocks engraved in the 2nd Year of
白紙 White Paper   "Kuang Hsü"

Accession No. 251ﾟA,B   Index No. 030-b0i

Title 古籀篇 篆文索引 附轉注假借説   *Ku Chou Pien*
Chuan Wên So Yin Fu Chuan Chu
隸文索引 附補遺   *Chia Chieh Shuo*
Li Wên So Yin Fu Pu I

Classification A-161

Subject

References

Author 竹田 高田忠周 *Chu Tien Kao Tien Chung Chou*

Edition 説文樓藏版（日本）
Block preserved in 2 *Shuo-Wên-Lou* ~~Tsang Pan~~ (Japanese) private-printed.

Index

Bound in 2 tao, 11 ts'ê

Remarks

The University of Toronto Chinese Library

．．．．．．．．．．．．．．．．．．．．

Accession No. 2515-A,B,C,D,E,F,G,H,I,J.   Index No. 030-boi

Title 古籀篇 Ku Chou Pien

Classification A-161

Subject

References

Author 高田忠周纂述 *Compiled & given in oral by* *Kao-Tien Chung-Chou*

Edition 說文樓藏版 (日本) *Shuo-Wên-Lou Tsang-Pan (Japanese)* *private printed.*
Block preserved in

Index

Bound in 10 tao, 50 ts'ê

Remarks

54

Accession No. 2517   Index No. 113-mc

Title 禮記 Li Chi

Classification A-56

Subject

References

Author

Edition 上海中華書局據相臺岳氏家塾本校刊
民國十三年七月再版
Shanghai, Chung-Hua Book Company according to Hsien-Tai-Yin-Shih
private-ed. revised ed.
Dated — Ming-Kuo 13/1924 July second edition

Index

Bound in 1 tao, 8 ts'ê

Remarks

. . . .

Accession No. 2518   Index No. 170·93gc

Title 陝西通志. Shan Hsi T'ung Chi

Classification B-192

Subject

References

Author 清 劉於義等奉勅纂修
Compiled, Amended by
Ching, Liu Yü-I and others
Edition 官版 雍正年刻 official ed.
Dated — Yung-Chêng period

Index

Bound in 10 T'ao   100 Chuan   100 Ts'ê

Remarks

The University of Toronto Chinese Library

. . . .

Accession No. 2519   Index No. 046-889ᶜ

Title 山西通志、 Shan Hsi Tung Chi

Classification B-192

Subject

References

Author 清 曾國荃 張煦 等奉旨修 Ch'ing, Tsêng Kuo-Chüan · Chang Hsu
Received an imperial
Edition 殿版 Palace ed.   decree to revise.
光緒壬辰年刻
Dated — Kuang-Hsü "Jên-ch'ên" 18/1892

Index

Bound in 19 t'ao   184 Chüan

Remarks

57

The University of Toronto Chinese Library

....

Accession No. 2520   Index No. 085-299c

Title 河南通志. Ho Nan Tung Chi

Classification B-192

Subject

References

Author 清田文鏡等奉敕修 續志 阿思哈等奉敕修
Ch'ing, Tien Wên-Ching and others) Hsü Chi was revised by A, Ssu-Ha and
(revised)   (others
Edition 殿版 光緒年重刊 Palace ed.
Dated — Kuang-Hsü period 1895 — 1908 second edition

Index

Bound in 12 T'ao (正編 8, 續編 4) 正志 80 chuan, 續志 80 chuan
(Chêng Pien 8, Hsü Pien 4) Chêng Chih 80 Chüan, Hsü Chi 80 Chüan
Remarks

Accession No. 2522   Index No. 085-gijc

Title 涇陽縣志. Ching Yang Hsien Chi.

Classification B-194

Subject

References

Author 清 劉懋官 周斯億等編纂 edited & Compiled by Ching, Liu Mao-Kuan and Chou Ssu-I

Edition 甲重修版 Revised edition 宣統年刻
光緒年刻 華新書局印

Index Dated — Hua-Hsin book Company print Hsüan-Tung period 1909—1911

Bound in 1 Tʻao   16 Chuan   4 Tsʻê

Remarks

The University of Toronto Chinese Library

. . . .

Accession No. 2523   Index No. 064-dzjc

Title 扶風縣志. Fu fêng Hsien Chi

Classification B-194

Subject

References

                                        edited & Compiled by
Author 清 宋世犖等編纂 Ching, Sang Shih-Lo and others

Edition 官版   嘉慶二十三年刻 Official ed.
Dated — Chia-Ching "Na-ying" 23/1818

Index

Bound in   1 t'ao   18 chuan   4 ts'ê

Remarks

60

Accession No. 2524   Index No. 189-孙ㄐc

Title 高陵縣志, 附續志八卷   Kao Ling Hsien Chih
                                 Fu Hsü Chih 8 Chüan

Classification B-194

Subject

References

Author 明 吕涇野編 清程維雍重修   edited by
                                    Ming. Lü Ching-Yeh
                                    Ching, Chêng Wei-Yung (revised)

Edition 官版   光緒年刻 Official ed.
Dated — Kuang-Hsü period 1875 — 1908

Index

Bound in   1 t'ao   15 Chüan (正志 7 Chüan, 續志 8 Chüan) 4 t'sè
Remarks   Chêng Chih   Hsü Chih

....

Accession No. 2525   Index No. 131-Kljc

Title 臨潼縣志. Lin Tung Hsien Chih

Classification B-194

Subject

References

Author 清 史傳遠重輯, *Recompiled by* Ching, Shih Chuan Yüan

Edition 乾隆四十一年刻
Dated — Chien-Lung "Ping-Shen" 41/1776

Index

Bound in 1 t'ao 9 Chüan 6 ts'ê

Remarks

The University of Toronto Chinese Library
....

Accession No. 2526   Index No. 001:6 2 jc

Title 三原縣志. San Yüan Hsien Chih

Classification B-194

Subject

References

Author 清 焦雲龍 賀瑞麟等編修. _Edited & Amended by Ching. Chiao Yün-Lung and Ho Jui-Lin_

Edition 學古書院藏版 光緒年刻
Block preserved Hsüeh-Ku-Shu-Yüan private printed ed.
Dated — Kuang-Hsü period 1875 — 1908

Index

Bound in 1 t'áo   8 Chuan   4 ts'ǔ

Remarks

63

The University of Toronto Chinese Library

....

Accession No. 2527   Index No. 001-bhjc

Title 三原縣志. *San Yüan Hsien Chih*

Classification B-194

Subject

References

Author 清 焦雲龍 賀瑞麟等編修 *edited + con Amended by Ching. Chiao Yün-Lung and Ho gui-Lin*

Edition 學古書院藏版 光緒年刻
Block preserved Hsüeh-Ku-Shu-Yüan private - printed
Dated — Kuang-Hsü period 1875 — 1908

Index

Bound in ● t'ao   8 Chuan   4 ts'ǔ

Remarks

The University of Toronto Chinese Library

. . . .

Accession No. 2528   Index No. 030-*jije*

Title 成陽縣志. 附教育統計表   *Hsien Yang Hsien Chih*
                              Fu Chiao Yü Tung Chi Piao

Classification B-194

Subject

References

Author 劉安國 吳延錫等修纂。 *Amended* Compiled by
                          Liu An-Kuo and Wu Yen-Hsi

Edition 鉛印版   民國二十一年 *Type-setting ed.*
Dated — Ming-Kuo 21/1932

Index

Bound in 1 *t'ao* 8 *chuan*   5 *tsʻ*

Remarks

The University of Toronto Chinese Library

....

Accession No. 2529   Index No. 168-3cc

Title 長安志，附長安志圖二卷   *Chāng An Chih*
                                      Fu Chāng An Chih Tu Ềⁿʰ *Chüan*

Classification B-174

Subject   •

References

Author 清 宋敏求撰 畢秋沅新校   *Written by*
                                Ching, Sung Min-Chiu   *Revised by*
                                                         Collated by Pi, Yüan-tsing
                                                         (revised).

Edition 民國二十年重印版
        長安縣志局印
        Chāng-An (Hsien Chih Chü) local government ed.

Index *Dated — Ming-Kuo 20/1931* *Reprinted ed.*
                                  second ed.

Bound in 1 *t'ao*   22 *Chuan*   4 *ts'e*

Remarks

The University of Toronto Chinese Library

....

Accession No. 2530   Index No. 040-P覍覍c

Title 寶雞縣志. Pao Chi Hsien Chih

Classification B-194

Subject

References

Author 清 鄧夢琴纂修. Compiled & Amended by Ching, Têng Mêng-Chin

Edition 乾隆五十年刻

本署藏版
Blocks preserved in Pên-Shu private-printed.
Index Dated — Ch'ien-Lung "I-Ssǔ" 50/1785

Bound in 1 t'ao   16 Chuan   4 ts'ê

Remarks

The University of Toronto Chinese Library

. . . .

Accession No. 2531   Index No. 085-ijjᶜ

Title 渭南縣志、 Wei Nan Hsien Chih

Classification B-194

Subject

References

Author 清畢沅 汪以誠等奉勅修 Ching, Pi Yüan, and Wang I-Chêng and others   revised by

Edition 官版 乾隆四十三年刻 official ed.
Dated — Chʻien-Kung "Wu-Hsü" 43/1778

Index

Bound in 1 tʻao   14 Chuan   8 tsʻü

Remarks

The University of Toronto Chinese Library

. . . .

Accession No. 2532   Index No. 085·djic

Title 沔縣新志. Mien Hsien Hsin Chih

Classification B-194

Subject

References

Author 清 張端卿 鑒訂 孫銘鐘華編輯
Ching, Chang Tuan Ching, edited & compiled by Sun Ming-Chung and others

Edition 官版 Official ed.
光緒癸年刻
Dated — Kuang-Hsü "Kuei-Wei" 9/1883

Index

Bound in   1 Tʻao   4 Chuan   4 tsʻè

Remarks

69

The University of Toronto Chinese Library

....

Accession No. 2533   Index No. 196-c88c

Title 鳳翔縣志 Fêng Hsiang Hsien Chih

Classification B-194

Subject

References

Author 清 羅鰲重修 Ching, Lo Ao (revised edition)

Edition 官版 official ed.
乾隆三十二年刻
Dated — Chien-Lung "Ting-Hai" 32/1769

Index

Bound in 1 t'ao   8 chuan   7 ts'ê

Remarks

The University of Toronto Chinese Library

· ·

Accession No. 2534   Index No. 040-kbcc

Title 寧羌州志. Ning Chiang Chou Chih

Classification B-194

Subject

References

Author 清 唐樹楠等重修 Ching, Tang Shu-Nan and others (revised ed.

Edition 官版 official ed.

Index

Bound in 1 t'ao   5 Chuan   5 ts'ê

Remarks

Accession No. 2535   Index No. 140-9夕jc

Title 蒲城縣志. P'u chêng Hsien Chih

Classification B-194

Subject

References

Author 清 張心鏡重修 Ching, Chang Hsin-Ching (revised ed.

Edition 官版 Official ed.
乾隆四十七年刻
Dated — Chien-Kung "Jen-ying" 47/1082

Index

Bound in 1 táo   15 Chuan   6 ts'ǎ

Remarks Mistakes in binding in 1st. ts'ǎ

The University of Toronto Chinese Library

. . . .

Accession No. 2536   Index No. 198·liuc

Title 麟麥遊新志· Lin Yu Hsin Chih

Classification B-194

Subject

References

Author 清 王贊襄 彭洵荤撰 ^Written by Chîng, Wang Tsan-Hsiang and Pêng Hsün

Edition 官版 official ed.

光緒九年刻

Doted— Kuang-Hsü "Kuei-Wei" 9//1883

Index

Bound in   1 táo   10 Chuan   4 tsè

Remarks

The University of Toronto Chinese Library

. . . .

36 ?

Accession No. 2537   Index No. 030-3Lkc

Title 咸淳臨安志. Hsien Chún Lin An Chih

Classification B-194

Subject

References

Author 清 宋 潛說友撰 *Written by* Sung, Chien Shuo-Yu

Edition 清 錢唐振綺堂汪氏仿宋本重雕雕精刻本
清道光年刊 Ching, Chien-Táng Chén-I-Táng Wang-Shih *imitated* *immetated Sung's copy fine—printed ed.*

Index *Dated — Ching, Tao-Kuang period — 1821—1850*

Bound in 3 t'ao 97 chuan 24 ts'è (附札記)

Remarks

Accession No. 2538   Index No. 151-尺jc

Title 豐縣志. fêng Hsien Chih

Classification B-194

Subject

References

Author 清 姚鴻杰重輯, Re-compiled by Ching, Yao Hung-Chieh

Edition 官版 Official ed.
光緒二十年刊
Dated — Kaang-Hsü "Chia-Wa" 20/1894

Index

Bound in 1 tᵃᵒ   16 Chuan   8 tsᵘ

Remarks

The University of Toronto Chinese Library

. . . .

Accession No. 2639   Index No. 154- 贛jc

Title 贛榆縣志. *Kan Yü Hsien Chih*

Classification B-194

Subject

References

Author 清 王文炳 張騫重修 *Ching. Wang Wên-Pin and Chang Chien(revised) ed.*

Edition 光緒戊子年刊
         Dated — Kuang-Hsü "Wu-Tzŭ" 14/1888

Index

Bound in 1 *t'ao* 18 *Chuan* 4 *ts'ê*

Remarks

o.k.

The University of Toronto Chinese Library
....

Accession No. 2540   Index No. 051-bjjc

Title 光緒
       山西 平遙縣志 Kuang Hsü P'ing Yao Hsien Chih
                    Shan Hsi

Classification B-194

Subject

References
                                                      revised by
Author 清 噶禮荃原修   林撰梅荃續修 Ch'ing Ko Li and others, Lin
                                          Kung-Shu and others

Edition 縣署藏版   劉潤平鐫字 Hsien Shu   Liu Jun-P'ing
         畢天臻訂裁刷印   光緒八年
publishedly Pi Tien-Chên

Index   Dated — Kuang-Hsü "Jên-Wu" 8/1882

Bound in 2 t'ao

Remarks

....

Accession No. 2541   Index No. 094. 上3 ℐᶜ

Title 雍正 山西 猗氏縣志. *Yung Chêng Shan Hsi* *I Shih Hsien Chih*

Classification B-194

Subject

References

Author 清 潘越纂輯 宋之樹重輯 *Compiled* *Ching, Pán Yüeh,* *rescompiled revised by* *Sung Chih-Shu*

Edition 官版 *Official ed.*
雍正己酉七年刊
Dated — Yung-Chêng "Chi-Yu" 7/1729

Index

Bound in 1 *t'ao* 4 *ts'ê* 8 *Chuan*

Remarks

The University of Toronto Chinese Library

....

Accession No. 2542   Index No. 163-jkjc

Title 民國 山西 鄉寧縣志. Ming Kuo Shan Hsi Hsiang Ning Hsien Chih

Classification B-194

Subject

References

Author 民國 趙祖抃等纂修 Compiled & amended by Republic, Chao Tsu-Pien and others

Edition 民國六年印
Dated — Ming-Kuo 6/1917 Printed.

Index

Bound in 1 táo 6 tsʻè

Remarks

Accession No. 2543   Index No. 085-gcgec

Title 乾隆 浦州府志 ChienLung Pu Chou Fu Chih
      山西   Shan Hsi

Classification

Subject

References

Author 清 喬光烈 周景柱等修 Amended by ↗ching, Chiao Kuang-Lieh and Chou
                                                    Ching-Chu

Edition 官版 official ed.
        乾隆二十年刊
        Dated — Chien-Lung "I-Hai" 20/1775

Index

Bound in 3 t'ao. 24 chuan 10 ts'ê

Remarks

oil

The University of Toronto Chinese Library

....

Accession No. 2544   Index No. 131- 木弓弓c

Title 乾隆 臨晉縣志 *Chien Lung*   Lin Chin Hsien Chih
       山西   *Shan Hsi*

Classification B-194

Subject

References

Author 清 王正茂纂著 Compiled by *Ching, Wang Chêng-Mao*

Edition 官版 *official ed.*
         乾隆癸巳年刊
         Dated — Chien-Lung "Kuei-Ssŭ" 38/1773

Index

Bound in 1 t'ao   6 Ts'ê   8 ts'ê

Remarks

81

The University of Toronto Chinese Library

· ·

Accession No. 2545   Index No. 109-ci3c

Title 光緒 山西 直隸澤州志 附外集 *Kuang Hsü Shan Hsi Chih Li Chiang Chou Chih*

Classification B-194

Subject

References

Author 清 李煥揚續修 *Amended ed. by Ching, Li Huan-Yang*

Edition 官版 *Official ed.*
光緒年刊
Dated — Kuang-Hsü period 1825—1908

Index

Bound in 2 *t'ao*   20 *chuan*   10 *ts'ê*

Remarks

82

The University of Toronto Chinese Library

· ·

Accession No. 2546   Index No. 085. a·n·j·c

Title 光緒
       山西 永濟縣志. *Kuang Hsü Shan Hsi Yung Chi Hsien Chih*

Classification B-194

Subject

References

Author 清 杜崧年 李榮和業修纂 *edited & Compiled by* *Ching, Tu Sung-Nien and Li Yung-Ho*

Edition 縣署藏版 光緒丙戌年鐫
Blocks preserved in Hsien-Shu local government ed.
Dated — Kuang-Hsü "Ping-Hsü" 12/1886

Index

Bound in 4 t'ao 24 chüan 14 ts'ê

Remarks

OK

Accession No. 2547   Index No. 085-888ᶜ

Title 民國 洪洞縣志、 Ming Kuo Shen Hsi Hung Tung Hsien Chih
       山西

Classification B-194

Subject

References

Author 民國 孫奐崙 韓坰等纂修. Compiled & edited by Republic, Sun Huan Lun and Han Chiung

Edition 民國六年
         上海商務印書館印
         Shanghai, Shang-Wu book company

Index Dated — Ming-Kuo 6/1919

Bound in 2 t'ao 18 chuan 10 ts'ê

Remarks

oll

The University of Toronto Chinese Library
....

Accession No. 2548   Index No. 131.kjc

Title 臨縣志、 Lin Hsien Chih

Classification B-194

Subject

References

Author 民國 胡宗虞 吳命新筆修纂 edited & Compiled by Republic, Hu Tsung-Yü and Wu Ming-Hsin

Edition 民國六年印
晉省大國民印刷廠印
Chin-Shêng, Ta-Kuo Min (Yin Shua Chang) press Co. printed.

Index Dated — Ming-Kuo 6/1917

Bound in 1 t'ao 4 ts'ê 20 Chuan

Remarks

Accession No. 2549   Index No. 073·bdjc

Title 光緒 曲沃縣志 *Kuang Hsü*
      山西   *Shan Hsi   Chü Wo Hsien Chih*

Classification B-194

Subject

References

Author 清 張鴻逵 茅玉熙 纂輯 *Compiled by Ch'ing, Chang Hung-Kúei and Mao Pêi-Hsi*

Edition 官版 *official ed.*
        光緒庚辰年印
        Dated — Kuang-Hsü "Kêng-Ch'ên" 6/1880

Index

Bound in 1 *t'ao*   6 *ts'ê*   32 *Chuan*

Remarks

The University of Toronto Chinese Library

. . . .

Accession No. 2550   Index No. 131-$k \bar{2} j^c$

Title 民國 山西 臨晉縣志, 附錄舊序   Min Kuo Shan Hsi Lin Chin Hsien Chih Fu Lu Chiu Hsü

Classification B-194

Subject

References

Author 民國 俞家驥 許鑑觀華修纂 *edited & Compiled by* Republic, Yü Chia-Chi and Hsü Chien-Kuan

Edition 民國十二年重修
Dated — Ming-Kuo 12/1913 (revised edition)

Index

Bound in 1 t'ao   4 ts'ê   16 Chuan

Remarks

The University of Toronto Chinese Library

....

Accession No. 2551   Index No. 075-jᵉjᶜ

Title 光緒 榮河縣志 *Kuang Hsü*
山西   *Shan Hsi Jung Ho Hsien Chih*

Classification B-194

Subject

References

Author 清 馬鑑 王希濂等修 *edited by*
                              Ching. Ma Chien and Wang Hsi-Lien

Edition 官版 *official ed.*
光緒七年重刊
Dated — Kuang-Hsü "Hsin-Ssü" 7/1881

Index

Bound in 1 *t'ao* 6 *ts'ê* 14 *Chuan*

Remarks

ok

The University of Toronto Chinese Library
. . . .

Accession No. 2552   Index No. 140-ie j c

Title 乾隆 山西 萬泉縣志 Chien Lung Shan Hsi Wan Ch'üan Hsien Chih

Classification B 194

Subject

References

Author 明, 等嘉訓傅修 清鄭章續修 畢宿壽增修

Edition Originally edited by Ming, Fu Chia-Hsün, revised edition by Ching, Chêng Chang, Amended edition by Pi Su-Tao.

木刻板 block printing edition

Index 乾隆戊寅二十三年刊 Dated - Chien-Lung "Wu-Ying" 23/1758

Bound in 1 t'ao 4 tsê 8 chuan.

Remarks

89

The University of Toronto Chinese Library

....

Accession No. 2553   Index No. 039·dgjc

Title 乾隆 山西 孝義縣志· *Chien Lung, Shan Hsi* # *Hsiao I Hsien Chih*

Classification B-194

Subject

References

Author 明 劉令譽原修 清鄧必安重修
Original edited by *Ming, Liu Ling-Yü, revised by, Ching, Teng Pi-An*

Edition 木刻版 ~~woodcuts~~ *blocks printing edition*
乾隆庚寅五年刊
Dated — Chien Lung "Kêng-Ying" 36/1770

Index

Bound in 1 *t'ao*   8 *ts'è*   19 *Chüan*

Remarks

90

The University of Toronto Chinese Library

．．．．．．．．．．．．．．．．．．．．．．．

Accession No. 2554   Index No. 120-88ᶜ

Title 光緒 絳縣志 *Kuang Hsü*
山西   *Shan Hsi Chiang Hsien Chih*

Classification B-194

Subject

References

Author 清 胡延重修 *Revised ed. by*
                Chʻing Hu Yen (revised)

Edition 光緒年刊
Dated — Kuang-Hsü period 1875—1908

Index

Bound in 1 *tʻao* 4 *tsʻê* 21 *Chüan*

Remarks

The University of Toronto Chinese Library

· ·

Accession No. 2555   Index No. 051-biec

Title 乾隆 山西 平陽 府 縣志 Chien Lung Shan Hsi Ping Yang Fu Chih

Classification B-194

Subject

References

Author 清 章廷珪等修 奉勅重 Ch'ing, Chang Yen-Kui and others received the order from Imperial to revised

Edition 木刻版 ~~wooden~~ block printing edition.
乾隆元年重刊
Dated — Chien-Lung "Ping-Chien" 1/1736

Index

Bound in 4 t'ao   36 chuan   18 ts'ê

Remarks

92

The University of Toronto Chinese Library

. . . .

Accession No. 2556   Index No. 124-2 Ø jc

Title 光緒 翼城縣志 Kuang Hsü I Chêng Hsien Chih
       山西   Shan Hsi

Classification B-194

Subject

References

Author 清 王耀章等重修 Revised by Ch'ing, Wang Yü Yao-Chang and others

Edition 官版 木刻版 official ed., Block-printing edition
         光緒辛巳年刊
         Dated — Kuang-Hsü "Hsin-Ssu" 7/1881

Index

Bound in 2 t'ao 28 chüan 8 ts'ê

Remarks

93

The University of Toronto Chinese Library

· ·

Accession No. 2557   Index No. 115-988c

Title 同治 山西 稷山縣志, 附山褚續志. Tūng Chih Shên Hsi   Chi Shan Hsien Chih
                                                           Fu Shan Hsü Hsü Chih

Classification D-194

Subject

References

Author 清 沈鳳翔修 續志.馬家鼎修 ^edited by Chʻing, Shên Fêng-Hsiang
                                                      "Hsü Chih" was revised by Ma Chia-

Edition 官版 同治四年刊 official ed. Ting
         續志 光緒十一年刊
         Dated — Tūng-Chih "I-Chʻou" 4/1865

Index   Kuang-Hsü "I-Yu" 11/1885

Bound in 2 t'ao   12 Chuan   10 ts'ê
Remarks   續志. 1 ts'ê 2 Chuan

94

Accession No. 2558   Index No. 145-大久大了ㄷ

Title   民國 襄陵縣志 (新志) Min Kuo Hsiang Ling Hsien Chih (Hsin
        山西   Shan Hsi   Chih)

Classification B-194

Subject

References

Author 民國 李世祐等修 edited by Republic, Li Shih-Yu and others

Edition 民國十二年刊
         Dated — Ming-Kuo 12/1923

Index

Bound in 2 t'ao   24 Chuan 8 ts'ê

Remarks

The University of Toronto Chinese Library

....

Accession No. 2559   Index No. 069-188c

Title 民國   新 絳 縣 志. Min Kuo
       山西   Shan Hsi Hsin Chiang Hsien Chih

Classification B-194

Subject   /

References

                        ed.
                  Revised by
Author 民國 徐昭儉等重修 Republic, Hsü Chao-Chien and others

Edition 太原崇實印刷所印 Tái-Yüan, Chúng-Shih Yin Shua So.
         民國十七年印
         Dated — Ming-Kuo 17/1928

Index

Bound in 2 t'ao   10 Chüan   10 ts'ê

Remarks

96

012

The University of Toronto Chinese Library
....

Accession No. 2560   Index No. 145-万 7 8c

Title 乾隆 山西 襄垣縣志 附續志. Chien Lung
Shan Hsi Hsiang Yüan Hsien Chih

Classification B-194

Subject

References

Author 清 李延芳等重修 Revised ed. by Ching, Li Yen-Fang and others (revised)

Edition 雜貨行存版 blocks preserved in Tsa-Tai-Hang
乾隆四十七年刊
Dated—Chien-Lung "Jên-Ying" 47/1982

Index

Bound in 2 T'ao   10 Chuan   10 Ts'ê

Remarks

97

012

The University of Toronto Chinese Library

....

Accession No. 2561   Index No. 168·3²J^C

Title 乾隆 山西 長治縣志 *Chien Lung Shan Hsi Chang Chih Hsien Chih*

Classification B-194

Subject

References

Author 清 吳九齡 張嶽拱 ~~等修~~ *edited by Ching, Wu Chiu-Ling and Chang Yü-Kung*

Edition 官版 *official ed.*

乾隆二十八年刊 *Dated — Chien-Lung "Kuei-Wei" 28/1763*

Index

Bound in 2 t'ao   28 Chuan   10 ts'ê

Remarks

O.K.

The University of Toronto Chinese Library
....

Accession No. 2562   Index No. 085-dcec

Title 乾隆 汾州府志 Chien Lung
      山西   Shan Hsi Fēn Chou Fu Chih

Classification B-194

Subject

References

Author 清 孫和相等纂修 Compiled & edited by Ching, Sun Ho-Hsiang and others

Edition 官版 official ed.
        乾隆辛卯年刊
        Dated — Chien-Lung "Hsin-Mao" 36/1771

Index

Bound in 3 t'ao   34 Chuan   16 ts'ə

Remarks

The University of Toronto Chinese Library

. . . .

Accession No. 2563   Index No. 037. a b j c

Title 道光 太平縣志 *Tao Kuang*
      山西   *Shan Hsi Tai Ping Hsien Chih*

Classification B-194

Subject

References

Author 清 王茂松 李炳彥等纂修 *Compiled. edited by*
                                Ching. Wang Mao-Sung and Li Ping-
                                Yen (revised)

Edition 官版 *official ed.*
        道光五年刊
        Dated — Tao-Kuang "I-Yu" 5 / 1825

Index

Bound in 2 t'ao   16 Chuan   8 ts'ü

Remarks

The University of Toronto Chinese Library

· ·

Accession No. 2564   Index No. 085-dijc

Title 光緒 山西 汾陽縣志. *Kuang Hsü Shan Hsi Fên Yang Hsien Chih*

Classification B-194

Subject

References

Author 清 慶文等續修 *Amended edition by Ching, Ching Wên and others (revised)*

Edition 官版 *Official ed.*
光緒八年刊
Dated — Kuang-Hsü "Jên-Wu" 8/1882

Index

Bound in 2 t'ao 14 Chuan 10 ts'è

Remarks

The University of Toronto Chinese Library

....

Accession No. 2565   Index No. 156-94jc

Title 道光 山西 趙城縣志. *Tao Kuang Shan Hsi Chao Chêng Hsien Chih*

Classification B-194

Subject

References

Author 明 賀國定劇   清楊延亮重修 *Revised ed. by Ming, Ho Kuo-Ting. revised by Ching, Yang Yen Liang*

Edition 官版 *Official ed.*
道光八年刊
Dated — Tao-Kwang "Wu-Tzŭ" 9/1828

Index

Bound in 2 t'ao   37 Chuan 8 ts'ê

Remarks

102

The University of Toronto Chinese Library

. . . .

Accession No. 2566   Index No. 085-988ᶜ

Title 光緒 浮山縣志 *Kuang Hsü*
         山西   *Shan Hsi, Fu Shan Hsien Chih*

Classification B-194

Subject

References

Author 清 潘廷候等創修（康熙十二年）   鹿學典 裴允莊等補修
Original edited by Ching, Pan Ting-Hou and others   revised by Lu Hsüeh-Tien and Péi

Edition 縣署藏版 (Hsien-Ya) Local government Chuang
         光緒六年刻   private ed.
                  Dated — Kuang-Hsü "Kéng-Chén" 6/1880

Index

Bound in 3 t'ao 34 Chuan 12 tsʾo

Remarks

The University of Toronto Chinese Library

. . . .

Accession No. *2567*   Index No. *067-337^c*

Title 文水縣志. *Wên Shui Hsien Chih*

Classification *B-194*

Subject

References

Author 清 傅星等原修　范啟塗 陰步霞等續修
Original edited *Ching, Fu Hsing and others,* ~~revised~~ *amended ed.* *by Fan Chi-Kun and Yin Pu-Hsia*

Edition 縣衙藏版 *(Hsien-Ya) local government ed.*

光緒九年重修
Dated — ~~Revised ed. in~~ Kuang-Hsü "Kuei-Wei" 9/1883

Index

Bound in *1 t'ao   12 Chuan   6 ts'e*

Remarks

Accession No. 2568   Index No. 033-美考记

Title 壺關縣志. Hu Kuan Hsien Chih

Classification B-194

Subject

References

Author 明 張西林原修 清 楊宸 秦之栖新修
Original edited Ming, Chang Hsi-Lin, revised by Ching, Yang Chên and Chin Chih-Ping
Edition 官衙藏版 Kuan-Ya private-printed ed.
乾隆三十五年刻
Dated — Chien-Lung "Kêng-ying" 35/1770

Index

Bound in 1 t'ao 18 Chuan 4 ts'ê

Remarks

The University of Toronto Chinese Library

. . . .

Accession No. 2569   Index No. 141-888ᶜ

Title 虞鄉縣志、 Yü Hsiang Hsien Chih

Classification B-194

Subject

References

Author 清 周大儒等修　崔鑄善等修續
edited by Ch'ing, Chou Ta-ju and others, revised by Ts'ui Chu-Shan and others
Amended ed.

Edition 官版 Official ed.
　　　　光緒十七年刻
　　Dated —— Kuang-Hsü "Hsin-Mao" 17/1891

Index

Bound in 1 t'ao   12 Chuan   4 ts'ê

Remarks

106

The University of Toronto Chinese Library

....

Accession No. 2570   Index No. 009-bdjc

Title 介休縣志, Chieh Hsiu Hsien Chih

Classification B-194

Subject

References

Author 清 葉澄芝等重修, Revised.by Ching, Yeh ju-Chih and others (revised)

Edition 官版 official ed.

嘉慶十九年刊
Dated — Chia-Ching "Chia-Hsü" 19/1814

Index

Bound in 1 t'ao 14 Chuan 9 ts'ê

Remarks

The University of Toronto Chinese Library

. . . .

Accession No. 2571   Index No. 173-hcc

Title 霍州志 Huo Chou Chih

Classification B-194

Subject

References

Author 明 褚相等原修   清 崔允昭等新修
Original edited by Ming, Ch'u Hsiang and others, revised by Ching, Tsui Yün-Chao
                                               amended ed.

Edition 官署藏版 Official ed.

道光五年重修
               Revised ed. in
Dated — T'ao-Kuang "1-Yu" 5/1825
       ∧

Index

Bound in 1 t'ao 25 Chuan 10 ts'e

Remarks

108

The University of Toronto Chinese Library

. . . .

Accession No. 2572   Index No. 077-nlec

Title 歸德府志. *Kuei Tê Fu Chih*

Classification B-194

Subject

References

Author 清 蔣炳 *edited by* 等修. *Ching. Chiang Ping and others*

Edition 官版 光緒十九年重刻 *Official ed.*
Dated —— *Re-engraved in Kuang-Hsü "Kuei-Ssŭ" 19/1893*

Index

Bound in 2 t'ao   36 Chuan   11 ts'ê

Remarks

....

Accession No. 2573   Index No. 085-zgec

Title 河南府志、 Ho Nan Fu Chih

Classification B-194

Subject

References

Author 宋 司馬光等原修　清施誠等重修
Original ed. by Sung, Ssŭ Ma Kuang and others, revised by Ching, Shih Chêng and others

Edition 官版 同治六年重刊 official ed.
Dated — Reengraved in Tung-Chih "Ting-Mao" 6/1867

Index

Bound in 4 t'ao   116 Chuan   24 ts'e

Remarks

. . . .

Accession No. 2574   Index No. 061-phec

Title 懷慶府志 *Huai Ching Fu Chih*

Classification B-194

Subject

References

Author 清 唐侍陛等重修 *Revised ed. by Ching, Tang Shih-Pi and others*

Edition 官版 乾隆五十四年重刊 *official ed.*
Dated — *Revised ed. in Chien-Lung "Chi-Yu" 54/1789*

Index

Bound in 2 t'ao   32 Chuan   15 ts'e

Remarks

The University of Toronto Chinese Library

....

Accession No. 2575   Index No. 152 . n LOC

Title 豫河續志 Yü Ho Hsü Chih

Classification B-194

Subject

References

Author 民國 陳善同等續修 *Amended ed. by* *Republic, Chên Shan-Tung and others (revised,*

Edition 木刻版 民國十五年刊 *Block-printing edition*
河南河務局印
Ho-Nan, Ho-Wu-Chü printed.

Index *Dated — Ming-Kuo 15/1926*

Bound in *2 t'ao   20 chüan   14 ts'ê*

Remarks

The University of Toronto Chinese Library

. . . .

Accession No. 2576   Index No. 169-d7jc

Title 開封縣志. 舊名祥符縣. *Kai fêng Hsien Chih (Chiu Ming Hsiang Fu Hsien)*

Classification B-194

Subject

References

Author 清 劉樹堂等修, *edited by* *Ching, Liu Shu-Tang and others*

Edition 官版 光緒二十四年刊 *official ed.*
Dated — *Kuang-Hsü "Wu-Hsü" 24/1898*

Index

Bound in 2 t'ao 24 Chuan 12 ts'ê

Remarks Some mis-binding.

Accession No. 2578   Index No. 075- cjc

Title 杞縣志. Chi Hsien Chih

Classification B-194

Subject

References

Author 清 周璣等重修. Revised edition by Ch'ing, Chou Chi and others (revised)

Edition 官版 乾隆五十三年刊 official ed.
Dated — Chien-Lung "Wu-Shen" 53 / 1788

Index

Bound in 2 t'ao   24 Chuan   12 ts'e

Remarks

Accession No. 2579   Index No. 162-gdjc

Title   通許縣志 *Tung Hsü Hsien Chih*

Classification B-194

Subject

References

Author 明 韓玉創修   清阮龍光莘重修
Original edited Ming, Han Yü, revised ed by Ching. Juan Lung. Kuang and others

Edition 官版 乾隆三十六年刊 *official ed.*
          Dated — Chien-Lung "Hsin-Mao" 36/1771

Index

Bound in 1 t'ao 10 Chuan 6 ts'ê

Remarks

The University of Toronto Chinese Library

....

Accession No. 2580   Index No. 091-ㄨㄐㄐᶜ

Title 尉氏縣志. Wei shih Hsien Chih
                        ⁿᵘ

Classification B-194

Subject

References

Author 明 齊勉等創修   清 楊國楨等重修
Original ed. by Ming, Chi Mien and others, revised by Ching, Yang Kuo-Chên and others
Edition 官版 道光十一年刊 official ed.
        Dated — Tao-Kuang "Hsin-Mao" 11/1831

Index

Bound in 1 t'ao 20 Chuan 8 ts'ê

Remarks

The University of Toronto Chinese Library

. . . .

Accession No. 2581   Index No. 085-88jc

Title 浦川縣志. Wei Chuan Hsien Chih

Classification B-194

Subject

References

Author 清 何文明纂修 Compiled & edited by Ching, Ho Wên-Ming

Edition 官版 嘉慶戊寅年刊 Official ed.
Dated —— Chia-Ching "Wu-Ying" 23/1818

Index

Bound in 1 t'ao 8 Chuan 4 ts'z

Remarks

117

Accession No. 2582   Index No. 163-_tz h j c_

Title 鄢陵縣志, _Yen Ling Hsien Chih_

Classification B-194

Subject

References

Author 清 何鄂聯等纂修。 _Compiled or ed. by Ching, Ho O-Lien and others_

Edition 官版 道光十二年刊 _official ed._
Dated — Tao-Kuang "jên-chên" 12/1832

Index

Bound in 1 t'ao   18 Chuan   8 ts'ê

Remarks

The University of Toronto Chinese Library
....

Accession No. 2583   Index No. 163-ㄗㄥㄕㄢ

Title 鄢陵文獻志 *Yen Lin Wên Hsien Chih*

Classification B-194

Subject

References

Author 清 蘇源生纂 *Compiled by* *Ching, Su Yüan-Shêng*

Edition 周治元年刊
Dated — Tung-Chih "Jên-Hsü" 1/1862

Index

Bound in 2 t'ao 40 Chuan 20 ts'ã

Remarks

The University of Toronto Chinese Library

· ·

Accession No. 2584   Index No. 002cbjc

Title 中牟縣志, Chung Mou Hsien Chih

Classification B-194

Subject

References

Author 清 吳若烺等重修, *Revised ed. by* Ching, Wu Jo-Lang and others (revised)

Edition 縣署衙藏版 同治九年重修, *Block preserved in* " Local government ed.

Dated — Tung-Chih "Kêng-Wu" 9/1870

Index

Bound in 1 táo   12 Chuan   6 ts'ê

Remarks

The University of Toronto Chinese Library

. . . .

Accession No. 2585   Index No. 163-scjc

Title 鄭州縣志, Chêng Chou Hsien Chih

Classification B-194

Subject

References

Author 清 張鉄等續修, *Amended ed. by* Ching, Chang Têh and others (revised,)

Edition 官版   乾隆年刻 *official ed.*
Dated — Chien-Lung period 1736—1795

Index

Bound in 1 t'ao   12 Chuan (only 4 Ts'ê on shelf)

Remarks Printing not clear. Possible missing tsê.
Very old prints.

The University of Toronto Chinese Library

· ·

Accession No. 2586   Index No. 085.2 h jc

Title 河 陰 縣志. 附金石考及文徵   Ho Yin Hsien Chih
                                          Fu Chin Shih Kao Chi Wên Chêng

Classification

Subject

References

                                    Compiled & edited by
Author 民國 田文烈等纂修 Republic, Tien Wên-Lieh and others

Edition 民國六年版
         Dated — Ming-Kuo 6 / 1917

Index

Bound in / t'ao   17 Chuan   12 ts'ê

Remarks

122

The University of Toronto Chinese Library
. . . .

Accession No. 2587   Index No. 090-h jc

Title 密縣志. Mi Hsien Chih

Classification B-194

Subject

References

Author 清 謝增 白景綸等纂 *Compiled by* Ch'ing, Hsieh Tsêng and Pai Ching-Lun

Edition 官版 嘉慶二十二年刊 Official ed.
Dated — Chia-Ching "Ting-Ch'ou" 22/1817

Index

Bound in 1 t'ao   16 Chuan   4 ts'ê

Remarks

123

The University of Toronto Chinese Library

....

Accession No. 2588   Index No. 069-ilja

Title 新鄭縣志. Hsin Chêng Hsien Chih

Classification B-194

Subject

References

Author 清 黄本誠等重修 Revised ed. by Chíng, Haung Pêng-Chêng and others (revised)

Edition 官版 乾隆四十一年刊 official ed.
Dated — Chien-Lung "Ping-Shen" 41/1776

Index

Bound in 2 t'ao 31 Chuan

Remarks

The University of Toronto Chinese Library

. . . .

Accession No. 2589   Index No. 030-Lejc

Title 商邱縣志. Shang Chiu Hsien Chih

Classification B-194

Subject

References

Author 清 劉德昌等重修, *Revised ed. by* Ching. Liu Tê-chang and others (revised)

Edition 官版 光緒年重印 Official ed.
Dated — Kuang-Hsü period 1875 — 1908 re-printed

Index

Bound in 1 t'ao 20 Chüan 6 ts'ê

Remarks

The University of Toronto Chinese Library

....

Accession No. 2590   Index No. 198.337ᶜ

Title 鹿邑縣志. Lu I Hsien Chih

Classification B-194

Subject

References

Author 清 餘慶 于瀾滄等修 ˄edited by Chíng. Yü Chíng ˄and Yü Lan-Tsang

Edition 官版 光緒二十二年刻 ˄Block-engraving in official ed.
Dated —— ˅Kuang-Hsü "Ping-Shen" 22/1896

Index

Bound in 1 t'ao 16 Chuan 6 tíᵃ

Remarks

The University of Toronto Chinese Library

....

Accession No. 2591   Index No. 085·a公jc

Title 永城縣志, Yung Chêng Hsien Chih

Classification B-194

Subject

References

Author 清 餘慶 岳廷階等重修 Ching. Yü Ching. and Yüeh Ting. Chieh revised by and others

Edition 官版 光緒二十七年刊 official ed.
Dated — Kuang-Hsü "Hsin-Chou" 27/1901

Index

Bound in 1 t'ao 38 Chuan 8 ts'ê

Remarks

The University of Toronto Chinese Library

. . . .

Accession No. 2592   Index No. 141·9 3̅ c

Title 虞城縣志. Yü Chêng Hsien Chih

Classification B-194

Subject

References

Author 清 李淇苹重修 *Revised ed. by* n Ching, Li Chi and others

Edition 官版 光緒二十一年刊 Official ed.
Dated — Kuang-Hsü "I-Wei" 21/1895

Index

Bound in 1 t'ao   10 Chuan   6 ts'e

Remarks

The University of Toronto Chinese Library

....

Accession No. 2593   Index No. 109 h
                                               472 tcc

Title 雎州志. *Chü Chou Chih*

Classification B-194

Subject

References

Author 清 餘慶 王枚莘重修 *Ching, Yü Ching. revised by Wang Mei and*
                                                    others
Edition 官版 光緒十八年刊 *official ed.*
    Dated — Kuang-Hsü "Jên-Ch'ên" 18/1892

Index

Bound in 1 t'ao 12 Chuan 8 冊

Remarks

The University of Toronto Chinese Library

. . . .

Accession No. 2594   Index No. 125-c ✗ jc

Title 考城縣志. *Kᵃo Chou Hsien Chih*

Classification B-194

Subject

References

Author 清 李國亮等重修ₙ *Revised ed. by Ch'ing, Li Kuo-Liang and others (revised)*

Edition 康熙三十七年刊 官版 *Official ed.*
Dated — Kang-Hsi "Wu-Ging" 37/1678

Index

Bound in 1 t'ao 4 Chuan 4 t's'e

Remarks *Printing not clear, mistakes in binding*

Accession No. 2595   Index No. 075.22jc

Title 柘城縣志, Chê Chéng Hsien Chih

Classification B-194

Subject

References

Author 明 李本固初修   清 劉樹堂重修
Original ed. by Ming, Li Pên-Ku, revised by Ching, Liu Shu-Táng

Edition 官版 光緒二十二年刊 official ed.
Dated — Kuang-Hsü "Ping-Shen" 22/1896

Index

Bound in 2 t'ao   10 Chuan   10 ts'é

Remarks

The University of Toronto Chinese Library

....

Accession No. 2596   Index No. 040-cijc

Title 安陽縣志. *An Yang Hsien Chih*

Classification 3-194

Subject

References

Author 清 貴泰芊纂修 Compiled & edited by *Ching, Kuei Tai and others*

Edition 官版 嘉慶二十四年刊 *official ed.*
Dated — *Chia-Ching "Chi-Hao" 24/1819*

Index

Bound in 1 t'ao 28 Chuan 10 ts'è

Remarks

Accession No. 2597   Index No. 131-后后jc

Title 臨漳縣志. Lin Chang Hsien Chih

Classification B-194

Subject

References

Author 清 陳燮龍 周秉彝等重修, *Revised ed. by* Ching, Chén Kúei-Lung and Chou Ping-I (revised)

Edition 官版 光緒三十年刊, Official ed. Dated — Kuang-Hsü "Chiq-Shen" 30/1904.

Index

Bound in 2 t'ao 18 Chuan 12 ts'ŏ

Remarks

The University of Toronto Chinese Library

. . . .

Accession No. *2598*   Index No. *075-djc*

Title 林縣志 *Lin Hsien Chih*

Classification *B-194*

Subject

References

Author 清 楊潮觀等重修。 *Revised ed. by Ch'ing, Yang Cháo-Kuan and others (revised)*

Edition 黃華書院藏板   乾隆十七年刋
Block preserved Huang Hua Shu Yüan private printed ed.
   Dated — Chien-Lung "Jên-Shen" 17/1752.

Index

Bound in *1 t'ao   10 Chuan   4 ts'è*

Remarks

The University of Toronto Chinese Library

. . . .

Accession No. 2599   Index No. 077-dcjc

Title 武安縣志 Wu An Hsien Chih

Classification B-194

Subject

References

Author 清 尹會一 蔣光祖等重修 *Revised ed. by* Ching, Yin Huei-I and Chiang Kuang-Tsu (*revised*)

Edition 官板 乾隆四年刊 *official ed.*
Dated — Chien-Lung "Chi-Wei" 4/1739

Index

Bound in 1 t'ao 20 Chuan 8 ts'e

Remarks

The University of Toronto Chinese Library

....

Accession No. 2600   Index No. 011-b3gc

Title 內黃縣志。 *Nei Huang Hsien Chih*

Classification B-194

Subject

References

Author 清 尹會一 李湞等重修。 ~Revised ed. by~ *Chíng, Yin Hui-I and Li Chêng (revised)*

Edition 官板　乾隆四年刊 *Official ed.*
Dated — Chien-Lung "Chi-Wei" 4/1739

Index

Bound in 1 t'áo   18 Chuan   6 ts'ê

Remarks

The University of Toronto Chinese Library
....

Accession No. 2601   Index No. 085-₤ajc

Title 洛陽縣志 Lo Yang Hsien Chih

Classification B-194

Subject

References

Author 清 乾隆 龔崧林等重修 *Revised ed. by* Ching, Chien-Lung period, Kung Sung-Lin ^(revised)^

Edition 民國十三年重印板 ~~Second edition~~ Reprinted edition.
Dated — Ming-Kuo 13/1924

Index

Bound in 2 t'ao   24 Chuan   20 ts'ih

Remarks

137

The University of Toronto Chinese Library

. . . .

Accession No. 2602   Index No. 009-ïgjc

Title 偃師縣志. *Yen Shih Hsien Chih*

Classification B-194

Subject

References

Author 清 孫星衍 湯毓倬同纂 *Compiled by* *Ching, Sun Hsing-Yen* *and* *Tang Yü-Cho*

Edition 官版 *Official ed.*

Index

Bound in 2 *T'ao*   30 *Chuan*   16 *ts'è*

Remarks

Accession No. 2603   Index No. 173-P?jc

Title 靈寶縣志 Ling Pao Hsien Chih

Classification B-194

Subject

References

                              Revised ed. by
Author 清 曾國荃 周溶等重修 Ch'ing, Tsêng Kuo Chüan and Chou Kan Chin (revised)

Edition 官板 光緒二年刊 Official ed.
        Dated — Kuang-Hsü "Ping-Tgx" 2/1826

Index

Bound in 1 t'ao   8 Chuan   8 ts'è

Remarks

The University of Toronto Chinese Library

. . . .

Accession No. 2604   Index No. 039-88c

Title 孟津縣志 Mêng Chin Hsien Chih

Classification B-194

Subject

References

Author 清 徐元燦等修 edited by Ching, Hsü Yüan-Tsan and others

Edition 官板 康熙年刻 official ed.
Dated — Kang-hsi period 1662—1722

Index

Bound in 1 t'ao 4 Chuan 4 ts'e

Remarks Some parts of the printing had fade away

Accession No. 2605   Index No. 177-8jc

Title 鞏縣志. Kung Hsien Chih

Classification B-194

Subject

References

Author 清 李述武纂修. Ching, Li Shu-Wu
Compiled & Amended edited by

Edition 官板 乾隆年刻 official ed.
Dated — Chien-Kung period 1736 — 1795

Index

Bound in 1 t'ao   20 Chuan   6 ts'ê

Remarks Some parts had fade away.

Accession No. 260**6**   Index No. 024-g ïjc

Title 南陽縣志. *Nan Yang Hsien Chih*

Classification B-194

Subject

References

Author 清 于蔭霖 潘守廉等新修 *new revised by Ching. Yü Yin-Lin and Pán Shou-Lien*

Edition 官板 光緒三十年刊 甲辰 *official ed.*
Dated — *Kuang-Hsü "Chia-Chen" 30/1904*

Index

Bound in 1 t'ao 12 Chuan 8 ts'é

Remarks

The University of Toronto Chinese Library

. . . .

Accession No. 2607   Index No. 024. gbjc

Title 南昌縣志. Nan Chao Hsien Chih

Classification B-194

Subject

References

                                    Compiled & edited by
Author 清 任應烈 陳之煥等纂修. Ching, Jen Ying- Lieh and Chên Chih- Yün
                                      兩寅
Edition 官板 乾隆十一年刊 Official ed.
         Dated — Chien-Lung "Ping-Ying" 11/1746

Index

Bound in 1 t'ao 4 Chuan 4 ts'ê   附手抄清冊一份 手繪地圖一份

Remarks

143

The University of Toronto Chinese Library

· ·

Accession No. 2608   Index No. 030-99ᶜ

Title 唐縣志, Táng Hsien Chih

Classification B-194

Subject

References

Author 清 吳泰來 黄文蓮等續修 , Ch'ing, Wu Tái-Lai and Huang Wên-Lien ⁽ʳᵉᵛⁱˢᵉᵈ⁾

        Amended ed. by

Edition 官板   乾隆五十二年刊 Official ed.
        Dated — Chien-Lung "Ting-Wei" 52/1787

Index

Bound in 1 táo   10 Chuan   4 ts'ê

Remarks

144

The University of Toronto Chinese Library

. . . .

Accession No. 2609   Index No. 167. jbjc

Title 鎮平縣志. Chên Píng Hsien Chih

Classification B-194

Subject

References

Author 清 李慶翱等重修 *Revised ed. by* Ching, Li Ching. Ao   and others (~~revised~~)

Edition 官板   光緒二年刊 Official ed.

Dated — Kuang-Hsü "Ping-Tzŭ" 2/1876

Index

Bound in 1 t'ao   6 Chuan   4 ts'ü

Remarks

Accession No. 2610   Index No. 163-1cc

Title 鄧州志, Tēng Chou chih

Classification B-194

Subject

References

Author 清 蔣炳 蔣光祖等纂修。 *Compiled & edited by* Ching. Chiang Pin and Chiang Kuang-Tsu

Edition 官板 乾隆二十年刊 *official ed.*
Dated — Chien-Lung "I-Hai" 20/1755

Index

Bound in 2 t'ao 24 Chuan 6 ts'ê

Remarks

146

The University of Toronto Chinese Library

. . . .

Accession No. 2611   Index No. 163-lcc

Title 登州志, Têng Chou Chih

Classification B-194

Subject

References

Author 清 蔣炳 蔣光祖等重修 *Revised ed. by* Ch'ing, Chiang Pin and Chiang Kuang-Tsu

Edition 官板 乾隆二十年刊 Official ed.
Dated — Ch'ien-Lung "I-Hai" 20/1755

Index

Bound in 1 t'ao 24 chüan 6 ts'ê

Remarks

148

The University of Toronto Chinese Library

. . . .

Accession No. 2613   Index No. 069-idjc

Title 新野縣志. Hsin Yeh Hsien Chih

Classification B-194

Subject

References

Author 清 蒋炳 徐金位等纂修. Compiled or edited by Ching, Chiang Pin and Hsü Chin-Wei

Edition 官板 乾隆十九年刊 官板 official ed.
Dated — Chien-Lung "Chia-Hsü" 19/1754

Index

Bound in 1 t'ao 9 chuan 4 ts'è

Remarks

The University of Toronto Chinese Library

. . . .

Accession No. 2614   Index No. 011-bjjc

Title 內鄉縣志. Nei Hsiang Hsien Chih

Classification B-194

Subject

References

Author 清 寶鼎望等纂修. Compiled & edited by Ching, Pao Ting-Wang and others

Edition 官板 康熙三十二年刊 official ed.
蔡唐 Dated — Kang-Hsi "Kuei-Yu" 32/1693

Index

Bound in 1 t'ao   12 Chuan   4 ts'ŏ

Remarks Faded prints

The University of Toronto Chinese Library

....

Accession No. 2615   Index No. 145-gcc

Title 裕州志 Yü chou Chih

Classification B-194

Subject

References

Author 清 宋名立等續修 ^(Revised ed. by) Ching, Sung Ming-Li and others (revised)

Edition 官板 乾隆五年刊 Official ed.
Dated — Chien-Lung "Kêng-Shen" 5/1740

Index

Bound in 1 t'ao 6 chuan 4 ts'e

Remarks

The University of Toronto Chinese Library

....

Accession No. 2616   Index No. 136-Lije

Title 舞陽縣志 Wu Yang Hsien Chih

Classification B-194

Subject

References

Author 清 王家相等纂修 Compiled & edited by Ching, Wang Chia-Hsiang and others

Edition 官板 道光十五年乙未刊 Official ed.
Dated — Tao-Kuang "I-Wei" 15/1835 —

Index

Bound in 1 t'ao 6 chuan 4 ts'a

Remarks

The University of Toronto Chinese Library

. . . .

Accession No. 2617   Index No. 140-ijc

Title 葉縣志, Yeh Hsien Chih

Classification B-194

Subject

References

Author 清 歐陽霖等重修, Revised ed. by Ching, Ou Yang Lin and others (revised)

Edition 宣板 同治十年刊 Official ed.
Dated — Tung-Chih "Hsin-Wei" 10/1871

Index

Bound in 1 t'ao   10 chuan   8 ts'e

Remarks

. . . .

Accession No. 2618   Index No. 085-cijc

Title 汝陽縣志 *Ju Yang Hsien Chih*

Classification B-194

Subject

References

Author 清 閻興邦 邱天英等續修 Revised ed. by *Ching, Yen Hsing-Pang and Chin Tien-Ying* (revised)

Edition 官板 康熙廿九年刊 *Official ed.*
Dated — *Kang-Hsi "Keng-Wu" 29/1690*

Index

Bound in 1 *t'ao* 10 *Chuan* 8 *ts'e*

Remarks

154

The University of Toronto Chinese Library

. . . .

Accession No. 2619   Index No. 077-aijc

Title 正陽縣志. Chêng Yang Hsien Chih

Classification B-194

Subject

References

Author 清 陳鍾璈 彭良弼莘重修. *Revised ed. by* Ching. Chên Chung.

Edition 縣署藏板 嘉慶元年丙辰刊 *Block preserved in Local government of.*
Dated — Chia-Ching "Ping-Chên" 1/1796

Index

Bound in 1 t'ao   10 Chuan   4 ts'ê

Remarks

155

Accession No. 2620   Index No. 069-ikjc

Title   新蔡縣志. Hsin Tsai Hsien Chih

Classification B-194

Subject

References

Author 清 莫璽章 王增蓉重修 Revised ed. by Ching, Mo Hsi-Chang and Wang Tseng (revised)

Edition 官板 乾隆六十年刊 Official ed.
Dated — Chien-Lung "I-Mao" 60/1795

Index

Bound in 1 t'ao 10 Chuan 4 ts'ê

Remarks

The University of Toronto Chinese Library

. . . .

Accession No. 2621   Index No. 146-3bjc

Title 西平縣志, Hsi Ping Hsien Chih

Classification B-194

Subject

References

Author 清 閻興邦等重修, Revised ed. by Ching, Yen Hsing-Pang and others (revised)

Edition 官板 康熙年刊 Official ed.
          Dated — Kang-Hsi peried 1662 — 1722

Index

Bound in 1 t'ao   10 chuan   4 ts'e

Remarks Some missing pages

The University of Toronto Chinese Library

. . . .

Accession No. 2622   Index No. 162-i↓jc

Title   遂平縣志. Sui Ping Hsien Chih

Classification B-194

Subject

References

                          Revised ed. by
Author 清 金忠濟等重修, Ching, Chin Chung Chi and others (revised)

Edition 官板 乾隆三十四年刊 official ed.
Dated — Chien-Lung "Chi-Mao" 24/1759

Index

Bound in 1 táo 16 Chuan 4 tsʻü

Remarks Mistake in binding

The University of Toronto Chinese Library

. . . .

Accession No. 2623   Index No. 085-djc

Title 汲縣志. Chi Hsien Chih

Classification B-194

Subject

References

Author 清 徐汝瓚等纂修 Compiled and ed. by Ch'ing, Hsü Ju-Tsan and others

Edition 官板 乾隆二十年刊 Official ed.
Dated — Chien-Lung "I-Hai" 20/1755

Index

Bound in 1 t'ao   14 chuan   6 ts'è

Remarks

The University of Toronto Chinese Library

· ·

Accession No. 2624   Index No. 069-ijjc

Title 新鄉縣志. *Hsin Hsiang Hsien Chih*

Classification B-194

Subject

References

Author 清 趙開元等重修, *Revised ed. by Ching, Chao Kai-Yuan and others (revised)*

Edition 官板 乾隆年刊 *official ed.*
Dated — Chien-Lung period 1736—1795

Index

Bound in 1 t'ao 34 Chuan 6 ts'e

Remarks

Accession No. 2625   Index No. 094-nkjc

Title 獲嘉縣志 Huo Chia Hsien Chih

Classification B-194

Subject

References

Author 清 吳喬齡等重修 Revised ed. by Ching, Wu Chiao-Ling and others (revised)

Edition 官板 乾隆二十一年刊 official ed.
Dated — Chien-Lung "Ping-Tzǔ" 21/1756

Index

Bound in 1 t'ao   16 Chuan   6 tsě

Remarks

Accession No. 2626   Index No. 085. kjc

Title   淇縣志. Chi Hsien Chih

Classification   B-194

Subject

References

Author   清 王南國 白龍躍等纂修 Compiled & edited by ∧ Ching, Wong Nan-Kuo and Pai Lung-Yao

Edition 官版   順治庚子年七年刊 official ed.
        Dated —— Shun-Chih "Kēng-Tsǔ" 17/1660

Index

Bound in   1 t'ao   10 Chuan   5 ts'ê

Remarks

Accession No. 2627   Index No. 159-と-jｃ

Title 輝縣志. Hui Hsien Chih

Classification B-194

Subject

References

Author 清 桂良 周際華等重修 Revised ed. by Ching, Chou Kui Liang and Chou Chi-Hua (revised)

Edition 百泉書院藏板 道光十五年重刊
Block preserved in Po Chuan Shih shu yuan. 光緒十四年補訂

Date — Tao-Kuang "I-Wei" 15/1835 re-published
Index   Kuang-Hsü "Wu-Tzü" 14/1880

Bound in 1 t'ao   20 Chuan   8 ts'ě

Remarks

Accession No. 2628   Index No. 105-g88c

Title 登封縣志. *Têng fêng Hsien Chih.*

Classification B-194

Subject

References

Author 清、洪亮吉 陸繼萼等纂   *Compiled by* *Ch'ing, Hung Liang-Chi and Lu Chi-O*

Edition 官板   乾隆壬子年刊 *official ed.*
Dated — Ch'ien-Lung "Ting-Chou" 22/1757

Index

Bound in 2 *t'ao*   32 *Chuan*

Remarks

164

The University of Toronto Chinese Library

. . . .

Accession No. 2629   Index No. 085-2bjc

Title 河内縣志. Ho Nei Hsien Chih

Classification B-194

Subject

References

Author 清 程祖洛 袁通等重修 Revised by Ching, Chêng Tsu-Lo and Yüan Tung (revised)

Edition 官板 道光五年刊 (Official ed.
Dated — Tao-Kuang⁵-Yn " 5/ 1825

Index

Bound in 2 t'ao   36 Chuan   10. t'sʽ

Remarks

165

The University of Toronto Chinese Library

. . . .

Accession No. 2630   Index No. 009-ᴸᵈʲᶜ

Title 修武縣志 Hsia Wu Hsien Chih

Classification B-194

Subject

References

Author 清 馮繼照等修 *edited by* ching. fêng Chi-chao and other

Edition 官板 道光十九年刊 official ed.
Dated — Tao-Kuang "Chi-Hai" 19/1839

Index

Bound in 1 t'ao   12 Chuan   12 tsʻê

Remarks

The University of Toronto Chinese Library

. . . .

Accession No. 2631   Index No. 077-d 武涉jc

Title 武涉縣志. Wu Shê Hsien Chih

Classification B-194

Subject

References

Author 清 王榮陞等修 edited by ^ Ch'ing, Wang Jung-Pi and others

Edition 官板 道光己丑年刊 Official ed.
Dated — Tao-Kuang "Chi-chóu" 9/1829

Index

Bound in 2 t'ao 60 Chuan (續志. 24 Chuan) 14 ts'ê

Remarks

Accession No. 2632   Index No. 085-ijc

Title 溫縣志. Wên Hsien Chih

Classification B-194

Subject

References

Author 清 王其華等纂修。 *Compiled & edited by* Ching, Wang Chi-Hua and others

Edition 官板 乾隆艺卬年刊 *official ed.*
         Dated — Chien-Lung "chi-Mao" 24/1759

Index

Bound in 1 t'ao 12 Chuan 4 ts'ê

Remarks

The University of Toronto Chinese Library

. . . .

Accession No. 2633   Index No. 085-ngjc

Title 濟源縣志, chi Yüan Hsien Chih

Classification B-194

Subject

References

Author 清 蕭應植等纂修 Compiled & edited by Ching. Hsiao Ying. Chih and other

Edition 官板 乾隆葉菫年刊 official ed.
Dated — Chien-Lung "Hsin-Ssu" 26/1061

Index

Bound in 2 t'ao 16 Chuan, 續志 12 Chuan

Remarks

The University of Toronto Chinese Library

· ·

Accession No. 2635   Index No. 046-98ᶜ

Title 嵩縣志. Sung Hsien Chih

Classification B-194

Subject

References

Author 清 康基淵等纂修. Compiled & edited by Ching, Kang Chi-yüan and others

Edition 官板 乾隆三十二年刊 official ed.
Dated — Chien-Lung "Ting-Hai" 32/1767

Index

Bound in 1 tao   30 Chuan   4 ts'è

Remarks

The University of Toronto Chinese Library

· ·

Accession No. 2636   Index No. 027-2 djc

Title 原武縣志, Yüan Wu Hsien Chih

Classification B-194

Subject

References

Author 清 茱瑋 吳文炘等纂修, Ching, Chai Chai Wei and Wu Wên-Hsin *Compiled & edited by*

Edition 官板 乾隆十二年刊 Official ed.
Dated — Chien-Lung "Ting-Mao" 12/1747)

Index

Bound in 1 t'ao   10 Chuan   5 ts'ê

Remarks

Accession No. 2637   Index No. 170-idjc

Title 陽武縣志. *Yang Wu Hsien Chih*

Classification B-194

Subject

References

Author 清 談諟礐等纂修. *Ching, Tán Fú-Tsêng and others*
Compiled & edited by Shih

Edition 縣署藏板 乾隆九年增修 *Local government ed.*
Blck Preserved in
Dated — *Chien-Lung "Chiǔ-Ngū" 9/1744*

Index

Bound in 1 *t'ao* 12 *Chuan* 8 *ts'è*

Remarks

The University of Toronto Chinese Library

．．．．．．．．．．．．．．．．．．．．．．．．．

Accession No. 2638   Index No. 085-Lijc

Title   淮陽縣志. Huai Yang Hsien Chih

Classification B-194

Subject

References

                              Revised ed. by
Author 民國 嚴緒釣等重修, Republic, Yen Hsü-Tiao

Edition 民國五年重刊 Re-printed edition
        Dated — Ming-Kuo 5/1916

Index

Bound in 2 t'ao   20 Chuan   13 ts'ē

Remarks

. . . .

Accession No. 2639   Index No. 030-kzjᶜ

Title 商水縣志, Shang Shui Hsien Chih

Classification B-194

Subject

References

Author 民國 楊凌閣等續修, Amended ed. by Republic, Yang Ling-Ko and others (revised)

Edition 民國七年刊
Dated — Ming-Kuo 7/1918

Index

Bound in 2 t'áo. 25 Chuan 10 t₅'è

Remarks

The University of Toronto Chinese Library

. . . .

Accession No. 2640   Index No. 146-ghjc

Title 西華縣志 Hsi Hua Hsien Chih

Classification B-194

Subject

References

Author 清 宋炯等纂修 *Compiled & edited by* Ch'ing, Sung Hsün and others

Edition 官板 乾隆年刊 Official ed.
Dated — Chien-Lung period 1736—1795

Index

Bound in 1 t'ao   14 Chüan   6 ts'ê

Remarks

Accession No. 2641   Index No. 085-dejc

Title 沈邱縣志, shên chiu Hsien chih

Classification B-194

Subject

References

Author 清 崔應階 何源洙等續修 ~~amended~~ Amended ed. by Ching, Tsui Ying-Chieh and Ho Yüan-chu (revised)

Edition 官板 乾隆丙寅刊 official ed
Dated — Chien-Lung "Ping-ying" 11/1746

Index

Bound in 1 t'ao   12 Chuan   4 ts'ê

Remarks

The University of Toronto Chinese Library

． ．

Accession No. 2642   Index No. 064-djjc

Title 抚溝縣志 Fu Kou Hsien Chih

Classification B-194

Subject

References

Author 清 熊燦等纂修 Compiled or edited by Ch'ing, Hsüng Tsan and others.

Edition 大程書館藏板 光緒十九年刊 plak preserved in
石 — Ch'ēng-Shu-Kuang private
Dated — Kuang-Hsü "Kuei-Chi" 19 / 1893

Index

Bound in 1 t'ao   16 Chuan   6 ts'ě

Remarks

177

The University of Toronto Chinese Library

....

Accession No. 2643   Index No. 149-dcc

Title   許州志 Hsü Chou Chih

Classification B-194

Subject

References

Author 清 蕭元吉等纂修 Compiled & edited by ^Ch'ing, Hsiao Yüan-Chi and others

Edition 官板 光緒 道光戊戌年刊 official ed.
Dated — Tao-Kuang "Wu-Hsü" 18/1838

Index

Bound in 2 t'ao 16 Chuan 10 ts'è

Remarks

178

The University of Toronto Chinese Library

. . . .

Accession No. 2644   Index No. 131- 志 jc

Title 臨潁縣志 Lin Ying Hsien Chih

Classification B-194

Subject

References

                              Compiled & edited by
Author 清 吳中奇等纂修 Ching. Wu Chung-Chi and other

Edition 官板   順治年刊 official ed.
        Dated — Shun-Chih period 1644—1661

Index

Bound in 1 t'ao 8 chuan 6 ts'ê

Remarks Printing is not clear

179

The University of Toronto Chinese Library

. . . .

Accession No. 2645   Index No. 168-ji jc

Title 長葛縣志 *Cháng Kó Hsien Chih*

Classification B-194

Subject

References

Author 清沉景威葺重修 *Revised ed. by Ching. Juan Ching-Hsien and others (revised)*

Edition 官板 乾隆十三年刊 *official ed.*
Dated — *Chien-Lung "Ting-1790" 12/1747*

Index

Bound in 1 *t'ao* 10. *Chuan* 4 *ts'è*

Remarks

180

The University of Toronto Chinese Library

....

Accession No. 2646   Index No. 163-i ɣ jc

Title 鄢城縣志 Yen chêng Hsien chih

Classification B-194

Subject

References

Author 清 傅豫等重修 Revised ed. by ching. Fu Yü and others (revised),

Edition 官板   乾隆十九年刊 official ed.
         Dated — "Ch'ien-Lung Chih - Hsü" 19/1054

Index

Bound in 1 t'ao   18 Chuan   6 ts'ê

Remarks

The University of Toronto Chinese Library

. . . .

Accession No. 2647   Index No. 040·fk jc

Title 寶豐縣志. Pao fêng Hsien Chih

Classification B-194

Subject

References

                              Compiled or edited by
Author 清 李佐梧 楊兆李莘纂修, Chíng, Li Fang-Wu and Yang Chao-Li

Edition 官板　道光十七年刊 official ed.
Dated — Tao-Kuang "Ting-Yu" 17/1837

Index

Bound in 1 táo 16 Chuan 6 tśě

Remarks

The University of Toronto Chinese Library

. . . .

Accession No. 2648   Index No. 040·ɣkjc

Title 寶豐縣志. *Pao fêng Hsien chih*

Classification B-194

Subject

References

Author 清 李傍棨 楊兆熒等纂修 *Compiled & edited by* *Ch'ing, Li Fang-Wu and Yang Chao-Li*

Edition

Index

Bound in 1 t'ao 16 Chuan

Remarks This seems to be a more recent edition than the previous one, judging from its appearance, although the date of printing was not given.

The University of Toronto Chinese Library

. . . .

Accession No. 2648 2649   Index No. 195-dzzc

Title 魯山縣志, Lu Shan Hsien Chih

Classification B-194

Subject

References

Author 清 董作棟等重修, *Revised ed. by* Ch'ing, Tung Tso-Tung and other (revised)

Edition 官板 嘉慶年刊 Official ed.
Dated — Chia-Ching period 1796 — 1820

Index

Bound in 1 t'ao 26 Chüan 6 ts'é

Remarks

The University of Toronto Chinese Library

. . . .

Accession No. 2649 2650   Index No. 170-9cc

Title 陝州志, Shan Chou Chih

Classification B-194

Subject

References

Author 清 趙希曾等重修, Revised ed. by Ching, Chao Hsi-Tsêng and others (revised)

Edition 官板   光緒十七年刊 official ed.
Dated — Kuang-Hsü "Hsin-Mao" 17/1891

Index

Bound in 1 t'ao 15 Chuan 12 ts'ê

Remarks

185

The University of Toronto Chinese Library

· ·

Accession No. 2651   Index No. 009·dijc

Title 伊 陽 縣 志 I Yang Hsien Chih

Classification B-194

Subject

References

Author 清 張道超等重修 Revised ed. by Ching. Chang Tao-Cháo and others (revised)

Edition 官板 道光未酉年 official ed.
Dated — Tao-Kuang "Wu-Hsü" 18/1838

Index

Bound in 1 táo   6 chuan   6 tsè

Remarks

Accession No. 2652   Index No. 169-hjjc

Title 閿鄉縣志. Wên Hsiang Hsien Chih

Classification B-194

Subject

References

Author 清 沈守廉 劉思恕等纂修 Compiled & ed. by Ch'ing, Shên Shou-Lien and Liu Ssŭ-Shu

Edition 官版 光緒二十年刊 official ed.
Dated — Kuang-Hsü "Kêng-Tzŭ" 20/1840

Index

Bound in 1 t'ao 12 Chuan 8 ts'ê

Remarks

The University of Toronto Chinese Library

. . . .

Accession No. 2653   Index No. 108-Lzjc

Title 盧氏縣志 Lu Shih Hsien Chih

Classification B-194

Subject

References

Author 清 郭光澍等重修 *Revised edition by* Ching, Kao Kuang-Chu and other (~~serial~~)

Edition 莘原書院藏板 四川楊清珊鐫刻 印刷 *Block preserved in* Hsin-Yuan-Shu-Yuan ~~private-printed.~~
光緒己亥年刊 Ssu-Chuan, Yang Ching-Shan
Dated — Kuang-Hsü "Chi-Hai" 18/1839

Index

Bound in 2 t'ao   18 Chuan   10 ts'e

Remarks

188

The University of Toronto Chinese Library

. . . .

Accession No. 2654   Index No. 010-dggc

Title 光山縣志。 Kuang Shan Hsien Chih

Classification B-194

Subject

References

Author 清 楊殿梓等纂修。 *Compiled & edited by* Ch'ing. Yang Tien-Tgǔ and others

Edition 自縣衙藏板 乾隆五十年刊 光緒年補刊 *Block preserved in Local government 土.*

Dated — Ch'ien-kung "l-Ssǔ" 50/1785 published Kuang-Hsü period 1825-1908 aud (Re-engraved)

Index

Bound in 3 t'ao 32 Chuan 12 ts'e

Remarks

The University of Toronto Chinese Library

. . . .

Accession No. 2655   Index No. 031-223c

Title 固始縣志 Ku Shih Hsien Chih

Classification B-194

Subject

References

Author 清 謝聘莘重修 *Revised ed. by* Ching, Hsieh Pin and others (revised)

Edition 官版 乾隆五十一年刊 official ed.
Dated — Chien-Lung "Ping-Wu" 51/1986

Index

Bound in 2 t'ao 26 Chuan 15 ts'i

Remarks Some missing pages. The table of content is not complete.

Accession No. 2656   Index No. 061-7jc

Title   息縣志、 Hsi Hsien Chih

Classification B-194

Subject

References

Author 清 劉光輝等重修, Revised ed. by Ching, Liu Kuang-Hui and others (seased)

Edition 官版 嘉慶己卯刊 Official ed.
Dated — Chia-Ching "Chi-Wei" 4/1789

Index

Bound in 1 t'ao 8 chuan 8 ts'o

Remarks

Accession No. 2657   Index No. 140-Lcec

Title 萊州府志, *Lai Chou Fu Chih*

Classification B194

Subject

References

Author 清 嚴有禧 張桐事重修 *Revised ed. by Ching, Yen Yu-Hsi and Chang Tung (revised)*

Edition 官版 乾隆庚申刊 *official ed.*
Dated — Chien-Lung "Keng-Shen" 5/1740

Index

Bound in 1 tao

Remarks

The University of Toronto Chinese Library

. . . .

Accession No. 2658   Index No. 010-gcec

Title 兗州府志 Yen Chou Fu Chih

Classification B194

Subject

References

Author 清　陳顧聯等纂修 *Compiled & edited by* Ching, chén Ku-Lien

Edition 官版　乾隆年刊 *official ed.*
Dated —— Chien-Lung period 1736 — 1795

Index

Bound in 1 tao　30 Chuan　12 ts'ê

Remarks

The University of Toronto Chinese Library

....

Accession No. 2659   Index No. 077-1?jc

Title 歷城縣志 *Li Chêng Hsien Chih*

Classification B194

Subject

References

Author 清 沈廷芳 胡德琳等纂修。 Compiled & edited by *Ching. Shên Ting-fang and Hu Tê-Lin*

Edition 官版 乾隆三十七年刊 *Official ed.*
Dated — Chien-Lung "Jên-Chên" 37/1772

Index

Bound in 2 tao 50 Chuan 16 tsê

Remarks *Worm holes in some of the pages*

The University of Toronto Chinese Library

. . . .

Accession No. 2660   Index No. 117-8 e jc

Title 章邱縣志 *Chang Chiu Hsien Chih*

Classification B194

Subject

References

Author 清 桑蟫荃纂修 *Compiled & edited by Ching, Wu Chang and others*

Edition 官版 道光癸巳年刊 *official ed.*
Dated — Tao-Kuang "Kuei-Ssu" 13/1833

Index

Bound in 2 *tao* 16 *chuan* 8 *ts'e*

Remarks

The University of Toronto Chinese Library

· ·

Accession No. 2661   Index No. 163-jbjc

Title 鄒平縣志 Tsou Ping Hsien Chih

Classification B194

Subject

References

Author 清 雒宗瀛等重修 Ching, Lo Tsung-Ying and others (revised)
               Revised ed. by

Edition 官庫藏版 道光十六年刊 Official ed. block preserved edition.
Dated — Tao-Kuang "Ping-Shen" 16/1836

Index

Bound in 1 tao   18 Chuan   8 ts'o

Remarks

Accession No. 2662   Index No. 168-338c

Title 長山縣志 *chang shan Hsien Chih*

Classification B194

Subject

References

Author 清 倪企望等續修 *amended ed. by* *Ching, Ni Chi-Wang and others (revised)*

Edition 官版 嘉慶六年辛酉刊 *official ed.*
Dated — Chia-Ching "Hsin-Yu" 6/1801

Index

Bound in 1 tao 16 Chuan 10 ts'e

Remarks

The University of Toronto Chinese Library

．．．．．．．．．．．．．．．．．．．．．．．．．．．

Accession No. 2663   Index No. 085-nijc

Title 齊陽縣志 Chi Yang Hsien Chih

Classification B194

Subject

References

                                    Compiled & edited by
Author 清 関鶯元 胡德琳等纂修 Ching, Min Ê-yüan and Hu Tê-Lin

Edition 官版 乾隆三十年刊 Official ed.
       Dated — Chien-Lung "I-yu" 30/1765

Index

Bound in 1 tao 14 Chuan 8 ts'ê

Remarks

198

The University of Toronto Chinese Library

. . . .

Accession No. 2664   Index No. 168-3 んうc

Title 長三清縣志 Cháng Chíng Hsien Chih

Classification B194

Subject

References .

Author 清 舒化民 等重修 Revised ed. by Ching, Shu Hua-Min and others (revised)

Edition 官版 道光十五年刊 Official ed.
Dated — Tao-Kuang "1-Wei" 15/1835

Index

Bound in 1 tao

Remarks

The University of Toronto Chinese Library

....

Accession No. 2665   Index No. 060-lcc

Title 德州志, Tê Chou Chih

Classification B194

Subject

References

Author 清 王道亨等重修, Revised ed. by ching. Wang Tao-Hêng and others (~~serinat~~)

Edition 官版 乾隆戊申五十三年刊 Official ed.
Dated — Chien-Lung "Wu-Shen" 53/1788

Index

Bound in 1 tao 12 chuan 8 ts'ê

Remarks

200

The University of Toronto Chinese Library

．．．．．．．．．．．．．．．．．．．．．．．

Accession No. 2666   Index No. 060-ℓ bjc

Title 德平縣志 Tê Ping Hsien Chih

Classification B 194

Subject

References

Author 清 凌錫祺等重修 *Revised ed. by* Ch'ing. Ling Hsi-Chi and others (revised)

Edition 官版 光緒癸巳年刊 Official ed.
Dated — Kuang-Hsü "Kuei-Ssu" 19/1893

Index

Bound in 1 tao 12 chuan 6 ts'ê

Remarks

The University of Toronto Chinese Library
. . . .

Accession No. 2667   Index No. 210-g-eg-c

Title 齊河縣志 Chi Ho Hsien Chih

Classification B094

Subject

References

Author 清 程開業等纂修 Compiled & edited by
                              ᴧ ching, chéng kai-yeh and others

Edition 官版 乾隆元年刊 official ed.
                  丙辰
Dated — Chien-Lung "Ping-Chén" 1/1736

Index

Bound in 1 tao 10 chuan 5 ts'ē

Remarks

The University of Toronto Chinese Library

....

Accession No. 2668   Index No. 051-bとjc

Title 平原縣志 *Ping Yüan Hsien Chih*

Classification B194

Subject

References

Author 清 黃懷祖等重修 *Revised ed. by Ching, Huang Hui-Tsu and others (revised)*

Edition 官版 縣庫藏版 乾隆十五年刊 *Official ed. Local government ed. Block Preserved in*

Dated — Chien-Lung "Kêng-Wu" 15/1750

Index

Bound in 1 tao   10 Chuan   4 ts'ê

Remarks

The University of Toronto Chinese Library
....

Accession No. 2669   Index No. 085-injc

Title 滋陽縣志 Tzǔ Yang Hsien Chih

Classification B.194

Subject

References

Author 清 伊勒通阿 李兆霖等續修 Amended ed. by Ching, I Lo-Tung and Li Chao-Lin (revised)

Edition 尊經閣藏板 光緒戊子四年刊 Block Preserved in Tsun-Ching-Ko private-printed
Dated—Kwang-Hsü "Wu-Tzǔ" 14/1888

Index

Bound in 1 tao   14 Chuan   10 ts's

Remarks

The University of Toronto Chinese Library

. . . .

Accession No. 2670   Index No. 073-bzjc

Title 曲阜縣志, Chü Fu Hsien Chih

Classification B194

Subject

References

Author 清 潘相菁新修 Ching, Pán Hsiang and others (new revised)

Edition 聖化堂藏板 乾隆卅九年刊 block preserved in Shen-Hua-Tang private printed
Dated — Ch'ien-Lung "Chia-Wu" 39/1774

Index

Bound in 2 tao 100 Chuan 12 tsê

Remarks

205

Accession No. 2671   Index No. 040-kioc

Title 寧陽續志 *Ning Yang Hsü Chih*

Classification B194

Subject

References

Author 清 高陞榮華續修 *Amended ed. by Ching, Kao Shêng Jung and others (revised)*

Edition 官衙藏板 光緒五年增刊 block preserved in Official ed.
Dated — Kuang-Hsü "Chi-Mao" 5/1879

Index

Bound in 2 tao   24 chuan   12 tsê

Remarks

The University of Toronto Chinese Library

....

Accession No. 2672   Index No. 163-gg c

Title 鄒縣志,又續志   Tsou Hsien Chih
                                          Yu Hsü Chih

Classification B192

Subject

References

                                    Revised ed. by
                                    Ching, Lou I-Chün and others
Author 清 婁一均等重修   續志 吳若灝等修   (revised) ed.
       康熙五十四年重修   光緒十八年修   "Hsü Chih" was revised by Wu
                                                           Jo-Hao
Edition 官板 邑廨藏板   光緒十八年刊 official ed.

Dated — Kǒng-Hsi "Chiǒ-Wu" 54/1714
        Kuang-Hsü "Jên-Ch'ên" 18/1892

Index

Bound in 1 tao   正志 3 Chuan 4 ts'ě   Total 8 ts'ě
Remarks   續志 12 chuan 4 ts'ě

The University of Toronto Chinese Library

. . . .

Accession No. 2673   Index No. 075·jcjc

Title 榮成縣志 Jung Chêng Hsien Chih

Classification B194

Subject

References

Author 清 李天騭等重修 Revised Ching, Li Tien-Chih and others (~~uunit~~)

Edition 官板 道光年刊 Official ed.
Dated — Tao-Kuang period 1821—1850

Index

Bound in 1 tao   10 Chuan   4 t,'è

Remarks

The University of Toronto Chinese Library

. . . .

Accession No. 2674   Index No. 085-jjc

Title 滕縣志, Têng Hsien Chih

Classification B194

Subject

References

Author 清 王政等重修 Revised edition by Ch'ing, Wang Chêng and others (revised)

Edition 官板 道光二十六年年刊 Official ed.
Dated — Tao-Kuang "Ping-Wu" 26/1846

Index

Bound in 1 tao   14 Chuan   8 tsê

Remarks

Accession No. 2675   Index No. 085-dbjc

Title 三文上縣志 Wên ß Shang Hsien Chih

Classification B194

Subject

References

Author 舊志明 粟可仕創修（萬曆三年） 續志清 聞元景修（康熙五十六年）
"Chiu Chih" ming was revised by Ming, Su Kó-Shih. "Hsü Chih" revised by Ching, Wên Yüan-Kuei

Edition 官板 康熙五十六年刻 official ed.
Dated — Kang-Hsi "Jing-gu" 56/1717

Index

Bound in 1 tao   舊志 8 Chuan 2 tsé   total 4 tsé
                  續志 6 Chuan 2 tsé

Remarks

Accession No. 2676   Index No. 085-ecjc

Title 泰安縣志 Tai An Hsien chih.

Classification B 194

Subject

References

Author 清黃鈐等新修 new revised by Ching, Huang Ling
+ others.

Edition 官板 official edition.

乾隆壬寅年刊 Block-engraving in Ch'ien Lung "Jên-
Ying" period.

Index
                                          1736-1795

Bound in 1 tao 12 chuan 14 tsê.

Remarks
.

The University of Toronto Chinese Library
....

Accession No. 2677   Index No. 075-dbcc

Title 東平州志. Tung Ping Chou Chih

Classification B194

Subject

References

Author 清 楊惠元 周雲鳳等重修 Revised ed. by Ching, Yang Huei-Yüan and Chou Yün-Fêng (revised)

Edition 官板 道光乙酉五年刊 official ed.
Dated — Tao-Kuang "I-Yu" 5/1825

Index

Bound in 1 tao 30 chüan 16 tsê

Remarks

The University of Toronto Chinese Library

. . . .

Accession No. 2678   Index No. 075.dbcc

Title 東平州志, *Tung Ping Chou Chih*

Classification B194

Subject

References

Author 清 楊惠元 周雲鳳等重修 ^Revised ed. by^ *Ching, Yang Hui-Yüan, and Chou Yün fêng*

Edition 州署藏板 道光五年刊 ^Block preserved in^ *Local government et.*

Date—*Tao-Kuang* "乙酉" 5/1825

Index

Bound in 1 tao   30 Chuan   16 ts'ê

Remarks

Accession No. 2679   Index No. 075-dejc

Title 東阿縣志、 Tung #A Hsien Chih

Classification B194

Subject

References

Author 清 楊惠元 李賢書等重修 *Revised ed. by* Ching, Yang Hui-Yüan and Li Hsien-Shu *(revised)*

Edition 官板 道光九年刊 official ed.
Dated — Tao-Kuang "Chi-Chóu" 9/1829

Index

Bound in 1 tao   24 Chüan   12 tsê

Remarks

The University of Toronto Chinese Library

. . . .

Accession No. 2680   Index No. 051-bzjc

Title 平陰縣志續刻 *Ping Yin Hsien Chih Hsü Kó*

Classification B194

Subject

References

Author 清 趙有燦補輯 日張撰著作碑記詩歌等一卷
De-compiled by King, Chao Yu-Ti

Edition 官板 道光廿八年刊 official ed.
Dated — Tao-Kuang "Wu-Shen" 28/1848

Index

Bound in 1 tao   1 chuan   1 tsè

Remarks

The University of Toronto Chinese Library

· ·

Accession No. 2681   Index No. 032-kggc

Title 堂邑縣志 *Táng I Hsien Chih*

Classification B194

Subject

References

Author 清 盧承琰等修 (康熙四十九年)   趙時熙等重刻 (道光)
                                    Re-engraved ed. by
edited by Chʻing, Lu Chʻêng-Yen and others   Chao Fang-Hsi and others (second)
                                    block-preserved in
Edition 崔城書院藏板 光緒年重刻. Chʻiao-Chʻêng-Shu-Yuan privately printed

Dated — Kuang-Hsü period 1875 — 1908

Index

Bound in 1 tao   20 Chuan   3 tsʻê

Remarks

The University of Toronto Chinese Library

. . . .

Accession No. 2682   Index No. 040-e.h.jc

Title 定陶縣志 *Ting Tao Hsien Chih*

Classification B194

Subject

References

Author 清 劉藻等續修 (乾隆十八年)
Amended ed. by Ching, Liu Tsao and others (several)
Edition 官板 康熙補刻板 光緒三年刊 official ed.
Dated — Kwang Hsü "Ping-Tzu" 2/1876

Index

Bound in 1 tao 10 Chuan 4 ts'e

Remarks

The University of Toronto Chinese Library

. . . .

Accession No. 2683   Index No. 024-jbjc

Title 博平縣志, Po Ping Hsien Chih

Classification D194

Subject

References

Author 清 楊祖憲等重修, Revised ed. by Ching, Yang Tsu-Hsien and others (revised)

Edition 縣庫存板 道光十一年刊, old block preserved in Local government ed.
Dated — "Tao-Kuang Hsin-Mao" 11/1831

Index

Bound in 1 tao   6 Chuan   6 ts'e

Remarks

The University of Toronto Chinese Library

. . . .

Accession No. 2684   Index No. 061- Lajc

Title 惠民縣志, (補正) Hui Min Hsien Chih (Pu Chêng)

Classification B194

Subject

References

Author 清 沈世銓等重修　柳堂補正重校
Revised ed. by Ching, Shên Shih-Chüan and others (revised) Liu Tang re(vised),

Edition 官板　光緒二十五年刊 official ed. amended & recollated edition.
Dated — Kuang-Hsü "Chi-Hai" 25/1899

Index

Bound in 1 tao　30 Chuan　7 ts'é

Remarks

The University of Toronto Chinese Library

· ·

Accession No. 2685   Index No. 167- e d j c

Title 鉅野縣志, Chü Yeh Hsien Chih

Classification B194

Subject

References

Author 清 黃維翰 袁傳裘等續修。 *Amended ed. by* Ch'ing, Huang Wei-Han and Yüan Chüan- Chiu (revised)

Edition 官板 道光庚寅年刊 official ed. Dated — Tao-Kuang "Kēng-Yü" 20/1840

Index

Bound in 2 tao   24 Chüan   16 ts'ê

Remarks

The University of Toronto Chinese Library

· ·

Accession No. 2686   Index No. 108-اذ ابعة

Title 益都縣志 ∧ I Tu Hsien Chih

Classification B 194

Subject

References

Author 清 陳食蒸纂修 楊浩助修 ∧ Compiled & edited by Ching, Chén Shih, and Yang Hao-chü yüan

Edition 官版 康熙年三年刊 official ed.
Dated — Kʻang-Hsi "Jên-Tʐŭ" 11/1672

Index

Bound in 1 tao   14 Chuan 6 tsʻê

Remarks The name of the editor is not clear due to poor printing

221

The University of Toronto Chinese Library

. . . .

Accession No. 2687   Index No. 075-Kcjc

Title 樂安縣志, Lo An Hsien Chih

Classification B194

Subject

References

Author 清 李方馨等重修。 Revised ed. by Ch'ing, Li Fang-Ying and others (revised)

Edition 官板 雍正十一年刊 Official ed.
Dated — Yung-Chêng "Kuei-Yu" 11/1733

Index

Bound in 1 tao 20 Chuan 4 ts'e

Remarks

Accession No. 2688   Index No. 149-i 8/c

Title 諸城縣志 Chu Chêng Hsien Chih

Classification B 194

Subject

References

Author 清 官懋讓等重修 Revised ed. by Ch'ing, Kuang Ma-jang and other (revised)

Edition 官板 official ed.

Index

Bound in 1 tao   46 Chuan   8 tsê

Remarks

Accession No. 2689   Index No. 012-dzjc

Title 昌樂縣志, Chang Lo Hsien Chih

Classification B 194

Subject

References

Author 清 魏禮焯 倪鏐 時銘等重修 Revised ed. by Ching, Wei Li Ch'o, I Huang and Shih Ming.

Edition 縣衙藏板 嘉慶己巳年刊 Block-preserved in Local government ed.
Dated — Chia-Ching "Chi-Ssŭ" 14/1809

Index

Bound in 1 tao 32 Chuan 6 ts'ê

Remarks

224

The University of Toronto Chinese Library

· ·

Accession No. 2690   Index No. 131-zzjc

Title 臨邑縣志 Lin I Hsien Chih

Classification B194

Subject

References

Author 清 沈淮葦重修 Revised ed. by Ch'ing, Shên and others (revised) Huai

Edition 縣街藏板 道光十七年刊 Block preserved in Local government ed. 正

Dated — Tao-Kuang "Ting-Yu" 17/1837

Index

Bound in 1 tao 16 Chuan 8 tiä

Remarks

The University of Toronto Chinese Library

· ·

Accession No. 2691   Index No. 131. 乚ㄜjㄷ

Title 臨朐縣志 Lin Chü Hsien Chih

Classification B 194

Subject

References

Author 清 姚延福等纂修 Compiled & edited by Ching, Yao Yen-Fu and others

Edition 官板 光緒十年刊 official ed.
Dated — Kuang-Hsü "Chia-Shen" 10/1884

Index

Bound in 1 tao 16 Chuan 6 tsê

Remarks

226

The University of Toronto Chinese Library

. . . .

Accession No. 2692   Index No. 170-iggc

Title 陽信縣志 Yang Hsin Hsien Chih

Classification B194

Subject

References

Author 清 王允深 李通甫等重修 Revised ed. by Ch'ing, Wang Yün-Shên and Chi Tung Pu [...]

Edition 官板 乾隆二十四年刊 Official ed.
Dated — Chien-Lung "Chi-Mao" 24/1759

Index

Bound in 1 tao   8 Chuan   5 ts'ê

Remarks Some mistakes in binding

The University of Toronto Chinese Library

. . . .

Accession No. 2693   Index No. 085.ncc

Title 濱州志 Pin Chou Chih

Classification B194

Subject

References

Author 清 李熙齡重修 Ching, Li Hsi-Ling (revised) — Revised ed. by

Edition 官板 咸豐十年刊 Official ed.
Dated — Hsien-Feng "Keng-Shen" 10/1860

Index

Bound in 1 tao 12 Chuan 4 ts'ŭ

Remarks

The University of Toronto Chinese Library

. . . .

Accession No. 2694   Index No. 072·dzjc

Title 昌邑縣志, *Cháng I Hsien Chih*

Classification B194

Subject

References

Author 清 周來邰重修 *Revised ed. by ching, Chou Lai-Tai (revised)*

Edition 官板 乾隆七年紙 *official ed.*
Dated — Chien-Lung "Jên-Hsü" 7/1742

Index

Bound in 1 tao 4 ts'ǎ

Remarks

The University of Toronto Chinese Library

· ·

Accession No. R695   Index No. 085-gkjc

Title 海豐縣志, Hai Fêng Hsien Chih

Classification B194

Subject

References

Author 清 胡公著等纂修, Compiled & edited by Ch'ing, Hu Kung-Chu and others

Edition 康熙年刊
Dated — K'ang-Hsi period 1662 — 1722

Index

Bound in 1 tao 12 Chuan 4 ts'ê

Remarks

The University of Toronto Chinese Library

. . . .

Accession No. 2696   Index No. 075- 九 九 夕 ＜

Title 樂陵縣志 Lo Ling Hsien chih

Classification B 194

Subject

References

Author 清 王謙益等重修 Revised ed. by ching, Wang ﹟ Chien-I and others (revised)

Edition 乾隆二十七年刊
Dated — Chien-Lung "Jen-Wu" 27/1762

Index

Bound in 1 tao   8 chuan   8 ts'e?

Remarks

The University of Toronto Chinese Library

. . . .

Accession No. 2697   Index No. 030-한지 c

Title 商河縣志 Shang Ho Hsien Chih

Classification B 194

Subject

References

Author 清 龔廷煌 王元濤 張楷纂修 Compiled & edited by Ching, Kung Ting-Huang, Wang Yüan-Tao and Chang Kai

Edition 道光乙未年刊 Dated — Tao-Kuang "I-Wei" 15/1835

Index

Bound in 1 t'ao   8 Chuan   8 ts'e

Remarks

The University of Toronto Chinese Library

....

Accession No. 2698   Index No. 018-23jc

Title 利津縣志 Li Chin Hsien Chih

Classification B194

Subject

References

Revised ed. by

Author 清 盛贊熙 等重修 Ching, Shêng Tsan-Hsi and others (revised)

Edition 光緒癸未年刊

Dated — Kuang-Hsü "Kuei-Wei" 9/1883

Index

Bound in 1 tao 10 Chuan 4 tsê

Remarks

233

The University of Toronto Chinese Library

· ·

Accession No. 2699   Index No. 173-hbjc

Title 靈化縣志 Chan Hua Hsien Chih

Classification B194

Subject

References

Author 清 聯印等重修 *Revised ed. by* Ching, Lien Yin and others (*revised*)

Edition 書院存板 光緒十七年刊 Shu-Yuen *preserved* edition
Dated — Kuang-Hsü "Hsin-Mao" 17/1891

Index

Bound in 1 套 16 Chuan 4 ts'ǔ

Remarks

The University of Toronto Chinese Library

....

Accession No. 2700   Index No. 085-dcc

Title 沂州志, H̶s̶i̶ Chou Chih

Classification B194

Subject

References

Author 清 邵士䇹奉勅修 received Commands to revise by Ching, & Shao Shih and others

Edition 康熙甲寅年刋 Dated — Kǎng-Hsi "Chia-Ying" 13/1684

Index

Bound in 1 tao 8 Chuan 8 Ts'è

Remarks

Accession No. 2701   Index No. 154-2jc

Title 費縣志 Fei Hsien Chih

Classification B194

Subject

References   Compiled ed. by

Author 清 黃學塾等纂修 ↖ Ch'ing, Huang Hsüeh-Chin and others

Edition 康熙三十八年刊
Dated — Kang-Hsi "Chi-Ssü" 28/1689

Index

Bound in 1 tao. 10 Chuan 4 ts'a

Remarks

Accession No. 2702   Index No. 140-khjc

Title 蓬萊縣志 *Pêng Lai Hsien Chih*

Classification B194

Subject

References

Author 清 王文燾重修 *Revised* ~~Amended~~ ed. by *Ching, Wang Wên-Tao (revised)*

Edition 縣署藏板 道光十九年刊 己亥 *Blocks preserved by* *Local government et.* *Dated — Tao-Kuang "Chi-Hai" 19/1839*

Index

Bound in 1 tao   14 Chuan   8 ts'ǎ

Remarks

Accession No. 2703   Index No. 026-gljc

Title 即墨縣志 *Chi Mo Hsien Chih*

Classification B194

Subject

References

Author 清 汪圻 尤淑孝等重修 *Revised ed. by Ching, Wang Chi and Yu Shu-Hsiao*

Edition 乾隆三十九年刊
Dated — Chien-Kung "Chia-Shen" 29/1764

Index

Bound in 1 *tao* 12 *Chuan* 6 *tsê*

Remarks

The University of Toronto Chinese Library

· ·

Accession No. 2704   Index No. 085-9 kcc

Title 濟寧州志. Chi Ning Chou Chih

Classification B.194

Subject

References

Author 清 藍應桂 胡德琳等重修 Ch'ing, Lan Ying-Kuei and Hu Tê-Lin (revised)

Edition 乾隆四十三年刊
Dated — Chien-Kung "Wu-Hsü" 43/1778

Index

Bound in 2 tao 34 Chuan 20 ts'ê

Remarks

239

Accession No. 2705   Index No. 167-308ᶜ

Title 金鄉縣志, Chin Hsiang Hsien Chih

Classification B194

Subject

References

                                    compiled ed. by
Author 清 宗稷辰 盧朝鳌等纂修 ᴧ Ching, Tsun Chi-Chên and Lu Chāo-An

Edition 同治元年刊   "Jên-Hsü"
       Dated — Tung-Chih 元 1/1862

Index

Bound in 1 tao   12 Chuan   4 tsʻe

Remarks

The University of Toronto Chinese Library

....

Accession No. 2706   Index No. 169-dcc

Title 開州志, Kái Chou Chih

Classification B194

Subject

References

Author 清　沈樂善等重修 (Ching, Shên Lo-Shan and others (revised)) Revised by

Edition 州署藏板　嘉慶十一年刊 Blocks preserved in Local government ed.
Dated ── Chia-Ching "Ping-Yin" 11/1806

Index

Bound in 1 tao　8 chuan　6 ts'ê

Remarks

The University of Toronto Chinese Library

. . . .

Accession No. 2707   Index No. 040-ecc

Title 定州志 Ting Chou Chih

Classification B194

Subject

References

Author 清 訥爾經額等重修 Revised by Ching. No.-Erh-Ching-O and others (revised)

Edition 道光卅年刊 庚戌
Dated — Tao-Kuang "Kêng-Hsü" 30/1850
1849

Index

Bound in 2 套 函 22 Chüan 12 tsè

Remarks

242

The University of Toronto Chinese Library

. . . .

Accession No. 2708   Index No. 163·2 l j c

Title 邯鄲縣志 Shan Tan Hsien Chih

Classification B194

Subject

References

Author 清 王炯等重修 *Revised by* Ching. Wang & Chiung and others (revised)

Edition 乾隆二十年刊 乙亥
Dated — Chien-Lung "I-Hai" 22/1755

Index

Bound in 1 tao   12 Chuan   6 ts'ê

Remarks

Accession No. 2709   Index No. 005-jiev

Title 乾隆府廳州縣圖志 Chien Lung Fu Ting Chou Hsien Tu Chih

Classification B187

Subject

References

Author 清 洪亮吉撰 Written by Ching, Hung Liang-Chi

Edition 乾隆五十三年刊起嘉慶八年工竣 Block print edition Shou-Ching-Tang ed.
光緒五年重刊 授經堂刊板

Dated — Started in Chien-Kung "Wu-Shen" 53/1788

Index   Finished in Chia-Ching "Kuei-Hai" 8/1813
Reprinted edition
— Re-printed in Kuang-Hsü "Chi-Mao" 5/1879

Bound in 2 tao   50 Chuan   20 ts'e

Remarks

244

The University of Toronto Chinese Library

· ·

Accession No. 2710   Index No. 085-gjic

Title 海塘新志、 Hai Tang Hsin Chih

Classification B194

Subject

References

Author 清 琅玕等奉敕纂 Compiled by Ching, Lang Kan and others

Edition 乾隆年刊 Block-engraving in
~~Dated~~ in Chien-Kung period 1736—1820
                                              1795

Index

Bound in 1 tao   6 Chuan   4 tsʼi

Remarks

The University of Toronto Chinese Library

· ·

Accession No. 2711   Index No. 168-3djc

Title 長沙縣志, Chăng Sha Hsien Chih

Classification B194

Subject

References
                              Amended ed. by
Author 清　劉采邦等續修 (Ching, Liu Tsai-Pang and others (revised)
                          廣年
Edition 同治九年刊 Block-engraving in
Dated Nung-Chi "Kěng-Wu" 9/1870

Index

Bound in 2 tao   36 Chuan 20 tsêi

Remarks

246

Accession No. 2712   Index No. 085-i.h.j.c

Title 湘陰縣志 *Hsiang Yin Hsien Chih*

Classification B194

Subject

References

Author 清 郭嵩燾纂 ∧ *Compiled by* *Ch'ing, Kuo Sung-Tao*

Edition 縣志局板 光緒六年刊 *康辰*
Block engraving in 已 *Kuang-Hsü "Kêng-Ch'ên" 6/1880*

Index

Bound in 2 tao   34 Chuan   14 tsê

Remarks

The University of Toronto Chinese Library

....

Accession No. 2713   Index No. 061-jaja

Title 慈利縣志 Tzŭ Li Hsien Chih

Classification B194

Subject

References

Author 民國 吳恭亨撰 Written by Republic, Wu Kung-Hêng

Edition 悔晦堂叢刻之十 民國十一年再版
→ Hui-Hui-Tâng
Republished in
Dated Ming-Kuo 11/1922

Index

Bound in 1 tao 7a Chuan 2 tsŭ
Remarks 8

The University of Toronto Chinese Library

. . . .

Accession No. 2714   Index No. 005.jcc

Title 乾州志、 *Chien Chou Chih*

Classification B194

Subject

References   *Revised ed. by*

Author 清 鑑懸業重修 ∧ *Ching, Chien Hsüan and others (revised)*

Edition *No indication of dates*

Index

Bound in 1 tao

Remarks

The University of Toronto Chinese Library

. . . .

Accession No. 2715   Index No. 085-chgc

Title 江陵縣志 *Chiang Ling Hsien Chih*

Classification B194

Subject

References

Author 清　倪文蔚等續修 *Amended by* *ed.* *Ching, Ni Wên-Wei and others (revised)*

Edition 賓興館藏板　光緒二年刊 *Block preserved in* "Ping-Hsing-Kuang private-printed-ed." *Dated — Kuang-Hsü "Ping-Tgü" 2/1876*

Index

Bound in 3 *tao*　65 *Chuan*　25 *tsê*

Remarks

The University of Toronto Chinese Library
....

Accession No. 2717   Index No. 040-9hgc

Title 寶華山志 Pao Hua Shan Chih

Classification B 207

Subject

References
                                    Compiled by
Author 清 定菴基祖 劉名芳等輯纂 Ching, Ting-An-Chi-Tsu and Liu Ming-Fang

Edition No. indication of date. Probably in 乾隆年

Index

Bound in 1 tao   15 Chuan   4 tse'

Remarks

The University of Toronto Chinese Library

....

Accession No. 2718   Index No. 031-63

Title 四書 *Ssŭ Shu*

Classification A-135

Subject

References

Author

Edition 山西濬文書局校刊   *Collated edition by*
Shan-Hsi, Chün-Wei Book Co.
清同治六年六月   *revised ed.*
Dated — Ching, Tung-Chi "Ting-Mao" 6/1867

Index

Bound in

Remarks *Missing 1-5 clmans in* 論語 *and 1-3 and 6,7 clmans*
in 孟子 *Meng-Tzu   Lun-Yu*

252

012

The University of Toronto Chinese Library

....

Accession No. 2719   Index No. 009-emzl

Title 佛學大辭典 Fo Hsüeh Ta Tzǔ Tien

Classification A-161

Subject

References

Author 疇隱居士 Chou-Yin-Chü-Shih

Edition 上海醫學書局 Shanghai, Medical Book Co. ed.
民國廿八年四月四版
Dated — Ming-Kuo 28/1939 April 4th ed.

Index

Bound in 4 tao, 16 ts'ê

Remarks

Accession No. 2720A,B   Index No. 009.83 ʒ²

Title 佩文韻府 附韻府拾遺   Péi Wên Yün Fu
                                    Fu Yün Fu Shih I

Classification A-166

Subject

References

Author

                              Block preserved by
Edition 嶺南潘氏海山書館藏版 Ling-Nan, Pan-Shih, Hai-San-
        康熙 己丑年   Shu-Kuang privated.
        Dated — Kang-Hsi "Kêng-Ying" 49/1710

Index

Bound in 33 Tao (正本 28 Tao, 拾遺 5 Tao); 正本 157 Ts'ê, 拾遺 20 Ts'ê
              lost   lost
Remarks

The University of Toronto Chinese Library

. . . .

Accession No. 2720   Index No. 072-db

Title 明史 Ming Shih

Classification B-12

Subject

References

Author 張廷玉等編, edited by. Chang Ting-Yü and others

Edition 光緒三年三月湖北崇文書局開周雕
Hupei, Chung-Wei Book Co,
Dated — Kuang-Hsü "Ting-Ch'ou" 3/1877 March
                                                    1876

Index

Bound in 8 tao

Remarks

The University of Toronto Chinese Library

· ·

Accession No. 2722   Index No. 072-gdbn

Title 晚明史籍考 Wan Ming Shih Chi Kao

Classification B-42

Subject

References

Author 安陽 謝國楨 輯 *Compiled by* An-Yang, Hsieh Kuo-Chên.

Edition 民國廿一年八月國立北平圖書館印
The National-Peiking-Library published
Dated — Ming-Kuo 21/1932 August.

Index

Bound in 1 套, 10 ts'ê

Remarks

Accession No. 2723   Index No. 112-7dib

Title 硃批諭旨 Chu Pi yü Chih

Classification B67

Subject

References

Author

Edition 清雍正十年
Dated — Ching, Yung-Chêng "jên-tzŭ" 10/1732

Index an index in details in the 1st tao

Bound in 18 tao, 110 tsʻê

Remarks

. . . .

Accession No. 2724   Index No. 085-北杏

Title 清初史料四種 Ching 8 Chü Shih Liao Ssŭ Chung

Classification B-52

Subject

References

Author 謝國楨輯 Compiled by Hsieh Kuo-Chên

Edition 國立北平圖書館印行
民國廿二年八月
National—Peiking—Library published
Index   Dated—Ming-Kuo 22/1933 August.

Bound in 1 tao, 2 ts'ê

Remarks

258

Accession No. 2725   Index No. 156-2 ㄎ ㄥ ㄅ

Title 越縵堂日記補 Yüeh Man T'ang Jêh Chi Pu

Classification B-107

Subject The Diary of Yüeh Man T'ang from 1854 – 1863, auditored
by Ts'ai Yüan P'ei

References

Author

Edition Shang-Wu Book Co. published. Collected & preserved in National-Peiking-Library
商務印書館印行，國立北平圖書館收藏，
民國廿五年十月初版
Dated—Ming-Kuo 25 / 1936 Oct.

Index

Bound in 1 tao, 13 ts'ê

Remarks

259

The University of Toronto Chinese Library

. . . .

Accession No. 2726   Index No. 002-chn7

Title 中國藏書家攷略 Chung Kuo Tsang Shu Chia Kao Lüeh

Classification B-117

Subject collected biographies of famous book collectors

References

edited & compiled by

Author 楊立誠 金步瀛 編纂 Yang Li-chêng and Chin Pu-Ying

Edition 浙江杭州省立圖書館四庫目略發行處發行
民國十八年四月初版
Chêkiang, Hang Chow-Provincial-Library San-Ku-Mu-
Lüeh-Fa-Hsin-Chü Fa-Hsin

Index Dated—Ming-Kuo 18/1929 April first ed.

Bound in 1 tao, 1 ts'ê

Remarks

The University of Toronto Chinese Library

....

Accession No. 2727   Index No. 163-9908

Title 邵亭知見傳本書目 Lü Tíng Chih Chien Chuan Pên Shu Mu

Classification B-~~337~~342

Subject

References

Author 莫友芝著 Mo Yu-Chih

Edition 上海掃葉山房版 Shanghai, Sao-Geh-Shan-Fang ed. *Lithographic*
民國十二年石印 ~~Lithographic Petin~~ Ming-Kuo 12/1923

Index An index in the 1st ts'e

Bound in 1 tao, 8 ts'e

Remarks

261

The University of Toronto Chinese Library

．．．．．．．．．．．．．．．．．．．．．．

Accession No. 2728   Index No. 031-b888

Title 四庫書目略 *Ssŭ Ku Shu Mu Lüeh*

Classification B-342

Subject

References

Author *Not given*

Edition 本宅藏板 *Private—printed ed.*
清同治庚午年鐫
Dated—Ching, Tǔng-Chi "Kǒng-Wu" 9/1870

Index

Bound in *1 t'ao, 12 ts'ê*
              2

Remarks

262

. . . .

Accession No. 2729   Index No. 140-nfzh

Title 藏書目錄三種 {
Tsang Shu Mu Lu San Chung

A. 汲古閣藏本書目 Chi Ku Kó Tsáng Pen Shu.
B. 李滄葦藏書目 Chi Tsáng Wei Tsáng Shu Mu
c. 藏書記要 Tsáng Shu chi Yao.

Classification

Subject B-337

References

Author   A. Mao I
          B. 黃丕烈 Huang Péi Lieh.
Edition   c. 孫從添 Sun Tsung Tien

Index   民國三年石印 Lithographic edition in the 3nd year
        of the Republic.

Bound in   1 tao, 3 tsè
           Printed in Shanghai, Sao-Yeh-Shan-Fang.
Remarks

263

The University of Toronto Chinese Library

. . . .

Accession No. 2730   Index No. 073-837

Title 書目答問 Shu Mu Ta Wên

Classification B-337

Subject

References

Author 張之洞 Chang Chih-Tung

Edition 光緒元年九月印 乙亥
Dated — Kuang-Hsü "I-Hai" 1/1875

Index

Bound in 1 tao, 3 ts'ê

Remarks

264

The University of Toronto Chinese Library

. . . .

Accession No. 2731   Index No. 012-3a§k

Title 八千卷樓書目 Pa Chien Chüan Lou Shu Mu

Classification B-337

Subject

References

Author 羅振玉 Lo Chên Yü

Edition 錢塘丁氏聚珍倣宋版 Chien-Tong, Ting-Shih pocketed
清光緒己亥年 ~~And the~~ imitation of
                                          Sung edition
Dated — Ching, "Kuang-Hsü" "I-Hai" 1/1875

Index

Bound in 1 tao, 10 ts'ê

Remarks

265

Accession No. 2732A   Index No. 058·7888

Title 彙刻書目 Hui Kʻo Shu Mu

Classification B-3#2

Subject

References

Author Not given.

Edition 光緒[丙戌]十三年 上海福三嬴書局版
Shanghai, Fu-Ying Book Co. ed.
Dated— Kuang-Hsü "Ping-Hsü" 12/1886

Index

Bound in 2 tao, 20 tsʻê

Remarks

Accession No. 2732 B   Index No. 120-07 58

Title 續彙刻書目 Hsü Hui Kʻo Shu Mu

Classification B-342

Subject

References

Author 羅振玉. Lo Chên Yü

Edition 連平范氏雙魚室刊
Block-printing edition Lien-Ping, Fan-Shih, Shuang-Yü-Shih published

Index

Bound in 1 tao, 8 tsʻê
                    10
Remarks

Accession No. 2733   Index No. 012-3a7k

Title 八千卷樓書目 Pa Chien Chüan Lou Shu Mu

Classification B-337

Subject

References

Author 羅振玉 Lo Chên Yü

Edition 錢塘丁氏聚珍倣宋版
Chien-Tong, Ting-shih procket ed & An imitation of Sung ed.

清光緒己亥年
Dated — Ching, Kuang-Hsü "Chi-Hai" 25/1899

Index

Bound in 1 tao, 10 ts'ê

Remarks

268

The University of Toronto Chinese Library

. . . .

Accession No. 2734   Index No. 030-ia88

Title 善本書室藏書志, *Shan Pên Shu Shih Tsáng Shu Chih*

Classification B-337

Subject

References

Author 錢塘丁丙松生甫輯, *Compiled by Chien-Táng (Ting-Ping) Sung Sháng-Fu*

Edition 清光緒辛丑季秋錢唐丁氏開周佳
Chien-Táng, Ting-Shih
Dated — Ching, Kuang-Hsü "Hsin-Chóu" 27/1901

Index

Bound in 2 tao, 16 ts'ê

Remarks

The University of Toronto Chinese Library

．．．．．．．．．．．．．．．．．．．．．．

Accession No. 2735⁻   Index No. 106-gdkn

Title 皕宋樓藏書志,目錄 Pi Sung Lou Tsang Shu Chih Mu Lu

Classification β-337

Subject

References

Author 歸安陸心源剛甫編 Edited by Kuei An Lu Hsin-Yüan, Kang Fu.

Edition 清光緒八年壬午冬月十萬卷樓藏版
Shih-Wan-Chüan-Lou private ed.
Block preserved in Dated — Ching, Kuang-Hsü "Jên-Wu" 8/1882 Winter

Index

Bound in 4 tao, 32 ts'ê

Remarks

270

Accession No. 2736   Index No. 029-P813

Title 叢書誼彙編 *Ts'un Shu Shu Mu Hui Pien*

Classification β - ~~337342~~

Subject

References

Author
Block preserved by
^Wu-Hsi, Ting-Shih private ed.

Edition 民國十八年十月上海醫學書局再版
無錫丁氏藏版 ∧ *Republished by* Shanghai Medical Book Co. second ed
~~Block preserved in~~ Ming-Kuo 18/1929 Oct. seconded.

Index

Bound in 1 tao, 4 tsê

Remarks

The University of Toronto Chinese Library

· ·

Accession No. 2737   Index No. 031. *h3cb*

Title 國立北平圖書館善本書目   *Kuo Li Pei Ping Tu Shu*
                              Kuan Shan Pên Shu Ma

Classification B-337

Subject

References

                          Written & collected by

Author 海寧 趙萬里 撰集 *↙ Hai-Ning, Chao Wan-Li*

Edition 民國廿二年十月刊印
Block-printing edition in ~~dated~~ Ming Kuo 22/1933 Oct. printed.

Index

Bound in *1 tao, 4 ts'e*

Remarks

where

The University of Toronto Chinese Library

....

Accession No. 2747   Index No. -~~076-bozh~~ 146-phbw

Title 西清古鑑 Hsi Ching Ku Chien

Classification B-347 譜錄 —— 器物 Pu Lu — Chi Wu

Subject -(Gest No. 1072-a) "Illustrations of ancient sacrificial
utensils and explanation of the inscriptions thereon."

References -160-lj 163-ggcj 9/9 031-bgld 12/14 012-zofk 12/1
031-bgdf 115/11 Gest Nos. 1072-a and 1865. Toronto Nos. 815-a)
Author - prepared by an Imperial commission headed by [2793,4,5 / 2815]
Edition Yün-lu 允祿

Index

Bound in 1 tao (Wooden Box), 22 ts'ê

Remarks

273

The University of Toronto Chinese Library

. . . .

Accession No. 2748   Index No. 085-大ㄷ大m

Title 清代禁燬書目 Chíng Tai Chin Hui Shu Mu

Classification B-337

Subject

References

Author 清 四庫館正總裁英廉奏呈所編應禁燬書目   乾隆四十五年
Ching Ssŭ Ku Kuan Chẽng Tsung Tsai Ying Lien Tsou Chẽng So

Edition 杭州抱經堂書局印行   民國二十年發行
Hang Chow, Pou-Ching-Tang Book Co. 印printed
Dated — Ming-Kuo 20/1931

Index

Bound in 1 t'ao   4 ts'e

Remarks

Accession No. 2755   Index No. 077-lccz

Title 國學基本叢書 歷代名人年譜 (Kuo Hsüeh Chi Pên Tsung Shu) Li Tai Ming gen Nien Pu

Classification

Subject

References

Author 吳榮光編 edited by Wu Jung-Kuang

Edition 商務印書館印   民國二十七年版
Shang-Wu Book Co. printed
Dated — Ming-Kuo 27/1938

Index

Bound in 1 tsʻe

Remarks

275

The University of Toronto Chinese Library

· ·

Accession No. 2756   Index No. 002-chzc

Title 中國人名大辭典 附 A Romanized Index to the Surnames in the
      Chung Kuo Jen Ming Ta Tzǔ Tien   Chinese Biographical Dictionary

Classification

Subject

References

Author 方賓觀等廿三人編 *edited by* Fang Pin-Kuan and others (23 writers)

Edition 商務印書館印　民國十九年版
        Shang-Wu Book Co. printed.
        Dated — Ming-Kuo 19/1920

Index

Bound in 1 tsǎ

Remarks

276

The University of Toronto Chinese Library
. . . .

Accession No. 2757   Index No. 032-cegl

Title 中國 古今 地名大辭典 (Chung Kuo Ku Chin) Ti Ming Ta Tzǔ Tien

Classification

Subject

References

Author 謝壽昌等編 edited by Hsieh Shou-Chǎng and others

Edition 商務印書館印 民國二十年版
Shang-Wu Book Co. printed
Dated —— Ming-Kuo 20/1931

Index

Bound in

Remarks

The University of Toronto Chinese Library

. . . .

Accession No. 2763   Index No. 144/KC 88

Title 衡齋金石識小錄
      Heng Chai Chin Shih Shih Shao Lu
Classification B 347

Subject

References

Author 黃濬撰集 Written & Collected by Huang Chün.

Edition 北平尊古齋發行   彩華珂羅甲印局印
        Published— Peiking, Tsun Ku Chi
        民國二十四年版
        Dated— The 24th year of the Republic

Index

Bound in 1 T'ao 2 Ts'é

Remarks

278

Accession No. 2764   Index No. 144/KC 衡齋

Title 衡齋覽見古玉圖 Heng Chai Tsang Tsang Chien Ku Yü Tu.

Classification B 347

Subject

References

Author 黃濬 撰集 Written & Collected by Huang chün

Edition 尊古齋 發行 Published — Pei-ping, Tsun Ku chi
何鑑樓印刷局印 Printing in Ke Lo Co.

Index

Bound in 1 Táo 2 Tsّ

Remarks

279

Accession No. 2825　　　　Index No. 070-3 c 3 x

Title 方志目錄 Fang Chih Mu Lu

Classification β - 3 3 7

Subject

References

Author

Edition 民國二十二年三月 國立北平圖書館印行
National Peiping Library printed
Dated — Ming-Kuo 22/1933 May

Index

Bound in 1 tao, 3 ts'e

Remarks

The University of Toronto Chinese Library

....

Accession No. 2826   Index No. 118-nick

Title 籌辦夷務始末 A, B, C,   Chou Pan I Wu Shih Mo A, B, C.

Classification B-277

Subject Documental record of Foreign affairs of Ching Dynasty
A, 4 Tao, 80 chuan, from 道光十四年 to 道光廿九年
B, 4 Tao, 80 chuan, from 道光三十年 to 咸豐十一年七月
C, 5 Tao, 100 chuan, from 咸豐十一年七月 to 同治十三年十二月

References

Author

Edition 清宮手抄稿 Ching Palace Manuscripts.
民國十八年故宮博物院用抄本影印
Ku-Kung-Po-Wu-Yuan lithographic ed from Manuscripts
Dated — Ming-Kuo 18/1929

Index

Bound in 13 tao, 260 chuan, 130 tsê

Remarks

281

The University of Toronto Chinese Library

. . . .

Accession No. 2827   Index No. 040-dicj

Title 宋會要稿 Sung Hui yao Kao

Classification β-282

Subject

References

Author

Edition 國立北平圖書館印
Nation/ Peiping library printed

Index

Bound in 16 tao, 200 ts'ê

Remarks

The University of Toronto Chinese Library

· ·

Accession No. 2828   Index No. 140-ik93

Title 萬壽盛典 初集 Wan Ch Shou Shêng Tien Chu Chi

Classification B-287

Subject

References

Author 清 大學士馬齊等 Ching, Ta Hsüeh Shih, Ma Chi and others

Edition 康熙五十六年纂修
Dated — Kang-Hsi "Hsin-Hai" 56/1791

Index

Bound in 4 Tao, 40 ts'ê

Remarks

283

The University of Toronto Chinese Library

. . . .

Accession No. 2929   Index No. 076-kebg

Title 欽定四庫全書總目

Classification β-342 目錄—經籍
                    Mu Lu   Ching Chi

Subject a descriptive catalogue of the Imperial Library
of the Ch'ing Dynasty.

References Wylie's Notes page 75   160-li; 163-28.e3 6/6
Author   012-3afk 9/15   Great Nos. 316, 449 and 821.
compiled on order of Emperor Chien-Lung by a
commission headed by Chi Yün 紀昀
Edition   the "Kuang-Tung-Shu-Chü" 廣東書局; dated
Tung-Chih 7/1868. Blocks, "fēn" paper.

Index a general table of contents (classifications) for 200
chüan.

Bound in 10 tao, 100 ts'e

Remarks

The University of Toronto Chinese Library

. . . .

Accession No. 2830 A, B, C, D   Index No. 002-chhi

Title 中華郵區地圖 Chung Hua Yu Chü Ti Tu

Classification B-232

Subject A: 山東, 貴州, 安徽 A: Shan-Tung, Kuei-Chou, An-Hui
         B: 山西, 四川, 雲南 B: Shan-Hsi, Ssŭ-Chuan, Yün-Nan
         C: 陝西, 山西, 江蘇 C: Shan-Hsi, Shan-Hsi, Chiang-Su
         D: 新疆, 浙江, 廣東 D: Hsin-Chiang, Chê-Chiang, Kuang-Tung
References E: 廣西, 福建, 湖北 E: Kuang-Hsi, Fu-Chien, Hu-Pei

Author

Edition

Index

Bound in 5 tao

Remarks

The University of Toronto Chinese Library

. . . .

Accession No. 2831
2931̶

Index No. 011-d07c

Title 全邊略記 *Chüan Pien Lüeh Chi*

Classification B 217

Subject

References

Author 方孔炤輯 *Fang Kung-Chao*

Edition 民國十九年六月國立北平圖書館印行
National Peiping Library printed
Dated — Ming-Kuo 19/1930 June
                    30

Index

Bound in 1 tao, 6 tsʻo

Remarks

The University of Toronto Chinese Library

. . . .

Accession No. 2832   Index No. 077-d'cze

Title 武夷山志、 Wu I Shan Chih

Classification B-207

Subject

References

Author 董天工 編 ∧ edited by Tung Tien-Kung

Edition 道光丙午年重刻 Wu-Fu-Chih-Mu-Hsüan private
玉夫尺木軒藏板 printed ed.
Dated — Tao-Kuang "Ping-Wu" 26/1846

Index

Bound in 1 tao, 24 chüan, 8 ts'ê

Remarks

<u>Accession No.</u> 2835   <u>Index No.</u> 085-271k

<u>Title</u> 汴京遺蹟志. *Pien Ching I Chi Chih*

<u>Classification</u> B-212

<u>Subject</u>

<u>References</u>

<u>Author</u> 李濂著 *Li Lien*

<u>Edition</u> 壬戌冬十二月河南官書局刊
Honan, Kuan-Shu-Chu published

<u>Index</u>

<u>Bound in</u> 1 tao, 6 ts'ê

<u>Remarks</u>

ok

The University of Toronto Chinese Library
....

Accession No. 2838   Index No. 031-hgcb

Title 國立北平圖書館善本書目   Kuo Li Pei Ping Tú Shu Kuan Shan)
丁文襄手札   Pên Shu Mu
肇止水齋藏書目   等   Ting Wên-jang Shou Cha
Classification B-337 (?)   Chien Chih Shui Chai Tsang Shu Mu

Subject

References

Author

Edition

Index

Bound in 1 tao, 6 ts'e

Remarks This is not a set of one book in sepperate 6 Ts'e, but
6 different books bound in one case which are not
in the same clasification.

Accession No. 2839A   Index No. 085-cpdz

Title 江蘇省立國學圖書館圖書總目
Chiang Su Shêng Li Kuo Hsüeh Tú Shu Kuan Tú Shu Tsung Mu

Classification B-337

Subject

References

Author

Edition 江蘇省立圖書館印   Kiangsu
                          Chiangsu Provincial Library printed
        癸酉年九月

Index
        6

Bound in 6 tao, 24 ts'e

Remarks

012

The University of Toronto Chinese Library

....

Accession No. 2839B   Index No. 085-cpdz

Title 江蘇省立國學圖書館圖書總目補編
Chiang Su Shêng Li Kuo Hsüeh Tú Shu Kuan Tú Shu Tsung Mu Pu Pien

Classification B-337

Subject

References

Author 刪 Unknown.

Edition 江蘇省立圖書館印 Kiang-Su Provincil Library printed.

Index

Bound in 2 tao, 6 tsǎ

Remarks

The University of Toronto Chinese Library

. . . .

Accession No. 2840   Index No. 076-Leah

Title 欽定天祿琳瑯書目 Chin Ting Tien Lu Lin Lang Shu Mu

Classification B-342

Subject

References

Author 乾隆四十年，于敏中等奉敕編校 Collated by Yü Ming-Chung and others

Edition 乾隆四十年 手抄本 Manuscripts ed.
Doted— Chien-Lung "I-Wei" 40/1775

Index

Bound in 2 tao, 12 ts'ê

Remarks

The University of Toronto Chinese Library

. . . .

Accession No. 2841   Index No. 167-m h g m

Title 鐵琴銅劍樓藏書目錄 Tieh Chin Tung Chien Lou Tsáng
                                               Shu Mu Lu

Classification B-342

Subject

References   名　字   Cháng-Shu, Chü Yung (Tzŭ-Yang)

Author 常熟瞿 鏞子雍   Cháng-Shu-Chü, Yung Tzŭ-Yung

Edition 光緒丁酉年誦芬室校刊
       Yung-Fēn-Tāng revised ed.
       Dated — Kuang-Hsü "Ting-Yu" 23/1897

Index

Bound in 1 tao, 10 ts'ê

Remarks

293

Accession No. 2842   Index No. 030-bɨ3ㄣ

Title 古逸書錄叢輯 Ku I Shu Lu Tsung Chi

Classification B-342

Subject

References

Author 貴陽 趙士煒 輯 Compiled by Kuéi-Yang, Chao Shih-Wei

Edition 國立北平圖書館印
National Peiping Library printed

Index

Bound in 1 tao, 4 tsʻê

Remarks

The University of Toronto Chinese Library

. . . .

Accession No. 2843   Index No. 073-833i

Title 書目長編 Shu Mu Cháng Pien

Classification B-342

Subject

References

Author 邵瑞彭等輯 *Compiled by* Shao Jui-Péng and others

Edition 戊辰正月印於京師 (民國) *Printed in Ching-Shih*

Index

Bound in 1 tao, 2 ts'é

Remarks

The University of Toronto Chinese Library

. . . .

Accession No. 2844   Index No. 031.bgld

Title 四庫簡明目錄標注 Ssŭ Ku Chien Ming Mu Lu Piao Chu

Classification B-342

Subject

References

Author 仁和 邵懿辰 位西 Jen-Ho, Shao I Chên Wei Hsi

Edition 清宣統三年
Dated — Ching, Hsüan-Tung "Hsin-Hai" 3/1911

Index

Bound in 1 tao, 6 ts'ê

Remarks

The University of Toronto Chinese Library

. . . .

Accession No. 2845   Index No. 069-ı l d g

Title 新鄭出土古器圖志全編   Hsin Chêng Chu Tu Ku Chi
Tü chih Chüan Pien

Classification B347

Subject

Cancel

References Toronto No. 2758

Author 陸軍第十四師司令部編 胡隸生製斯
Edited by Lu Chün Ti Shih Ssu Shih Ssü Ling Pu Pien, Hu Ti-shêng
Edition 漢口新鄭出土古器圖志總發行所發行 民國十二年版
Hankow, Hsing-Chêng, Chu-Tu-Ku-Chi-Tu-Chih Chung-Fa-
Hsin-So, published.

Dated — Ming-Kuo 12/1923 first ed.

Index

Bound in 1 t'ao 3 ts'e

Remarks

The University of Toronto Chinese Library

....

Accession No. 2851   Index No. 085-kchi

Title 漢代婚喪禮俗考 Han Tai Hun Sang Li Su Kāo

Classification B-287

Subject

References

Author 楊樹達 Yang Shu-Ta

Edition 商務印書館發行 Shong-Wu Book Co. published
民國二十二年十月初版
Dated — Ming-Kuo 22/1933 Oct. first ed.

Index

Bound in 1 tao, 1 ts'ê

Remarks

The University of Toronto Chinese Library

· ·

Accession No. 2853   Index No. 160-1949

Title 辦理四庫全書檔案 Pan Li Ssŭ Kŭ Chüan Shu Tang An

Classification B-342 經籍

Subject

References

Author 陳援菴 Chên Yüan-An

Edition 珍藏本 Fine private edition
          民國廿三年六月 dated Republic 23. June/1934
          錦連紙. "Mien-Lien" paper

Index

Bound in 1 táo 2 ts'ê

Remarks

The University of Toronto Chinese Library

. . . .

Accession No. 2854   Index No. 120-gndb

Title 經籍訪古志 Ching Chieh Fang Ku Chih

Classification 雜部 (經文8集) B342

Subject

References

Author 蓂庭 Tai Ting

Edition 珍版印行 Chên-Pan printed
光緒十一年 dated Kuang-Hsü 11/1885

Index

Bound in 1 táo 8 tsè

Remarks

The University of Toronto Chinese Library
. . . .

Accession No. 2855   Index No. 162-lej

Title   遼居稾 Liao Chü Kao

Classification B-107 獨錄 (碎序)

Subject

References

Author 羅振玉 Lo Chên-Yü

Edition 民國己巳 dated Republic I "Chi-Ssŭ" /1929

         綿連紙 "Mien-Lien" paper

Index

Bound in 1 t'ao 2 ts'ê

Remarks

The University of Toronto Chinese Library

. . . .

Accession No. 2856   Index No. 069-imlg

Title 新學偽經考 Hsin Hsüeh Wei Ching Kao

Classification B-42 引文

Subject

References

Author 南海 康有為, Nan-Hai, Kang Yu-Wei

Edition 重刊於京城 Revised at Peking ~~period (~~
光緒丁巳冬重刊 dated ~~Kuang-Hsü "Ting 55th"~~ /1918

萬木草堂叢書 Wan-Mu-Tsao-Tang edition
Index 民國戊午年 dated Republic "Wu-Wu" /1918

Bound in 1 tao, 6 tsê

Remarks

302

The University of Toronto Chinese Library

. . . .

Accession No. 2857   Index No. 162-9c93

Title 通志條格 Tung Chih Tiao Ko

Classification B-77 公文

Subject

References

Author 劉正等 Liu chêng and others

Edition 國立北平圖書館題印 National Peiping Library printed
民國十九年 dated Republic 19/1930
竹紙 Bamboo paper

Index

Bound in 1 Hao 2-9
13-22 Chüan, 6 tsê
Remarks 27-30

303

The University of Toronto Chinese Library

....

Accession No. 2858   Index No. 077-Lcbg

Title 歷代軍事分類詩選 Li Tai Chun Shih Fên Lei Shih Hsüan

Classification D-68 總集一輯

Subject a general collection of the ancient poems writing about military affairs + life.

References

Author 新生 張紡陵 輯 Selected & Compiled by Hin-An, Chang Fang

Edition 民國九年夏季

Dated Republic 9/1920 summer.

Index A general table of contents for 8 Chüan and separate table of contents for each chüan

Bound in 1 套, 8 Chüan, 8 冊

Remarks

304

The University of Toronto Chinese Library

· ·

Accession No. 2859   Index No. 166- b n p l

Title   重纂三遷志 Chúng Tsuan San Chien Chih

Classification   B 3 2 紀言本末
事

Subject

References

Author   張曜. 孟廣均纂 Chang Yao, and Mêng Kuang - Chün

Edition   殿版 Palace edition
光緒十三年丁亥 dated Kuang Hsü 13 "Ting-Hai"/1887
綿連紙 "Mien - Lien" paper

Index

Bound in   1 táo   10 Chüon, 6 tsè

Remarks

o l L

The University of Toronto Chinese Library

. . . .

Accession No. 2860   Index No. 031- h z c b

Title 國立北平圖書館 方志目錄   Kuo Li Pei Ping Tú Shu Kuan Fang Chih Mu Lu

Classification 8-337 目錄

Subject

References

Author 嘉興, 譚其驤   Chia-Hsing, Tán Chí-Hsiang

Edition 國立北平圖書館 印行   National Peking Library
民國二十二年五月 . dated Republic 22, may /1933
毛邊紙 "Mao-Pien" paper

Index

A general table of contents

Bound in

1 táo , 4 tsê

Remarks

The University of Toronto Chinese Library
....

Accession No. 2861   Index No. 039-ghcb

Title 孫淵如外集 Sun Yüan Ju Wai Shih

Classification C-303 雜家

Subject

References

Author 孫星衍撰, 王重民輯 ∧Sun Hsing-Yen (撰) *Written by*
                              ∧Wang Chung-Min (輯) *Compiled by*
Edition 民國廿一年 dated Republic 21/1932

Index

Bound in 5 chuan 1 t'ae

Remarks

307

The University of Toronto Chinese Library

· ·

Accession No. 2862   Index No. 085. ㄥㄉㄥㄅ

Title   清開國史料考 Ching Kai Kuo Shih Liao Kao

Classification   B-42 別史

Subject

References

Author   謝國楨 Hsieh Kuo-Chên

Edition

     民國廿年元月 dated Republic 20, June /1931
     綿連紙 "Mien-Lien" paper

Index

Bound in   2 本

Remarks

olk

The University of Toronto Chinese Library

. . . .

Accession No. 2863   Index No. 031-Lzcb

Title 國立北平圖書館目錄 Kuo Li Pei Ping Tu shu Kuang Mu Lu

Classification B-337 目錄

Subject

References

Author 蕭璋 Hsiao Chang

Edition 國立北平圖書館 National Peiping Library
         民國廿三年 dated Republic 23/1934

Index 毛籩紙 "Mao-Pien" paper
       邊

Bound in 2 Ai, 1 tao

Remarks

. . . .

Accession No. 2864   Index No. 106-dhcb

Title 皇朝中外壹統輿圖 Huang Chao Chung Wai I Tung Yü Tu

Classification B-194   地理-省志

Subject

References

Author 嚴樹森 Yen Shu-So Sên

Edition 藏板 Private edition blocks preserved in
同治二年 dated Tung-chih 2/1863

Index

Bound in 1 t'ao 2 ts'ê

Remarks

The University of Toronto Chinese Library

· ·

Accession No. 2865   Index No. 168-3dbd

Title 長沙古物聞見記 Cháng Sha Ku Wu Wên Chien Chi

Classification B-212 地理-古蹟

Subject

References

Author 承祚 Chêng-Tso

Edition 金陵大學中國文化研究所 Nanking University, Chung-Kuo-Wên Hua Yen Chiu So.
民國廿八年
dated Republic 28/1939

Index

Bound in 1 tâo 2 tsê

Remarks

Catalogued.

The University of Toronto Chinese Library

. . . .

Accession No. 2866   Index No. 032-赳c m

Title   埋劍記 Mai Chien Chi

Classification   C-368 小說家

Subject

References

Author   繼志參 Chi Chih-Tsan

Edition 不登大雅元庫藏本 Pu-Têng-Ta-Ya-Wên-Ku edition preserved
         國立北平圖書館借 National Peking Library borrowed
         民國十九年八月 dated Republic 19, August /1930

Index

Bound in   1 táo   2 ts'è

Remarks

312

The University of Toronto Chinese Library

. . . .

Accession No. 2867   Index No. 002-chcm

Title 中國地學論文索引續編 Chung Kuo Ti Li Hsüeh Lun Wên
                                    So Yin Hsü Pien

Classification B-337 目錄

Subject   Index to Chinese Geographical Literature

References

Author 王庸，茅乃文 合編 ∧ Wang Yung and Mao Nai-Wên
                        edited

Edition
    國立北平師範大學，國立北平圖書館出版
    National Peiping Normal & University and National Peiping Library edition
    洋白紙 ~~Western white paper~~ imported white paper

Index 民國廿五年六月 dated Republic 25. June/1936

    A general table of contents for 2 tsê
Bound in
    2 tsê

Remarks

The University of Toronto Chinese Library

. . . .

Accession No. 2868   Index No. 002 - chcm

Title 中國地理學論文索引 Chung Kuo Ti Li Hsüeh Lun Wên So
Yin

Classification
B- 337 目錄

Subject
Index to chinese geographical Literature

References

Author
王庸, 茅B文合編 edited by
Wang Yung and Mao Nai-Wên

Edition
國立北平師範大學, 國立北平圖書館出版
洋白紙 National Peiping Normal University and National Peiping Library edited
Western white paper imported white paper
民國廿三年六月 dated Republic 23, June /1934
a general table of contents for 2 tsê

Bound in
2 tsê

Remarks

The University of Toronto Chinese Library

. . . .

Accession No. 2869   Index No. 067-3m23

Title   文學論文索引續編 Wén Hsüeh Lun Wén So Yin Hsü Pien

Classification   B-337 目錄

Subject

References

Author   劉修業 Liu Hsiu-Yeh

Edition 國立北平圖書館 National Peiping Library
         民國廿二年 dated Republic 22/1933
         粉白紙竹紙 Bamboo paper

Index

Bound in   1 册

Remarks

The University of Toronto Chinese Library

．．．．．．．．．．．．．．．．．．．．．．．

Accession No. 2870   Index No. 067-3mんз

Title 文學論文索引三編 Wên Hsüeh Lun Wên So Yin San Pien

Classification B-337 目錄

Subject

References

Author 錢亞新 張陳卿, 陳璧如, 李維墀
chang Chên-Ching, Chên Pi-ju and Li Wei-Hsü

Edition 國立北平圖書館 National Peiping Library
民國廿一年 dated Republic 21/1932

Index 粉白紙 ~~Fên Pai~~ paper Powder White Paper

Bound in 1 册

Remarks

The University of Toronto Chinese Library

· ·

Accession No. 2871   Index No. 170-1931

Title   陽羨茗壺系 Yang Hsien Ming Hu Hsi

Classification   乙-275 食譜
                 乙-258 譜錄

Subject

References

Author   江陰 周高起伯高著 Chiang-Yin, Chou Kao-Chi (Po-Kao

Edition   光緒庚寅 dated Kuang-Hsü "Kêng-Yin"/1890
          粉白紙 powder white fên-pai paper

Index

Bound in   1 本

Remarks

The University of Toronto Chinese Library

....

Accession No. 2872   Index No. 194-2331

Title 魏書校勘記 Wei Shu Hsiao Kanchi

Classification B-42 別史

Subject

References

Author 長沙王氏□ Chang-Sha, Wang-Shih

Edition

　　　　光緒癸未 dated Kuang-Hsü "Kui-Wei"/1883

　　　　粉連紙 fen-lien paper
Index 　　　　Powder-like cotton paper

Bound in 1 冊

Remarks

The University of Toronto Chinese Library

. . . .

Accession No. 2873   Index No. 094-乙夕长3

Title 猛悔樓詩 Mêng Hui Lou Shih

Classification D-33 別集 詩文

Subject

References

Author 華陽 喬大壯撰 Written by Hua-Yang, Chiao Ta-Chuang

Edition

民國卅二年八月 dated Republic 32, August
毛邊紙   "Mao-Pien" paper   /1943

Index

Bound in 1 册

Remarks

Accession No. 2874   Index No. 038-ck2

Title   如夢錄   Ju Mêng Lu

Classification   B-212   地理古蹟

Subject

References

Author   河南官書局朱常茂徐秋壓氏．
Edition   Pien Chang, Mao-Lai-Chin Ya-Shih

重番
咸豐二年   dated Hsien-Fêng 2/1852

Index   河南官書局重刊   Ho-Nan Kuan-Shu-Chü revised

Bound in   1 fâo

Remarks

The University of Toronto Chinese Library

. . . .

Accession No. 2875   Index No. 119-hegd

Title   精神教育 Chīng Shēn Chiao Yü

Classification   B-289 教育

Subject

References

Author   蔣介石（中正）
         張人傑 Chang jên-chieh

Edition 中國國民黨陸軍軍學校 Chung Kuo Kuo Ming Tang Lu Chün
                                Chün Hwa Hsüeh Hsiao
         民國十四年 dated Republic 14/1925

Index

Bound in

Remarks

The University of Toronto Chinese Library

．．．．．．．．．．．．．．．．．．．．．．．．．

Accession No. 2876   Index No. 009-mm

Title   儀禮 I Li

Classification   A751 儀礼

Subject

References

Author   長沙葉氏觀古堂 Chang-Sha, Yeh-Shih Kuan-Ku-Tang

Edition   觀古堂藏本 preserved in, Kuan-Ku-Tang edition

Index

Bound in   1 册

Remarks

323

The University of Toronto Chinese Library

. . . .

Accession No. 2878   Index No. 066-ℓ9ℓ9

Title 故宮名畫信片第一集 . Ku Kung Ming Hua ~~I~~ Hsin Pien Ti
                                              I Chi

Classification C-223- 藝術一書畫

Subject ₍famous₎
         ∧ Pictures of from Tang Danays Dynasty to Ching Dynasty

References

Author 易培基 I Pei-Chi

Edition
        故宮博物院古物館印行
        Ku Kung Po Wu Yüan Ku Wu Kuan printed
        硬紙卡片 hard papered cards
Index
        a table of titles of the picture

Bound in
        1 box

Remarks

324

The University of Toronto Chinese Library

. . . .

Accession No. 2901   Index No. 075-jjc

Title 榮縣志 Jung Hsien Chih

Classification B-194

Subject

References

Author 總纂 趙熙 *Compiled by* Chao Hsi, Yü Shao Ching.

Edition 纂輯: 虞兆清

民國十七年縣志成 the 17th years of the Republic

Index 約出版於次年

Bound in 15 Chüan 8 Tsê

Remarks

The University of Toronto Chinese Library

. . . .

Accession No. 2902   Index No. 002-CCJC

Title 中江縣志 Chung Chiang Hsien Chih

Classification B-194

Subject

References

Author 陳敦甫 總纂 Compiled by Chên Tun Pu

Edition 民國十九年 Nineteen Year of the Republic

Index

Bound in 23 Chüan 8 Tsê

Remarks

012

The University of Toronto Chinese Library

. . . .

Accession No. 2903   Index No. 040-CᵍOC

Title 安 縣 續 志   An Hsien Hsü Chih

Classification 志.   An Hsien Chih
B-194

Subject

References

Author 陳紹欽 撰（安縣鐘志）, 劉公旭 撰（安縣志）
An Hsien Hsü Chih was Written by Chen Shao Chin, An Hsien Chih was Written by

Edition 中華民國二十七年 安縣鐘志   Liu Kung Hsu

中華民國二十二年 安縣志. (An Hsien Hsü Chih)
Index The 27th year of the Republic (An Hsien Hsü Chih)
The 22nd year of the Republic (An Hsien Chih)

Bound in 安縣志 60 Chüan 12 Tsé.

Remarks 安縣續志. 1 Tsé

327

The University of Toronto Chinese Library

. . . .

Accession No. 2904   Index No. 140-hiie

Title 華陽縣志
       Hua Yang Hsien Chih
Classification B-194

Subject

References

Author 曾鑑署嵩 Tseng Chien

Edition 甲戌九月 Sept., Chia-Hsü

Index

Bound in 36 chüan 16 Tsé

Remarks

The University of Toronto Chinese Library
. . . .

Accession No. 2905   Index No. 166-b.h.b.i.

Title 重修成都縣志
Chung Hsiu Chʻêng Tu Hsien Chih
Classification B-194

Subject

References

Author 夔玉, 羅廷權等 Kʻuei Yu, Lo Wang Chʻuan

Edition 同治十二年歲次癸酉重修 Revised edition in the twelfth of Tung Chih
節孝祠藏板 Blocks preserved in Chieh Hsiao Tzu.

Index
                                        1862-1874

Bound in 16 Chüan 16 Tsê.

Remarks

The University of Toronto Chinese Library

. . . .

Accession No. 2906   Index No. 162-ife

Title 達縣志 Ta Hsien Chih

Classification B-194

Subject

References

Author 吳德識 Wu Te Shih

Edition 中華民國二十二年三月
          March, 22nd Year of the Republic

Index

Bound in 14 Chüan 5 Tsé

Remarks

The University of Toronto Chinese Library

. . . .

Accession No. 2907   Index No. 137-RijC

Title 豐都縣志 Feng Tou Hsien Chih

Classification B-194

Subject

References

Author 黃光輝   Huang Hsien Hui

Edition 中華民國十六年 the sixteen year of the Republic
新文化社代印 Printed in Hsin Wen Hua She.

Index

Bound in 14 Chüan 6 Tsê.

Remarks

331

Accession No. 2908   Index No. 140 - k j d c

Title 蓬溪近志縣志, 續志
Péng Ch'i Chin Chih, Hsien Chih, Hsü Chih.

Classification B-194

Subject

References

Author 清, 潘之彪, 周學銘, Ching, P'an Chih Piao,
          Chou Hsueh Ming.

Edition 民國二十四年(近志) Twenty-four year of the Republic (Chi Chin)
          道光甲辰年 重修 (縣志) Revised ed. in "Tao-Kwang" "chia-chên" (Hsien Chih)
          光緒二十三年 (續志)

Index 25 year of Kwang Hsü (Hsü Chih)

Bound in 近志 (13 Chüan, 7 Tsé)

Remarks 縣志 (18 Chüan, 8 Tsé)
          續志 (4 Chüan, 4 Tsé)

Accession No. 2909   Index No. 085-i c j c

Title 溫江縣志
        Wen Chiang Hsien Chih
Classification B-194

Subject

References

Author 曾學傳纂修
        Compiled by Tsêng Hsueh Chuan

Edition
        民國十年 Tenth Year of The Republic

Index 溫江縣圖書館藏板
        Blocks preserved in Wen. Chiang library

Bound in

Remarks 12 Chuan 8 Tse

333

The University of Toronto Chinese Library

. . . .

Accession No. 2910   Index No. 085—*h h j o*

Title 涪陵縣續修涪州志

Fou Ling Hsien Hsü Hsiu Fou Chou Chih

Classification B-194

Subject

References

.

Author 明夏國孝編纂（原本）

Edition Compiled & edited by Ming, Hsia Kuo Hsiao
Original edition

Index 民國十七年（續修本）
Seventh year of The Republic
(Amended edition)

Bound in

Remarks 27 Chüan, 5 Tsê

334

The University of Toronto Chinese Library

. . . .

Accession No. 2911   Index No. 059-ijc

Title 彭縣志 P'eng Hsien Chih

Classification B-194

Subject

References

Author 王鍾釪總纂 (舊志) Original edition:
Compiled by:
張龍甲 " " (纂修) Wang Chung Fang

Edition   Revised edition:
Compiled by:
光緒四年重修 Chang Lung Chia

Index Revised in the 4th year of
"Kuang-Hsü"

Bound in   1877 1909

Remarks 14 Chüan, 10 Tsê

335

Accession No. 2912   Index No. 093 — ihjc

Title 犍為縣志   Chien Wei Hsien chih

Classification B-194

Subject

References

Author 嘉慶十九年王夢庚修纂 Revised & compiled by Wang Meng K'êng in the 19th Year of "Chia-Ching"

Edition 民國廿三年重修本出版 Revised edition was published in the 23rd Year of The Republic

Index

Bound in 14 Chüan, 8 Tsé

Remarks

336

Accession No. 2913   Index No. 162-ikjc

Title 遂寧縣志 Sui Ning Hsien Chih

Classification B-194

Subject

References

Author

Edition

Index

Bound in Chüan 4, 5, 6, 7, 8.

Remarks

Accession No. 2914   Index No. 041-9FjC

Title 射洪縣志 She Hung Hsien Chih

Classification B-194

Subject

References

Author 謝廷鈞等總核 (續修本)
Supervised by Hsieh Ting Chün & others

Edition (Amended edition)
光緒十年 (續修本)
The Tenth Year of "Kuang-Hsü"
1875-1909

Index

Bound in 18 Chüan 10 Tsé

Remarks

338

The University of Toronto Chinese Library

. . . .

Accession No. 2915   Index No. 069-ifjʒ

Title 新津縣縣志 Hsin Chin Hsien Hsien Chih

Classification B-194

Subject

References

Author 王夢庚纂修 (舊志)
   Compiled & amended by Wang Meng Kêng (Original edition)

Edition 嘉慶十七年
   The 17th Year of "Chia-Ching"
                  1796 - 1820

Index

Bound in 40 Chüan, 6 Ts'e

Remarks

339

The University of Toronto Chinese Library

. . . .

Accession No. 2916   Index No. 018-m f j o

Title 劍閣縣續志 Chien Ko Hsien Hsü Chih

Classification 8-194

Subject

References

Author 張政編次 Edited in order by Chang Cheng.

Edition 民國十六年 The sixteen of the Republic.
成都協昌公司代印
Printed in Hsieh Chang, Chengtu.

Index

Bound in 10 Chüan 8 Tsé

Remarks

The University of Toronto Chinese Library

· ·

Accession No. 2917   Index No. 024-gc jc

Title 南江縣志 Nan Chiang Hsien Chih

Classification B-194

Subject

References

Author 董珩監修 阿耀祖 岳永武 岳鎮東 纂修 Compiled & Amended by Yueh Yung Wu, He Yueh Tsu, Yueh Chen Tung.

Edition 民國十一年 Amended by Tung Heng Chien. The 11th year of The Republic.

成都聚昌公司代印 Printed in Chu Chang Co., Chengtu.

Index

Bound in 4 Tsé

Remarks

The University of Toronto Chinese Library

． ． ． ． ． ． ． ． ． ． ． ． ． ． ． ． ． ． ． ．

Accession No. 2918　　　　　Index No. 040-icjc

Title 富順縣志 Fu Shun Hsien Chih

Classification B-194

Subject

References

Author 段君齊纂定 Compiled by Chia Faans Jê Ying.

Edition 光緒八年 The 8th year of Kuang-Hsü

Index

Bound in 5 Chüan, 5 Tsé

Remarks

Accession No. 2919   Index No. 069-ㄴㄴㄱㄷ

Title 新都縣志.
        Hsing Tu Hsien Chih
Classification B-194

Subject

References

Author 張奉書纂修
        Compiled & amended by Chang Fêng Shu
Edition 道光廿四年
        The 24th year of "Jao-Kuang"
                                    1821-1850

Index

Bound in 18 Chüan 12 Tsé

Remarks

The University of Toronto Chinese Library

. . . .

Accession No. 2920   Index No. 167-zhj⁸

Title 金堂縣續志 Chin Tang Hsien Hsü Chih

Classification B194

Subject

References

Author 曾茂林總纂 Compiled by Tsèng Mao Lin

Edition 民國拾歲次辛酉鐫板
The 10ᵗʰ year of the Republic.

Index

Bound in 10 Chuan 8 Tsè

Remarks

Accession No. 2926   Index No. 039-mf ch

Title 學津討原 第四四 Hsueh Chin T'ao Yüan

Classification C 338

Subject

References

Author 清張海鵬輯 Compiled by Ching, Chang Hai Peng.

Edition 涵芬樓影印照曠閣本
   Photo-lithographic ed. by Han Fen Lou

Index

Bound in

Remarks 毛邊紙 Mao-pien paper

Accession No. 2927   Index No. 030-bb Rf

Title 古今圖書集成 Ku Chin Tu Shu Chi Chêng

Classification C 338

Subject

References

Author

Edition

Index

Bound in 150 Han,

Remarks

The University of Toronto Chinese Library

. . . .

Accession No 2928   Index No. 128-gike c

Title 聖諭廣訓序 Sheng Yu Kuang Hsun Hsu

Classification C 13

Subject

References

Author 清康熙帝御製 Made by Ching, K'ang Hsi Emperor

Edition 官板大本 official printed edition.

Index

Bound in 三冊 3 tsé

Remarks 綿連紙 Mein lien paper

347

The University of Toronto Chinese Library

....

Accession No. 2929   Index No. 059-L d a d

Title 影宋百衲本史記 一百三十卷 Ying Sung Po Na Pen Shih Chü.

Classification B 12

Subject

References

Author not given

Edition 涵芬樓借涉陽陶氏本影印.
初印本 first printing edition

Index ~~Han I~~ Photo-lithographic Edition by Han Feng Lou.

Bound in 一百三十卷 二十四册, 一期.

Remarks 綿建紙 Mein-Lien paper.

348

Accession No. 2930   Index No. 075 — ì ʒ ga

Title 楊文弱集 Yang Wén jè chì

Classification D 43

Subject

References

Author 明 武陵楊 嗣昌文著 Ming, Wu Ling Yang,
　　　　　　　　　　　　　　　　Szu Chang Wên

Edition 民國十九年 The 19ᵗʰ year of the Republic.

Index

Bound in 20 Tsê, 2 Vol.

Remarks

The University of Toronto Chinese Library

. . . .

Accession No. 2931   Index No. 195—d T d m

Title 魯巖所學集 Lu Yen So Hsueh Chi

Classification D 43

Subject

References

Author 張宗泰著 Chang Tsung Tan.

Edition 民國二十年重刊
Reprinted in the 12th year of the Republic

Index

Bound in 15 Chüan 11 Tsê

Remarks

The University of Toronto Chinese Library
....

Accession No. 2932   Index No. 167-8 f g

Title 金瓶梅 Chin P'ing Mei

Classification (古本) c 387

Subject

References

Author 明, 王鳳洲著 Ming, Wang Feng Chou

Edition 民國十五年 The 15th year of the Republic

Index

Bound in 4 Tze

Remarks

Accession No. 2924   Index No. 085-a k 3 f

Title 永樂大典 Yung Le Ta Tien

Classification C 348

Subject

References

　　　瞿景淳 Chu Ching Chün

Author 高拱 重錄 Recopied by Kao Kung

Edition

Index

Bound in 1 tsé

Remarks

Accession No. 2935   Index No. 096-3 d k b

Title 王忠慤公遺書
       Wang Chung Chueh Kung I Shu

Classification

Subject

References

Author

Edition

Index

Bound in

Remarks

Accession No. 2936   Index No. 031-b h p c

Title 四部叢刊續編集部
                    Szu Pu Ts'ung K'an Hsu Pien Chi Pu
Classification c 338

Subject

References

Author 呂才君撰 Written by Lü

Edition 上海涵芬樓景印專嘉興瞿氏鐵琴銅劍樓
藏明刻本 Printing in Han Fen Lou Ching.
                                              Shanghai.

Index

Bound in 15 tsè

Remarks

Accession No. 2937   Index No. 167—hcii

Title 錢志新編 Chien Chih Hsin Pien

Classification c 263

Subject

References

Author 張業懇撰輯 Collated & compiled by Chang

Edition   Ch'ung I

內春堂藏版— blocks Preserved in Cho Ch'un Tang.

Index

Bound in 18 chüan 7 ts'e

Remarks

357

. . . .

Accession No. 2942   Index No. 085 - h g p f

Title 涵海叢書 Han Hai Tsung Shu

Classification C 338

Subject

References

Author 李雨村編 Edited by Lî Yü Tsun.

Edition

仿萬卷樓原本 ~~2nd~~

According to the original edition of Wan Chüan
Lou.

Index 光緒丑午年 Kuang-Hsü "Chou Wu" period.

Bound in 160 ts'e

Remarks

Accession No. 2946   Index No. 002—chmm

Title 中國戲劇史 Chung Kuo Hsi Chu Shih.

Classification C368

Subject

References

Author 徐慕雲著 Hsü Mu Yün

Edition 世界書局印 Printing in Shih Chieh Book Co.
民國二十七年十二月初版.

Index First edition publishing in the 27th year of the
Republic.

Bound in 1 tse

Remarks

蓬萊慕氏藏書目

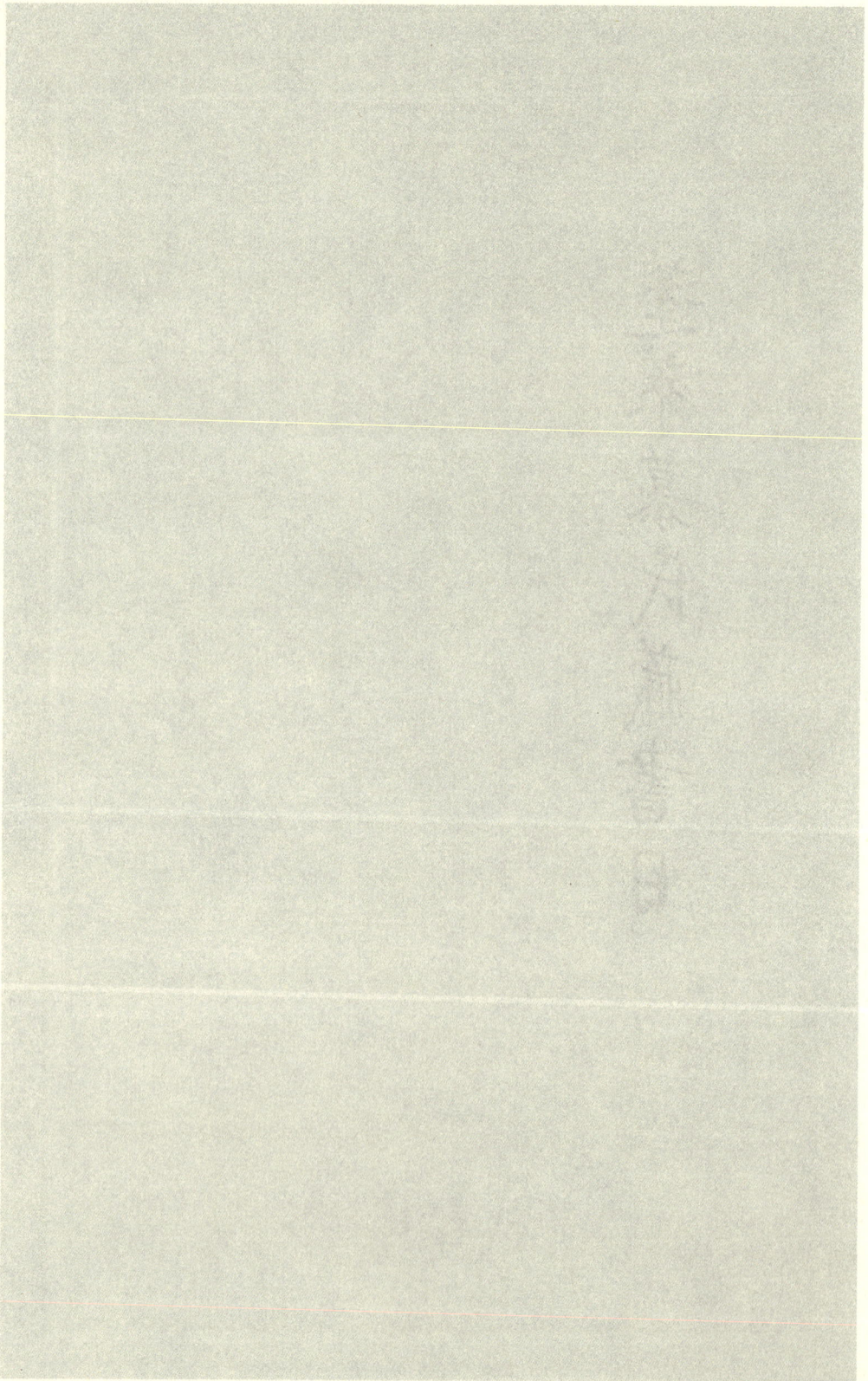

書名	著者註	版本	冊數	函數	備考	編列號數
四書說約	清鹿善繼著	家藏版	四冊	壹	貴州綿紙夾版 道光戊申年重刻	壹
奎壁禮記	清陳皓集說	善成堂藏版 正韻字體	十卷 十冊	壹	光緒辛卯年刻 竹紙	壹
四書朱子本義匯參	清王步青輯	敦復堂藏版	四十卷 四十七冊	五	江蘇學院頒行 毛太紙	貳
羣經義証		李渡校 家藏版	八卷 二冊	一	連史紙	貳
大學古本質言	清劉沅著	鈔印本	一冊	一	北京道德學社印 有光紙	貳
爾雅讀本	清周梫輯	家藏版	四集 二冊	一	竹紙	貳
文成字彙	清梅膺祚音釋	經綸堂刊	十二卷 十四冊	一	毛邊紙	貳
四書古註九種羣義彙解		石印袖珍本	十六冊	一	油光紙夾板	貳
四書味根錄	清金秋澄著	點石齋石印	上下二冊	一	光緒癸未年印 白綿紙	叁

書名	著者・版本	卷冊	部數	紙・刊記	類
周禮正義	清孫貽讓學粉印本	八十六卷二十冊	二	光緒乙巳年出版	叁
音韻註略約編	清張彭緒輯 家藏版	四冊	一	咸豐元年刊褧員 白堂藏版毛太紙	叁
小學集解	清張伯行纂輯 家藏版	六卷四冊	一	竹紙	叁
春秋穀梁傳註	柯劭忞學粉印本	十四卷四冊	一	洋毛邊紙	叁
周易	宋朱熹本義 摹宋刻大字本	二冊	一	宋咸淳乙丑吳革原刊本綿連紙	肆
爾雅音圖	晉郭璞註 影宋大字本	二冊	一	嘉慶六年藝學軒摹刊	肆
經字正蒙	清李文沂纂 家藏版	八卷八冊	一	光緒乙酉年刻廣東羊城萃經堂刻毛邊紙	肆
四書	高麗國仿宋刻大字本	十六本	三	高麗箋紙 夾板	肆
五經	江南書局刻本	二十九本	六	綿連紙	肆
釋名	漢劉熙撰 明刻本	八卷二冊	一	竹紙	肆

直省釋奠禮樂記	春秋分國左傳	禮記	十三經	左傳拾遺	臨文便覽	臨文便覽	夏小正	劉氏家塾四書解	儀禮釋官
	清盧元昌評閱	清陳澔集說		清朱師晦著	清龍翰臣等撰	清龍翰臣等撰	清王筠集傳	清袁文煥校訂	清胡匡衷著
廣東富文齋刊印	思美廬版	浙江書局刊	金陵書局刊	家藏版	松林齋刊		賀惠等校刊本	本塾藏版	研六閣藏版
四冊	十六卷 六冊	十卷 十冊	共五十四冊	上下二冊	上下二冊	二冊	一冊	八冊	九卷 二十九冊
一	一	一	十二	一	一	一			
夾板綿連紙 光緒十七年刻	毛太紙 硃點	竹紙 光緒癸巳年刻	大版連史紙 同治五年刻	夾板 竹紙	粉紙 光緒年刻	綿連紙 同治甲戌年刊	綿連紙	竹紙 光緒丙子年刻	竹紙 嘉慶丙子年刊
伍	伍	伍	伍	伍	伍	伍	伍	伍	伍

經部

書名	著者/輯註	版本	卷冊		紙張/印行	價
禮記正義	吳興劉氏四卷 嘉業堂刊		一冊	一	毛邊紙	伍
欽定篆文四書		古今圖書局 仿原本影印	六冊	一	廣益書局 連史紙 民國三年再版	陸
篆文論語	清吳大澂篆書	振新書肚影印	四冊	一	篤素堂張曉滄藏 竹紙	陸
檀弓考工二通	清徐穆如輯註	家藏版	八卷 八冊	一	綿連紙	陸
三禮圖	宋聶崇義輯註	上海同文書局石印本	共八冊 二十卷 二十冊	一	綿連紙	陸
詩韻全璧		暢愹書尾校本 鴻寶齋印	全六冊	一	光緒年印 綿連紙	柒
詩韻全璧		惜陰書宝藏版 積山書局石印	全六冊	一	光緒十七年印 綿連紙	柒
四書偶談續編	清戚翰芳著	家藏版	一冊	一	毛邊紙	柒
考工記圖	清戴震著	鏗石山館藏版	四冊	一	宜秋館藏 白紙	柒
張氏說文發疑	浙張乳伯述	家藏版	六卷 二冊	一	朱欄之藏 光緒九年刻 綿連紙	柒

三

書名	著者	版本	卷冊	部數	紙張・年代	類
說文通檢	清黎永椿編	崇文書局刊	二十四卷 十四冊	一	綿連紙 光緒二年刻	柒
十一經音訓	清楊國楨等編纂	大梁書院版	十六卷 共計二十六冊	六	毛邊紙	柒
欽定書經圖說	清孫家鼐徐鄘等奉勅纂輯 官版 大學堂編書局		五十卷 十六冊	四	單宣紙 光緒三十一年印	捌
四書典故辨正	清周理裏著	敬義齋藏版	二十卷 四冊	一	竹紙	捌
草字彙	清石梁著	精刻本	六冊	一	乾隆戊申年刻	捌
四書集註		李氏珍藏大字	六冊	一	白毛邊紙 金陵狀元閣印	捌
尚書約註	清任啟運纂	家藏版	二冊	一	毛邊紙	捌
說文解字註 附說文提要	清段玉裁註	湖北崇文書局重刻	三十二卷 三十八冊 又附一冊	二	綿連紙 同治壬申年刻	捌
經典釋文	唐陸德明釋	湖北崇文書局刊本	三十卷 十二冊	二	綿連紙 同治八年刊	捌
周易傳義大全	宋程頤傳 宋朱熹本義		二十四卷 十二冊	二		捌

経部

書名	著者	版本	冊・卷		刻・紙	
韻籟	清華長忠著	松竹齋版	二册 四卷	一	光緒年刻 連史紙	玖
詩經去疑	清王逐升編輯	三樂齋刊	四册 八卷	一	毛邊紙	玖
四書地理攷	清王亮生著	智靜齋刊	六册 十五卷	一	光緒年刻 連史紙	玖
四書經史摘証	清宋飜種輯著	隱芝堂藏版 廣州將軍署重刊	四册 七卷	一	光緒元年刻 夾板綿連紙	玖
說文眞本	漢許愼撰	北宋本校刊 汲古閣藏版	六册 八卷	一	連史紙	玖
字林攷逸	清任大椿學	江蘇書局刊本	三册 八卷	一	光緒庚寅年刊 棉連紙 夾板	玖
倉頡篇補本	清陶方琦學	江蘇書局刊本	一册 二卷	一	光緒十六年刊 綿連紙	玖
九經圖	清楊魁植編輯	翁園藏版	十册	一	乾隆壬辰年刻 連史紙	玖
漢印分韻	清袁予三編	漱藝堂版	四册 四卷	一	嘉慶年刻 一粉紙夾板	玖
古今韻略	清邵長蘅纂	家藏精刻本	五册 五卷	一	毛邊紙	拾

部一 四一

經書字音辨要	五經旁訓	尚書札記	御纂周易折中	欽定書經傳說彙纂	欽定詩經傳說彙纂	欽定春秋傳說彙纂	欽定周官義疏	欽定儀禮義疏	欽定禮記義疏
清楊名颺撰	宋朱熹等註	清許鴻磐著	清康熙帝纂 李光地等校對	清康熙帝欽定 王頊齡等纂輯	清康熙帝欽定 王鴻緒等纂輯	清康熙帝欽定 王掞等纂輯	清乾隆帝欽定 允祿等纂輯	清乾隆帝欽定	清乾隆帝欽定
令德堂刻本	家藏版	學海堂藏版 皇清經解本	湖北崇文書局 仿殿版	湖北崇文書局 仿殿版	湖北崇文書局 仿殿版	湖北崇文書局 仿殿版	湖北崇文書局 仿殿版	湖北崇文書局 仿殿版	湖北崇文書局 仿殿版
九卷 二冊	八冊	四卷 四冊	二十二卷 十二冊	二十一卷 十二冊	二十三卷 十八冊	三十八卷 二十冊	四十八卷 四十冊	四十八卷 三十二冊	八十二卷 四十八冊
一	一	一	二	一	二	二	四	四	五
綿連紙	竹紙	夾連紙	夾綿板連紙 同治十年刊	夾綿板連紙 同治十年刊	夾綿板連紙 同治十年刊	夾綿板連紙 同治十年刊	夾綿板連紙 同治十年刊	夾綿板連紙 同治十年刊	夾綿板連紙 同治十年刊
拾	拾	拾	拾	拾	拾	拾	拾	拾	拾

四書改錯	四書集註直解說約	書經	康熙字典	小學句讀記	禮記體註大全合參	春秋律身錄	鄉黨圖考	羣經字詁	四書字詁
清毛奇齡稿	明張居正著	宋蔡沈集傳	敕纂	清王仲復記	清范子登輯	清楊長年著	清江永著	清段謞廷纂	清段謞廷纂
學蔀 西河合集本	清八旗經正書院翻刻本	宋刻本	清張玉書等奉敕纂重刊 湖北崇文書局重刊	三原劉傳經堂版	文成堂版	家藏版	滙德堂版	黔陽楊氏存版	黔陽楊氏存版
八冊	十二冊	六卷 八冊	四十冊	五卷 六冊	四卷 四冊	二十二卷 八冊	四卷 四冊	七十二卷 十三冊	七十八卷 十五冊
一	二	二	六	一	一	一	一	一	一
綿連紙	毛邊紙		光緒元年刊 綿連紙	粉紙	竹紙	光緒年刻 粉紙	乾隆年刻 毛邊紙	道光己酉年刻 毛太紙	道光己酉年刻 毛太紙
拾貳	拾貳	拾貳	拾貳	拾壹	拾壹	拾壹	拾壹	拾壹	拾壹

經部

五一

書名	撰者	版本	卷冊	部	紙・年代	櫃
撫本禮記	清鄭康成註	張敦仁仿宋本刻	二十卷 附考異	一	同治九年刻 綿連紙	拾貳
方言疏証	清戴震著	漢青籍刊微波榭本 崇文書局重刊	八冊	一	光緒年刻 綿連紙	拾貳
公穀合刊	清王崑繩詳訂	仿宋刻本	共六冊	一	乾隆年刻 毛邊紙	拾貳
隸辨	清顧南原撰	玉原堂	八卷 八冊	一	嘉慶甲子年刻 毛邊紙	拾貳
說文聲系	清姚文田撰	粤東省學使署刻	二冊	一	連史紙	拾貳
新定三禮圖	宋聶崇義輯註	家藏版	二十冊	一	康熙丙辰年刻 毛邊紙	拾貳
駢雅訓纂	明朱謀㙔撰 魏笛生纂	知不足齋刊	七卷 六冊	一	光緒十二年刻 粉紙	拾叄
文字蒙求廣義	清王筠原本	江楚書局刊	五卷 四冊	一	竹紙	拾叄
四書代言	明方應祥纂	明刊本	四冊	一	竹紙	拾叄
四書圖考	清杜炳撰	鴻文書局石印本	四冊	一	光緒丁亥年印 綿連紙	拾叄

經部

書名	撰述・校訂	版本	卷冊	部數	紙張・刊年	價
說文篆韻譜	清徐鉉述	綿州李氏用吳縣翡氏本校	五卷 二冊	一	官堆紙 夾板	拾叄
小學鈎沈	清任大椿學 王念孫校正	青華閣藏版	二冊	一	光緒丁亥重刊 毛邊紙 附在前書內	拾叄
五經		金谷園藏版	十六冊	二	雙白毛邊紙 道光二十二年刊	拾叄
毛詩辨韻	清趙似祖撰	家藏版	四冊	一	白竹紙 嘉慶年刊	拾叄
禮記省度	清彭頤纂	家藏版	四卷 四冊	一	綿連紙	拾叄
考工記 附檀弓	明郭正域撰	明萬曆版 硃批評點	二卷 三冊	一	竹紙	拾叄
經書字音辨要	清楊名颺編輯	令德堂刊	九卷 一冊	一	毛邊紙 光緒癸巳年刊	拾叄
四書成語集對	清揚裕忱輯	昭然堂藏版	二冊	一	毛邊紙 道光年刊	拾肆
小學集註	宋朱熹撰 明崇禎皇帝御製序	明崇禎八年刊本	六卷 四冊	一	白紙	拾肆
爾雅直音	清孫保輯	崇德書院藏版	上下二卷 二冊	六 一	毛邊紙 光緒乙未年刊	拾肆

書名	著者	版本・刊行	卷冊	部	紙張	定價
小學集解	宋朱熹撰	湖北崇文書局刻本　同治六年刊	六卷 三冊	一	綿連紙	拾肆
小學集解	清張伯行輯註	吳與劉氏校刊本　民國辛酉年刊	四冊	一	綿連紙	拾肆
四書說約	清鹿善繼著	本　光緒丁酉年印	三卷 三冊	一	夾板綿連紙	拾肆
爾雅圖音註（通）	晉郭璞註	慎記書莊石印　袖珍本　光緒乙酉年刊	八卷 八冊	二	毛邊紙	拾肆
經字正蒙	清李文沂纂	本　粤東萃經堂刊	二冊	一	洋毛邊紙	拾肆
易通釋（通例）	清陳啟彤著	家藏版	三十冊	一	毛邊紙　夾板	拾肆
詩經集傳音釋	宋朱熹集傳　清許謙名音釋	家藏版	四卷 二十冊	一	白紙	拾肆
篆文四書	清李光地等奉勒撰	殿版	十冊	二	毛邊紙	拾肆
四書考輯要	清陳宏謀輯	培遠堂藏版　乾隆三十六年刻	二十卷 十冊	一	毛邊紙	拾肆
四書便蒙	清焦袁熹等定	立本齋藏版　道光五年刻	十四冊	二	白綿紙	拾肆
四書說苑	清琇廕科輯	家藏版	十一卷 四冊	一	毛邊紙	拾肆

經部

書名	著者	版本	卷冊	數	刊印・紙	價
論語淺解	清喬松年註	強恕堂藏版	四卷 一冊	一	光緒三年刻　綿連紙	拾肆
明本排字九經直音		清吳興陸氏十萬卷樓刻本	四冊	一	光緒七年刊　夾板　綿連紙	拾肆
儀禮圖	清張惠言述	湖北崇文書局　重刻本	六卷 三冊	一	同治九年刻　毛邊紙	拾肆
萬言肆雅	清屈曾發撰	亦園藏版	六冊	一	同治庚午年重刻　綿連紙　夾板	拾肆
御製日講四書解義	清喇沙里等奉勅纂	殿版	八冊	二	毛邊紙	拾伍
四書圖考	清杜炳學家藏	賞奇閣藏版	十二冊	二	綿連紙	拾伍
四書典故辨正	清周炳中著	掃葉山房映寫原本校刻本	二十卷 五冊	一	同治丙寅年重刊本　毛邊紙	拾伍
古本尚書	元金履祥表註	原本校刻本	二卷 二冊	一	光緒甲申年刻　綿連紙	拾伍
篆文孝經	清吳大澂寫	上海同文書局　石印本	一冊	一	光緒乙酉年印　綿連紙	拾伍
經韻集字析解	清熊守謙參訂	天津分司署藏版	二冊	一	道光壬午年刻　綿連紙	拾伍

書名	撰輯者	版本	卷冊	部數	紙張・刊年	價
疏堂韻同	清趙校輯	進一堂藏版	五冊	一	道光元年刻 綿連紙	拾伍
四聲易知錄	清姚文田輯	廣州修補印行	四卷 二冊	一	光緒八年印 綿連紙	拾伍
古籕拾遺	清孫貽讓記	永嘉戴鍾毓劉本	二卷 二冊	一	竹紙	拾伍
樂律全書	明朱載堉撰	明萬曆年刊本大開本	四十冊	四	明綿紙 夾板	拾伍
小四書	明方逢辰撰	明嘉靖二十六年刊本大字精刻	三卷 三冊	一	明綿紙	拾伍
文字蒙求	清蔡友篛撰	學務局精刻大字本	四卷 一冊	一	光緒三十年刻成 綿連紙	拾伍
爾雅音圖	晉郭璞註	曾氏刊本藝學軒藏版	三卷 三冊	一	嘉慶六年影宋繪圖本重摹刊 綿連紙	拾伍
宋紹熙本公羊傳注		清汪喜孫等重校刊本	十二卷 二冊	一	道光四年刊 毛邊紙	拾伍
小學集註	宋朱熹撰	吳棠仿殿版重刊	六卷 四冊	一	同治二年刊 毛邊紙	拾伍
草韻彙編	清陶南望輯	乾隆二十年刊本	十冊	一	毛邊紙	拾伍

書名	著者・編者	版本	卷冊	部	紙張・刊年	價
四聲精辨		袖珍本	五卷	一	白紙	拾伍
禮記通識	嚴尹邡城著	宣統年刻	四卷	一	竹紙版 火竹紙版	拾陸
檀弓述註	明孟鳴父纂述	芮惇叙堂刊	上下二冊	一	竹紙 夾板	拾陸
五雅	晉郭璞註 明葉字本重訂	明天啟丙寅年 剩本	十二冊	二	竹紙	拾陸
說文解字義證	清桂馥撰	湖北崇文書局 刊本	五十卷 三十二冊	四	同治九年刊 毛邊紙	拾陸
小學纂註	宋朱熹著 清高愈纂註	浙江書局刊本	六卷 二冊	一	綿連紙 火板 同治十一年刊	拾陸
左粹類纂	明施仁編輯	明萬曆十一年 刊本	十二卷 八冊	一	白紙	拾陸
詩經		明凌杜若刊本 硃批評點	六冊	一	綿連紙	拾陸
論孟集註	明鍾惺 批點	寶恕堂版	十一冊	一	厚白毛太紙 夾板	拾陸
駁呂留良四書講義	清朱軾等輯	官版	八冊	一	毛邊紙	拾陸

八一

書名	著者	版本	卷・册	部	紙張・刊記	價
字鑑	元李文仲編	蔣氏精刻本	五卷 一册	一	綿連紙 光緒甲申年刻	拾陸
周易逢原	清馮光炳著	寫本	十册	一	綿連紙	拾陸
小四書	宋方逢辰等撰	鋤經閣重刊本	六卷 四册	一	白毛太紙	拾陸
書經	宋蔡沈集傳	湖北崇文書局版	六册	一	綿連紙 同治七年刊	拾陸
秦書八體原委	清華嵒疏輯	天津博物院影印版	二册	一	綿連紙 同治甲戌年刊	拾陸
增廣字學舉隅	清嵒珊輯	蘭州郡署刊版	四册	一	綿連紙	拾陸
鄭志	漢鄭康成撰		三卷 三册	一	毛邊紙	拾陸
欽定各郊壇廟樂章	清張樂盛譜	原刻本	二册	一	毛邊紙	拾陸
春秋四傳		明刻本	三十八卷 八册	二	綿連紙 漢陽周貞亮藏	拾柒
周易集義		明刻本	二十四卷 六册	一	綿連紙 漢陽周貞亮藏	拾柒

書名	著者	版本	卷／冊	部數	紙／藏	價
書經集傳		明刻本	六卷 六冊	一	漢陽周貞亮藏 綿連紙	拾柒
禮記集傳		明刻本	三十卷 八冊	一	漢陽周貞亮藏 綿連紙	拾柒
詩經·集傳		明刻本	三十六卷 六冊	一	漢陽周貞亮藏 綿連紙	拾柒
欽定春秋左傳讀本		武英殿版	三十卷 十六冊	二	道光二年刻 太史連紙	拾柒
大戴禮記	漢戴德著	元撫宋版 懷德堂	十三卷 四冊	一	吳廣霈藏 夾竹紙	拾柒
聯經	清李學禮述	補過堂藏版	四卷 四冊	一	乾隆年刻 竹紙	拾柒
詩三家義集疏	清王先謙著	盧受堂刊本	二十八卷 十二冊	一	毛邊紙	拾柒
文字蒙求	清莫友芝纂	原刻本	四卷 四冊	一	綿連紙	拾柒
欽定清音字式		官版	一冊	一	綿連紙	拾柒
四書類考	清陳愚谷纂	蘄州陳氏家塾本	三十卷 十八冊	二	嘉慶辛酉年刻 士綿連紙	拾捌

九一

書名	著者	版本	卷冊	部	紙／刊年	價
經書字音辨要	清楊名殿編輯	令德堂重刻本	九卷一冊	一	道光丁未年刊 綿連史紙	拾捌
禹貢本義	清楊守敬撰	刊於鄂城菊灣	一冊	一	光緒丙午年刊 洋紙	拾捌
此木軒四書說	清焦袁熹著 家藏版	日本版	四卷九冊	一	清翰林院藏本 毛邊紙	拾捌
論語解註合編	清姚永樸註	秋浦翰墨林 石印	二十卷十冊	一	毛邊紙	拾捌
毛詩品物圖考	浪華岡元鳳纂輯	日本版	七卷四冊	一	高麗綿紙	拾捌
四書註疏大全合纂	明張溥纂	明崇禎九年精刻本	十八冊	四	竹紙	拾玖
五經萃室		奉新宋氏卷雨樓影印清 武英殿仿宋本	四十四冊	八	白毛邊紙	拾玖
尚書因文	清武士逵學	約六山房刻	六卷四冊	一	竹紙	貳拾
字系	清夏日瑑學	琴絲匣鏡軒稿	十五卷附錄一卷 四冊	一	連史紙	貳拾
說文引經考證	清陳瑑學	三益廬刊	七卷附異說二卷 四冊	一	光緒年刻 連史紙	貳拾

項目	大學論語中庸傳註	春秋取義測	四書	五經三傳讀本	廣金石韻府	周禮	禮記鄭氏註	禮記	四書提耳	佩文詩韻
著者	明李塨傳註	清法坤宏撰			明朱時望原輯 清周亮工校刊	漢鄭康成註 唐陸德明音義	漢鄭康成註		清耿坑著	
版本	粵省西湖齋精印本	六書齋刻本 精寫刻本	殿版	濕陽萬氏蓮峰書屋藏版 精刻本	大菜堂藏版	崇文書局刊	味經書院刊	抄寫本 硃批點	屏山堂藏版	明善堂藏
卷冊	四冊	十二卷	五冊	四十冊	四冊	十二冊	二十卷	二冊	共十九冊	五卷 五冊
函	十	一	一	四	一	一	一	一	一	一
用紙	綿連紙	綿連紙 乾隆甲寅年刻	毛邊紙 清國子監藏版	易經書經禮記春秋三傳詩經 綿連紙	綿連紙	連史紙 同治七年刻	夾板白綿紙 光緒年刻	竹紙	夾連史紙 乾隆元年刻	連史紙
價	貳壹	貳拾	貳拾	貳拾	貳拾	貳拾	貳拾	貳拾	貳拾	貳拾

書名	撰者	版本	卷數	冊數	部	紙張・刊年	號
洪武正韻	明宋濂等奉勅撰	精刊本	十六卷	一冊	一	明隆慶元年 白紙 夾板	貳貳
欽定春秋傳說彙纂	清王掞等奉勅撰	清殿版 開化版	三十八卷	二十四冊	二	康熙六十年印 夾板	貳叁
欽定四書圖說		原延呈御覽 抄寫底本 隋寫繪圖		十九冊	四	宣紙硃絲欄黃綾書皮 及套裝潢	貳叁
四書字詁	清段諤廷原稿 黃本驥編訂	黔陽楊氏存版	七十八卷	七十六冊	二	光緒己酉年刊 毛邊紙	貳叁
羣經字詁	清段諤廷原稿 黃本驥編訂	黔陽楊氏存版	七十二卷	十六冊	二	光緒己酉年刊 毛邊紙	貳叁
大戴禮記斠補	清孫詒讓撰	石印本	三卷	三冊	二	連史紙	貳叁
千文六書統要	清李登等撰	十竹齋版本 精刻初印		六冊	一	康熙癸卯年刻 竹紙	貳叁
孫氏說文（附說文通檢）	清孫星衍輯	番禺陳昌治校刊 精刻版本	共三十卷	十冊	一	同治十二年刊 綿連紙	貳叁
論孟精義	清李日烓輯	家藏精刻本		十三冊	一	龍門紙	貳叁
易經通註	清傅以漸添勅撰	舊精抄巾箱本 原紅格底本	九卷	八冊	一	龍門紙 夾板	貳叁

書名	著者	版本	卷冊	部數	紙張・年代	價
校字錄	清史評等撰	巾箱本	二冊	一	道光七年刊 毛邊紙	貳叁
正韻辨字全書		舊抄本	上下二卷 二冊	一	白紙	貳叁
隸書大字典	清翟雲升等輯	上海掃葉山房影印原本	二十冊	四	計二百四十六種漢碑精華 民國十三年印綿連紙	貳肆
千文六書統要	明胡正言輯篆	十竹齋藏版	二卷 四冊	一	竹紙	貳肆
四音釋義	清鄭長庚輯	束鹿堂藏版	十二冊	一	道光十一年刻 竹紙	貳肆
毛詩學	馬其昶著	聚珍仿版	十三卷 一冊	一	龍門紙	貳肆
全補五經諸史海篇直音 讀史雜字	明酒齋先生輯	明萬曆版	二冊	一	竹紙 熙俊藏	貳肆
古本尚書	元金仁山表註	原本刊	上下二冊	一	光緒年刊 綿連紙	貳肆
寫定尚書	清吳汝綸錄	桐城吳氏家塾本	一冊	一	光緒十八年印 綿連紙	貳肆
周易費氏學	馬其昶撰	豫章饒氏等刊	八卷 四冊	一	龍門紙 夾板	貳肆

經部 十一

御製繙譯四書	音韻逢原	四書釋地補	四書成語對	助字辨略	爾雅直言	四書正蒙	六經圖	四書一貫講	經傳釋詞
乾隆帝御製 鄂文泰籌定	清裕恩撰定	清閻若璩原本 樊廷枚校補	清揭裕忱輯	清劉淇選	清孫俌輯		清鄭之僑編輯	清顧天健著	清王引之著
聚珍堂刊	聚珍堂刊	梅陽海涵堂刊本	昭然堂藏版	長沙楊氏校刊	天心閣藏版本 嘉慶巳未增訂	仿明刻本 文盛堂藏版	逃堂藏版 精刻本	啟後堂藏版	文學山房 聚珍版印
六冊	十二卷 四冊	五冊	二冊	五冊 卷	上下二卷 二冊	八冊	十二冊	十六冊	四卷 十冊
一	一	一	一	一	一	一	二	二	一
竹紙 光緒年重刊	毛邊紙 道光年刻	竹紙 嘉慶丙子年刊	毛邊紙 光緒癸巳年刻	竹紙	綿連紙	綿紙 光緒戊子年刻	綿連紙	竹紙 乾隆癸未年鐫	綿連紙
貳肆	貳肆	貳肆	貳肆	貳肆	貳肆	貳伍	貳伍	貳伍	貳伍

書名	著者	版本	卷冊	函	紙／刊年	價
萬壽衢歌樂章	清彭元瑞撰	聚珍版印 朱墨套印	六卷 四冊	一	竹紙	貳伍
同音字辨	清劉維坊彙輯	重訂善成本 京師善成堂藏版	四冊	一	同治十二年刊 竹紙	貳伍
經字辨體	清邱家煒學	京都二酉齋刊版	八卷 四冊	一	光緒辛巳年重刊 綿連紙	貳伍
經韻集字析解	清彭良敞集註	長臻重刊本	二卷 二冊	一	綿連紙	貳伍
說文通訓定聲	清朱駿聲輯	家藏版 進呈本	三十二冊	四	同治八年刻本 竹紙	貳陸
九經談	日本太田元貞著	日本四書房藏版	十卷 一冊	一	東洋綿紙	貳陸
詩經音韻解（附解觸）	清甄士林音釋	家藏版 精刻本	四卷 五冊	一	綿連紙	貳陸
十三經挈本	清彭玉雯纂	彭氏刊本	八冊	一	夾板 綿連紙	貳陸
詩經緝	宋嚴粲述	雙闈重校刊宋本	三十六卷 十二冊	一	光緒庚寅年刊 毛邊紙	貳陸
易經通註	清傅以漸撰	雙闈校刊小箱本	四冊	一	光緒丙戌年刊 綿連紙	貳陸

十二

書名	著者	版本	卷數	冊數	套	紙張・刊印	編號
批點尚書讀本	清王言綸批點	精鈔原刻底本 硃批點	六卷	一冊	一	山西紙	貳陸
爾雅音圖		影宋繪圖本重摹刊	三卷	一冊		綿連紙 嘉慶六年初印	貳柒
御纂周易折中	清康熙帝纂	殿版 開化紙初印	二十二卷	一冊	一	刻絲套 黃絹書皮 綿連紙	貳柒
特別左傳	晉杜預註釋 宋林堯叟見	細紅格板套印 巾箱本精刊	五十卷	十六冊	一	石經山房藏本	貳柒
字典考證	清突榆等輯錄	進呈日本堂藏版		八冊	一	毛邊紙	貳柒
經言拾遺	清徐文靖學	志寧堂藏版	十四卷	四冊	一	竹紙 乾隆丙子年刊	貳柒
同聲韻學便覽	清删德懋編輯	家藏版	四卷	四冊	一	油光紙 光緒年刊	貳捌
春秋左傳杜註補輯	清姚培謙學	梅墅石渠開刊	十三卷	三十冊	二	白紙 光緒九年刊	貳捌
詩經講意鐸振	清江環輯著 徐奮瑞刪補		八卷	八冊	一	竹紙	貳捌
聖門樂誌	清孔尚任原纂	闕里倪寬亭藏版		一冊	一	油光紙 光緒年重刊	貳捌

書名	著者	版本	冊卷	數量	刊刻/紙張	編號
望門禮誌	清孔令貽輯	闕里硯寬亭藏版	一冊		光緒年重刊 油光紙	貳捌
蘇老泉批評孟子眞本	宋蘇洵原本	懊詁堂藏版硃批本	上下二冊	一	嘉慶年刻 竹紙	貳捌
廣韻新編	勉學堂編	家藏版	一冊		康熙年刻 榜紙	貳捌
左繡	清鴈李驛評輯	華川書屋刊本	三十卷 十四冊	二	龍門紙	貳捌
古樂經傳	清李光地計	家藏版	五卷 四冊	一	毛邊紙	貳玖
經籍纂詁	清阮元譔集 孫淸楨輯	阮氏小嫏嬛仙館刊本	一百零六卷 四十八冊	五	嘉慶年刻 綿連紙	貳玖
四書讀本		明刻本	五冊	一	綿連紙	貳玖
詩韻辨字略		沈定夫原刻 黃倬重刊	五卷 一冊		光緒三年刻 竹紙	叁拾
字錄	清李調元撰	家藏版	上下二冊		竹紙	叁拾
論語要略	清許玨輯	無錫許氏刊	一冊		連史紙	叁拾

經部

十三

書名	著者	刊印	卷冊	種	紙・刻	價
詩傳傍通 附三續 千文註	清梁益輯	武進盛氏刊	十五卷 附千文註一冊	一	毛邊紙	叁拾
子夏易傳		通志堂經解本 廣東書局重刊	四卷 一冊	一	同治十二年刻 毛邊紙	叁拾
漢上易傳	清朱震集傳	通志堂經解本 廣東書局刊	四卷 二冊		毛邊紙	叁拾
春秋公羊穀梁傳	漢何休學 晉范寗集解	金陵書局重刊	共二十四卷 四冊	一	光緒二十年刻 毛邊紙	叁拾
論語管見	日本龜谷省軒著	日本吉川半七刊印	一冊		明治十年印 白紙	叁拾
三經誼詁	馬其昶學	民彝叢刊之一 中央訓經院印	三卷 一冊		民國年印 平粉連紙	叁拾
春秋左傳	宋岳珂刊補	江西書局刊	三十卷 十六冊	一	同治十三年刻 夾綿板連紙	叁拾
易經		江西書局刊	四卷 六冊	一	同治十三年刻 夾綿版連紙	叁拾
書經		江西書局刊	六卷 四冊	一	同治十三年刻 夾綿版連紙	叁拾
禮記		江西書局刊	十卷 十冊	一	同治十三年刻 夾綿版連紙	叁拾

書名	編著・版本	卷數	册數／箱	年代・附記	紙	價
經義考	清朱彝尊錄　曝書亭藏版	三百卷	一箱		毛邊紙	叁壹
	廬見曾編　精刻初印本	六十册				叁壹
康熙字典（敕纂）	清凌紹雯等奉　殿版初印	十二卷	四十册　六	康熙五十五年印　毛邊紙		叁壹
樂書	宋版　朱蝴蝶裝	卷三十八至四十二册　二册		共計二十七頁　麻沙紙		叁壹

以上共計貳百陸拾貳種

書名	著者註	版本	冊・卷數	函數	備考	編列號數
二十四史	馮沈德潛等編	殿版	三百七十八冊 八十四	壹	竹紙 漢陽周貞亮藏本	壹
舊五代史	宋薛居正等撰	吳興劉氏嘉業堂四 明輯抱經樓依舊禮抄 本校刊	一百五十卷 三十二冊	四	秀水莊氏藏書	壹
甲子會紀	明薛應旂編輯	玄津草堂版 明嘉靖戊午五	五冊	壹	明綿紙	壹
元聖武親征錄	何秋濤校正	家藏本	二冊	壹	小琨巢	壹
海錄	楊炳南著	家藏本	一冊	壹	黃毛邊紙	壹
白雲仙表	清完顏崇實著	家藏本	上下二冊	壹	白連紙 培經堂藏書	壹
欽定光祿寺則例	清光祿寺修纂	官版	九十四卷 五十四冊	四	咸豐五年刊 夾板 夾連紙	壹
洪憲元年曆書	教育部 中央觀象台	觀象台製	一冊	壹	白綿紙	壹
陳氏中西回史日曆	陳垣撰	叢書 國立北京大學研究所國學門	二十卷 五冊	壹	朱墨兩色鉛印 洋平面粉連紙	壹

書名	著者	版本	卷冊	部數	紙張・刻印	等級
彙纂功過格		澱西蘭室唵館重梓	十二卷 附感應篇頌等一卷 一冊	一	白綿紙 光緒五年刻	壹
念昔齋囈言圖纂	清黃雲鵠撰	家藏本	四冊	一	竹紙	壹
景教碑文紀事考証	清楊棨著	楊大本堂刊	三卷 一冊	一	綿連紙夾板 光緒二十一年	壹
詞林典故	清朱珪等纂	官版	六十四卷 三十四冊	四	連史紙 光緒十三年重刻	貳
詞林典故	清張廷玉等修	殿版	八卷 十冊	二	厚竹紙 乾隆戊辰年刻	貳
張文襄公四種	清張之洞著 無錫許同莘編輯	鉛印	共一百五十一卷 七十五冊	八	竹紙鉛印 白蘭言藏書	貳
古方略	明張自烈述	忠貞堂版	五十六冊	二	夾板 白蘭言藏書	貳
史筌	清楊銘枻編著 寄雲書屋	家藏版	二冊	一	竹紙 道光年刻	貳
郎潛紀聞	清陳康祺著	校經山房刊	共三十卷 八冊	一	毛太紙 光緒十年刻	貳
二十一史約編	清鄭子唯述	魚計堂藏版	八冊	一	補前後二編 毛太紙	貳

書名	著者	刊本	卷冊	部數	備考	等第
御製古稀說	清乾隆帝製	殿版	一冊	一	鈐有御寶 開化榜紙	貳
佛學地理志	張相文撰	鉛印本	三卷 一冊	一	民國十四年出版 毛邊紙	貳
開禧德安守城錄	明王致遠編	永嘉劉本	一冊	一	闞味軒藏本 竹紙	貳
東華錄	清王先謙撰	京都善成堂刊	共四百九十四卷 計一百四十冊	二十四	光緒丁亥年重刻 共十種 連史紙	貳
東華錄	清蔣良驥著	寫本	計十六冊	二	楷書 白竹紙 硃點 二夾板	貳
大清光緒新法令	譯所編輯	商務印書館編 商務印書館鉛印	二十三冊 四類	四	宣統元年八月再版 油光紙	貳
史學疆珠	清周贇纂輯	家藏版	四十卷	一	光緒七年刊 毛邊紙	叄
郡齋讀書志	宋晁公武撰	靈石楊氏刊本	十四卷 六冊	一	道光二十七年刊 竹紙	叄
元朝祕史		石印	十五卷 二冊		連筠簃叢書本	叄
鳳洲綱鑑會纂	明王世貞撰	石印本	七十六卷 十六冊	一	光緒庚寅上海鴻文書局刊 資治通鑑綱目三編四卷二冊 綿連紙夾版	叄

書名	撰者	版本	卷／冊	函	刊刻・用紙	等第
求闕齋弟子記	清王定安譔	京都龍文齋藏版	三十二卷	二	光緒二年刊 綿連紙	叁
進脩堂奏稿	清白恩佑撰	家藏版	十六冊	二	光緒二十三年刊 綿連紙	叁
聖門諸賢輯傳	清查光泰輯	家藏版	一二冊卷	一	綿連紙	叁
歷代循吏傳	清朱軾輯	家藏版	一冊	一	夾連紙	叁
文廟通考	清唐啟祖等輯	家藏版	六八冊卷	一	岳邑朱文亮重刊 白毛邊紙	叁
大清律例	清唐紹祖等奉勅纂修	殿版	二六冊卷	二	綿夾連紙	叁
西審等處軍務紀略	清奎順述	石印	四十七卷	二	白綿紙	叁
明紀	清陳鶴纂	家藏版	二六十冊卷	一	白連紙 二夾板	肆
裕莊毅公年譜		家藏版	二十冊	一	同治九年刊於廣州 夾連紙	肆
四裔編年表	美國林樂知譯 中國嚴良勳譯 李鳳苞校編	木刻本	四冊	一	毛邊紙	肆

史部

書名	著者	版本	卷册	函	紙張・刊年	部
開國方略	清伯麟等奉敕撰	抄寫大字本	三十二卷 十六册	一	白綿紙	肆
欽定四庫全書簡明目錄	清紀昀等奉敕撰	廣東書局重刊本	二十卷 十二册	一	綿連紙 同治七年刊	肆
洪武聖政記	明宋濂撰	明刻版	一册	一	夾板 光緒丁丑年刻	肆
史外	清汪有典撰	家藏版	八卷 八册	一	綿連紙 光緒十三年刻	肆
高厚蒙求	清徐朝俊纂	同文館聚珍版	四册	一	綿連紙	肆
史通削繁	清紀昀纂	初印本／硃印本	四册／四册	一	毛邊紙	肆
霞客遊記	明徐宏祖著	水心齋葉氏刻本	十册	一	嘉慶戊辰校補本	肆
澳門紀略	清印光任等纂	家藏版	二卷 二册	一	嘉慶五年刻 綿連紙	肆
高氏戰國策（附向歆大傳三卷一冊）	漢高誘註	雅雨堂刻本	三十三卷 六册	一	乾隆丙子年刻 綿連紙	肆
戰國策去毒	清陸闓其評選	重刊本	二册	一	同治庚午年刊 綿連紙	肆

十七 一

書名	撰著	版本	卷册	數	紙張・刊年	
朱伯廬先生編年毋欺錄	金吳·瀾編	家藏版	三卷附觀復堂稿一卷鶴雲川年譜一卷順亭林年譜一卷 六册	一	毛邊紙	肆
熙朝紀政	清王慶雲逃	石印	六卷 二册	一	連史紙 光緒年印	肆
英法俄德四國志略	清沈敦和輯譯	四明耳學廬刻	二册	一	連史紙 民國八年印	肆
金石萃編	清王昶著	掃葉山房石印	一百六十卷 三十二册	四	毛邊紙	肆
欽定理藩院則例	清托津等奉勅撰	活字排版印本	十六册	二	毛邊紙 光緒三十四年	肆
原修回疆則例	清托津等奉勅撰	活字板排印本	二八册	二	毛邊紙 光緒三十四年	肆
永樂大典目錄	明姚廣孝奉勅撰	靈石楊氏刊本	六十册	一	連箋匧叢書本	肆
續通鑑類纂		上海和記書莊 石印本	二十册	二	洋粉連紙 光緒壬寅年印	肆
增兩朝御批正	清馬佳松椿纂	石印本	二十二卷 十二册	一	綿連紙 光緒甲午印	肆
路史	宋羅泌著	校宋本縮印	六十六卷 十册	一	竹紙	肆
國史略	日本松苗編	日本刻版	二八册	一	明治戊辰年刻本	肆

書名	著者	版本	卷	冊	部	紙	等
國朝先正事略	清李元度纂 校印本	山東官印書局	六十卷	十本		洋粉連紙	肆
甲子會紀	明陳應旂輯	明朝嘉靖年刊本	五卷	四冊	一	竹紙	肆
宸垣識略	清吳太初輯	池北草堂版	十六卷	八冊	一	光緒年刊 白綿紙	伍
明會要	清龍文彬纂	永懷堂版	八十卷	十冊	二	毛太紙 二夾板	伍
帝鑑圖說	明張居正著	江陵鄧氏藏版	四卷	四冊	一	白綿紙	伍
十六國春秋	魏崔鴻撰	家藏版	四卷	四冊	一	毛太紙	伍
三史拾遺	清錢大昕著	嘉興郡版	四卷附諸史拾遺五卷	四冊五冊	一	嘉慶十二年刊 連史紙	伍
紀元編	清六承如集錄	叢學齋刊	三卷	四冊	一	道光辛卯刊 毛邊紙	伍
元朝名臣事略	元蘇天爵撰	清武英殿聚珍版	十五卷	四冊	一	白毛邊紙 一夾板	伍
清嘉慶二年時憲書	清欽天監編	官版	一	一冊		白竹紙	伍

史部

十八一

清光緒年時憲書	清同治年時憲書	清咸豐年時憲書	欽定修造吉方立成	岑勤襄公年譜	徵君孫先生年譜	明儒學案	隸續	史外	廿一史彈詞
清欽天監編	清欽天監編	清欽天監編	清欽天監編	清岑毓英趙藩編輯	明孫奇逢清湯斌編次	明黃宗羲著	宋洪适撰	清汪有典著	明楊慎纂
官版	官版	官版	官版	家藏版	懷遠堂梓	國學研究會重刊本	日本浪華書林翻刻	家藏版	玲瓏山館藏版
計二四六(二)九十四八(二)前一(二)前三十四年各一册共計十六册	十三年各一册共計十三册	十八冊計九冊	一冊	五十册	四册	三十二册	二十一卷四册	八卷八册	二册
				一	一	二	一	一	一
粉紙	粉紙	粉紙	稿連紙清光緒三十年製	光緒巳亥年刊附遊記中州人物考	年到康熙壬寅綿連紙	毛邊紙民國元年刊	文化紀元甲子梓竹紙夾板	朱懷之藏毛太紙光緒丁丑年刻	乾隆年刻朱黃運紙氏藏鐵
伍	伍	伍	伍	伍	伍	伍	伍	伍	伍

書名	著者	版本	卷數	册數	部數	紙張	價
歷代名人年譜	清吳榮光著	樵山草堂版	十卷附存疑一卷	一册	一	光緒元年刻毛邊紙	伍
廿一史四譜	清沈炳宸鈔	吳氏清來堂刊	五十四卷	四十四册	四	同治辛未年刻	伍
國朝御史題名錄	清黃玉圃編輯	京畿道藏版	五卷	五册	一	竹紙	伍
明清題名碑錄	清國子監編	官版	十四卷	十四册	一	毛太紙一夾板	伍
天聖明道本國語	吳曾昭注	湖北崇文書局刊	二十一卷考異四卷	二十一册	一	竹紙	伍
歷代地理志韻編今釋	清李兆洛輯	家藏版	五種計二十七卷	十册	二	同治己巳年刻毛邊紙	伍
史記狐白	明湯賓尹選	明刻本	四卷	四册	一	明竹紙	伍
孔孟編年	清狄子奇輯	浙江書局刻本	八卷	二册		光緒丁亥年刊惜陰軒叢書本毛邊紙	伍
京畿金石考	清孫星衍撰	李熙齡校刊本	二卷	二册		毛邊紙	伍
新疆建道志	清宋伯魯撰	海棠仙館紛印本	四卷	四册		有光洋紙	伍

史部　十九　一

書名	著者	版本	卷冊	部數	紙張	價
雲南水道考	清李誠撰	吳興劉氏嘉業堂刊	二卷 二冊	一	毛邊紙	伍
顧閣年譜	清張穆編	家藏版 道光二十四年刊	二冊	一	綿連紙	伍
史略	宋高似孫輯	仿宋一廎本刊	六卷 二冊	一	洋粉連紙	伍
淮安府志	清衛哲治訂正	公局版	三十二卷 十三冊	二	毛邊紙 咸豐壬子重刻	陸
關帝聖蹟圖志	清盧湛彙輯	于成龍鑒定本	五冊	一	毛邊紙	陸
說嵩	清景東暘著	嶽生堂版	三十二卷 十六冊	一	竹紙	陸
圓明園圖詠	清帝御製	天津石印書屋 石印硃點	二冊	一	連史紙 一夾板	陸
滿文避暑山莊圖詠	清帝御製	木版	一冊	一	連史紙	陸
圓明園圖詠	清帝御製	石印硃墨原寫本	二冊	一	竹紙	陸
養正圖解	清焦竑恭進	原刻本	四卷附圖詩一卷 圖說一卷 六冊	一	綿連紙	陸

史部

書名	著者／版本	版本	卷・冊	紙・刊	陸
萬國公法	清丁韙良譯	鉛印本	四卷 一冊	粉連紙 夾板	陸
水利書	清孫承澤輯	抄寫本	二冊 一	竹紙 珠墨	陸
聖諭廣訓疏義	清聖祖仁皇帝 版 兩粤廣仁善堂		十六條 一	珠墨 夾板	陸
長編總檔	清聖祖仁皇帝	寫本	十二卷 六冊 一	珠格綿紙 東昌 清同治十年	陸
長編總檔	清聖祖仁皇帝	寫本	十二卷 六冊 一	珠格綿紙 東昌 清同治十一年	陸
大清世祖章皇帝聖訓	清 敕修	寫本	二六卷 二冊 一	粉紙 珠格 清同治十一年	陸
史眷	明王木仲著	明版	十五冊 二	竹紙	陸
百將圖傳	清丁日昌著	家藏版	上下二冊 一	竹紙	陸
廣百將譜	明黃道周註斷 明崇善堂版		二十卷 二十冊 二	毛邊紙	陸
三續疑年錄	清陸心源編 家藏版		二十冊 一	白紙 光緒年刊	陸

二十

書名	著者	版本	卷冊	數	紙	類
庚子西行紀事	清唐晏纂	求恕齋刊	一冊	二	竹紙	陸
渤海·國志	清唐晏纂	求恕齋刊	十四卷　四冊	六	竹紙	陸
欽定國史忠義傳	清曹振鏞等奉敕輯	抄寫本	卷三十二至四十八　一百六十一冊	六	硃色格開化紙	陸
光緒台州府志	清王舟瑤輯	台州旅杭同鄉會館鉛印	一百六卷　六十冊	二	毛邊紙	陸
平定回疆方略	敕撰	殿版	八十卷　八十五冊	六	白紙	陸
歷代名臣傳	清朱軾等訂	世恩堂刊本	三十五卷　二十五冊	六	毛邊紙（光緒二十三年刊）	陸
山東通志	清岳濬等監修	官版	四十二冊	四	洋紙	陸
歷代名臣言行錄	清朱桓編輯	上海商務印書館（鉛印本）	二十四卷　九冊	四	洋紙	陸
御批歷代通鑑輯覽	清傅恒等奉敕纂	鉛印本	一百二十卷　四十冊	一	洋紙夾板	陸
者獻類徵（附賢媛類徵）	清李桓錄	湘陰李氏藏版	三百六十卷　四百九十冊	二十八	毛邊紙夾板	柒

書名	著者	版本	卷／冊	部數	紙張・刊年	編號
東觀漢紀	漢班固等撰	上海埽葉山房版	二十四卷 四冊	一	毛邊紙 乾隆乙卯年刻	柒
易知摘要類編	清富俊編	紹衣堂藏版	十二卷 四冊	二	綿連紙 同治甲戌年刻	柒
皇清開國方略	清阿桂等奉敕撰	上海廣百宋齋校印	三十二卷 六冊	一	洋粉連紙	柒
聖廟祀典圖考 附聖蹟圖	清顧沅輯	上海同文書局縮印本	四冊	一	綿連紙	柒
元史·新編	清魏源譔	邵陽魏慎微堂刊本	九十五卷 三十二冊	二	光緒乙巳年刊 綿連紙	柒
續藏書	明李贄編	明刻本	二十七卷 四十冊	四	竹紙	柒
清凉山新志	清朱奎刻	十卷 十冊		一	毛邊紙	柒
元朝祕史	靈石楊氏刊本	十五卷 四冊		一	毛邊紙 道光二十七年刊	柒
大清會典	清雍正年修殿版	二百五十卷 計一百冊	十四冊	十四	綿連紙	柒
廿二史言行略	清過元歐輯 家藏版	四十二卷 三十六冊	六冊	六	毛邊紙	捌

二十一

書名	著者	版本	卷冊	部數	紙	
元西域人華化考（稿本）	陳垣撰	膠寫版印本	二冊	一	毛邊紙	捌
明季國初進士履歷跋後	清邵懿辰撰	任和邵氏牛巖廬所著書刊本	一冊	一	宣紙　牛巖廬所著書之七	捌
御批歷代通鑑輯覽	清乾隆帝御批	仿殿本	一百二十卷　五十八冊	八	綿連紙　硃批	捌
明季南略	清計六奇編輯	牛松居士排字本	十八卷　十二冊	二	毛邊紙	捌
明季北略	清計六奇編輯	牛松居士排字本	二十四卷　十二冊	二	毛邊紙	捌
春秋世族譜	清陳厚耀撰	維揚寶翰樓藏版	二冊	一	道光庚子年刻　竹紙	捌
淳化閣帖釋文	清朱家標校定	綱錦堂刊本	二十卷冊	一	毛邊紙	捌
盛京典制備攷	清崇厚纂輯	原刻本	六卷　八冊	一	綿連紙	捌
瘞鶴銘攷補	清翁方綱撰	硃印本	二冊	一	綿連紙	捌
書目答問（附識軒齋）	清張之洞撰	諸家寫刻本	二冊	一	綿連紙	捌

史部

書名	著者	版本	卷册	部數	紙/刻年	類
四裔編年表	美國林樂知中國嚴良勳同譯 清李鳳苞嚴復編	原刻本	四册	一	綿連紙	捌
彭剛直公奏稿 附詩集八卷	清彭玉麟撰	俞樾刻本 又附八卷	八卷 六册 二册	一	光緒十七年刻 綿連紙	捌
顧閤年譜合刻	清張穆訂 祁氏刊本	山西壽陽祁氏刊本	二册	一	道光二十四年刊 綿連紙	捌
御製圓明園避暑著山莊圖詠	清徐氏摹	大同書局石印本	二册	一	綿連紙	捌
安陽縣金石錄	清武虛谷著	消貴泰校梓	十二卷 四册	一	洋紙	捌
包孝肅奏議	宋包拯撰	清李瀚章重刊省心閣藏版	十卷 四册	一	綿連紙	捌
國語校註本三種	清汪遠孫輯	振綺堂汪氏刊本	六册	一	道光丙午年刻 綿連紙	捌
劉川姚氏本戰國策	漢高誘注	湖北崇文書局重刊本	三十三卷 四册 又策扎三卷一册	一	同治己巳年刻 毛邊紙	捌
歷代史表	清芮斯同撰	廣雅書局刻本	五十三卷 十二册	一	光緒十五年刻 毛邊紙	捌
鐵琴銅劍樓宋金元本書影	清瞿良士輯影印本		九册 二十二一	一	毛邊紙	捌

書名	編著者	版本	卷冊		紙張	
史記評林	明李宗諤集評	明萬歷年刻本	二十四冊	四	竹紙	玖
漢書評林	明凌以棟集評	明萬歷年刻本	二十冊	四	竹紙	玖
南北史楂華	清周嘉猷著	家藏版	八卷四冊	一	白紙	玖
歷代史案	清洪亮吉編	聚奎閣版	六十卷二十冊	一	毛邊紙一夾板	玖
歷代史略		江楚書局刊	八卷六冊	一	毛邊紙	玖
宋岳忠武王金陀全編	清岳士景編	家藏版	二十八卷續編二十八卷四冊	一	綿連紙乾隆年刻	玖
金陀粹編	清岳珂編	浙江書局刊	二十八卷六冊	一	毛邊紙光緒九年刻	玖
金陀續編	清岳珂編	浙江書局刊	三十卷六冊	一	毛邊紙光緒九年刻	玖
續漢志	梁劉昭註補	浙江書局刊	三十卷二冊	一	毛邊紙	玖
聖武記	清魏源撰	古微堂版	十四卷十二冊	一	白紙	玖

書名	著者	版本	卷冊	部數	刊年・用紙	價
稽古錄	宋司馬光撰	崇文書局版	二十卷	一	同治十一年刻 粉紙 揕卿藏 夾板	玖
小腆紀年 附攷	清徐鼒譔	扶桑使館版	二十二卷	一	光緒年鉛印 綿連紙	玖
五種紀事本末	宋袁樞等編輯	湖南思賢書局 校刊本	一百二十冊	十六	內有通鑑 宋 元史 明史五種 竹紙 光緒戊戌年刊	玖
稽古錄	宋司馬光撰	家藏版	四十卷 二十冊	一	連史紙	玖
漢書評林	明茅坤評釋	明崇禎乙亥年刻	九十三卷 二十二冊	四	毛邊紙	玖
百將圖傳	清丁日昌輯	家藏版	六冊	一	綿連紙	玖
廿一史約編	清鄭芷畦述	魚計亭藏版	八冊	一	竹紙	玖
二十二史感應錄	清彭希涑輯	棃儀重刊本	二卷 二冊	一	宜統元年刊 連史紙	玖
古今列女傳	明解學士撰	積秀堂版	四卷 四冊	一	嘉慶年刻 毛邊紙	玖
十七史蒙求	清王逢原著	文奎堂版	十六卷 李氏蒙求補註六卷 六冊	一	道光年刻 白紙	玖

史部 二十三

407

書名	著者	版本	卷數・冊數	數	紙張・刊刻	價
讀史管見	清齊文庵著	家藏版	八十四卷 四冊	一	竹紙 光緒年刻	玖
綏寇紀略	清吳駿公纂輯	照曠閣版	十二卷補遺三卷 八冊	一	竹紙	玖
西漢會要	宋徐天麟撰	江蘇書局版	七十卷 十冊	一	夾竹板 光緒年刻	拾
東漢會要	宋徐天麟撰	江蘇書局版	四十卷 八冊	一	夾竹板 光緒年刻	拾
唐會要	宋王溥撰	江蘇書局版	一百卷 二十四冊	四	夾竹板 光緒年刻	拾
五代會要	宋王溥撰	江蘇書局版	三十卷 六冊	一	夾竹板 光緒年刻	拾
通鑑輯覽	清乾隆帝御批	官版	一百二十卷 六十冊	八	竹紙 乾隆年刻	拾
通鑑韻書	清沈炳仁編註	綠陰堂藏版	三十二卷 五冊	一	毛邊紙 康熙四十四年刊	拾壹
史記集解抄	明茅坤抄	明萬曆乙亥年精刊本	九十一卷 二十四冊	二	明白綿紙 夾板	拾壹
校刊史記集解索隱正義札記	清張文虎校	金陵書局刊本	五卷 二冊	一	官堆紙 同治壬申年刊	拾壹

書名	著者	版本	卷冊	部數	紙／刊印	價
淳化閣帖釋文	清郎師韓等	敦教堂刻本 朱欄大字寫刻	二十卷 一冊	一	夾連紙	拾壹
宋元舊本書經眼錄	清莫友芝輯	家藏版	五卷 二冊	一	連史紙	拾壹
皇清職貢圖	清傅恒等纂	官版	十二冊	二	竹紙	拾壹
南史識小錄	清沈潤芳 朱文益 合輯	清來堂版	十四卷 八冊	二	竹紙 康熙年刻	拾壹
理學宗傳	清孫奇逢輯	家藏版	二十六卷 十二冊	二	竹紙 同治年刻	拾壹
碧血錄	清莊芝階著	同文書局石印	五卷 五冊	一	連史紙 光緒八年印	拾壹
叢書書目彙編	沈博元編纂	無錫丁氏藏版	四冊	一	平粉連 民國十七年印	拾壹
中州人物攷	清孫奇逢輯	家藏版	八卷 八冊	二	毛邊連 道光二十四年刊	拾壹
宋本韓柳二先生年譜	宋呂大防輯	小玲瓏山館 仿宋重刊	共八冊	一	竹紙 雍正年刻	拾壹
樞垣紀略	清梁茝林著	家藏版	二十八卷 六冊	一	粉紙 海桌圖藏刻 光緒年	拾壹

書名	著者	版本	卷·册	部	刻印·紙張	價
舒氏族譜	舒氏宗祠紀	家藏版	一册	一	光緒年刻 連史紙	拾壹
還讀我書室老人年譜	自訂	家藏版	二卷 二册	一	竹紙	拾壹
竹書紀年校正	梁沈約附注	東路廳署刊	二卷 二册	一	光緒五年刻 竹紙	拾壹
史記菁華錄	清姚苧田氏著	舒外艸堂藏本	六卷 六册	一	光緒九年刻 連史紙	拾壹
唐鑑	清范祖禹撰	廣州翰墨園刊	二十四卷 四册	一	竹紙	拾壹
史通削繁	清紀昀著	兩廣節署	四卷 四册	一	道光年刻 硃批翰墨園藏版白紙	拾壹
頤齋四譜	清丁晏編	家藏版	上下兩册	一	道光年刻 竹紙	拾壹
史鑑節要便讀	清鮑古邨編輯	崇文書局	十卷 補四道四卷 二册	一	同治年刻 粉紙夾板	拾壹
盤山山志	清釋智朴輯		十卷 補四道四卷	一	道光年刻 連史紙	拾壹
盧山小志	清蔡小霞纂	娜嬛別館版	六卷 二十四册	一	道光年刊 綿連紙	拾壹

411

書名	著者	版本	卷册	部	紙／刊年	價
大義覺迷錄	清帝上諭	仿殿版	八册	一	竹紙	拾貳
稽古錄	宋司馬光撰	清初刻本	二十卷册	二	毛邊紙	拾貳
路史	宋羅泌纂	明萬曆年刻	十六册	二	毛邊紙	拾貳
季漢書	明謝陞撰	明刻本	十册	二	竹紙	拾貳
兩漢刊誤	宋吳仁傑撰	金陵書局刊本	二十卷册	一	補連紙	拾貳
史略	宋高似孫綴古	崑山鮑氏刊本	六卷册	一	光緒癸未年刻	拾貳
包孝肅公奏議	宋包拯撰	省心閣藏版	四册	一	綿連紙	拾貳
讀史鏡古編	清潘世恩輯	冶城飛霞閣重刻	三十二卷册	一	毛邊紙 同治甲戌年刻	拾貳
讀史碎金註	清胡虎臣輯	家藏版	八十卷册	十	連史紙 光緒年刻	拾叁
十七史蒙求	清王逢源原著 金三俊輯	大文堂刊	六十六卷册	一	白紙 道光年刻	拾叁

史部

書名	著者	版本	卷數	冊數	部數	紙張刊刻	定價
歷代名臣傳節錄	清崇厚增輯	雲陰堂藏版	三十卷	十三冊	一	綿連紙 道光年刻	拾叁
野獲編	清沈德符著	錢塘姚氏鑒藏	三十卷	二十冊	二	竹紙 道光年刻	拾叁
弇山畢公年譜	清史善長撰	家藏版		一冊	一	夾板竹紙舟刻 同治年刻	拾叁
綱目嶺言	清柯曉崗著	問心堂版		上下二冊	一	毛邊紙 光緒二十八年印	拾叁
寰宇分合志	明徐樞編輯 湘潭楊氏 家藏縮本		八卷	九冊	一	毛太紙 嘉慶丁巳年刻	拾叁
歷代名臣言行錄	清朱桓輯	蔚齋藏版	二十四卷	二十六冊	六	綿連紙 同治庚午年刊	拾叁
藏書	明李戴贄輯著	副本 明萬歷巳亥年	六十八卷	十四冊	一	竹紙 夾板	拾叁
戰國策去毒	清陸隴其輯	重刊本		二十二冊	一	綿連紙 光緒乙未年刊	拾叁
駱文忠公自訂年譜	清駱秉章撰	思賢書局重刊本	二卷	二冊	一	毛邊紙 光緒乙未年刊	拾叁
邵亭知見傳本書目	清莫友芝撰	上海埽葉山房石印本	十六冊	二十六	一	綿連紙 民國十七年印	拾叁

書名	著者	版本	冊卷	函	刻印年/印行	紙	類
河南通志 纂	清孫灝等奉敕	官版	八十八卷	六	光緒年刻 六夾板	油光紙	拾叁
續河南通志	清阿思哈等輯	官版	八十六冊	二	光緒二十八年刻 二夾板	油光紙	拾叁
濟南府志	清王贈芳等輯	官版	七十二冊	四	道光己亥年刻	竹紙	拾叁
史記通註	唐劉知幾著 明陳懿儒註	明刻本	二十冊	一		竹紙	拾肆
史記狐白	明湯賓尹精選	明刻本	六冊	一		竹紙	拾肆
史懷	明鍾惺輯	餘草堂藏版	二十冊	一	光緒辛卯年刻	竹紙	拾肆
逆臣傳	清國史館原本	松居士排字本	十六冊	一		竹紙	拾肆
西域記	清七十一著	家藏版	八冊	一		竹紙	拾肆
道藏目錄詳註 附大明國道藏經目錄	明道士白雲霽撰	退耕堂景印文津閣四庫全書本	四冊		中華印刷局印	綿連紙	拾肆
古今偽書攷攷釋	清姚首源原著 金受申攷釋	鉛印本	二冊		民國十三年初版	厚毛邊紙	拾肆

414

書名	編著者	版本	卷冊	部數	刊年／用紙	定價
皇朝謚法表	清 楊樹編次	家藏版	二冊	一	光緒二十八年刊　綿連紙	拾肆
神僧傳	明 西天笠青河　髮僧梓	明刻版	九卷　十冊	一	毛邊紙	拾肆
大清律例增修統纂集成	遊武林清來堂　吳氏原本增修	錯銅版	四十卷　二十四冊	四	光緒二十年印　綿連紙	拾肆
讀史方輿紀要	清 顧祖禹著	敷文閣藏版	一百三十卷　七十二冊	一	毛邊紙	拾肆
天下郡國利病書	清 顧炎武輯	蜀南桐華書屋　薛氏家塾本	一百二十卷　五十冊	一	毛邊紙	拾肆
欽定天祿琳琅書目	清 于敏中等　奉敕編校	長沙王氏刊	前編十卷　後編二十卷　十二冊	一	粉紙一夾板　光緒甲申年刻	拾肆
百將圖傳	宋 張預撰　清 丁日昌輯刊	家藏版	二卷　四冊	一	白紙　同治年刻	拾肆
潭柘山岫雲寺志	神穆德編訂	家藏版	二卷　二冊	一	竹紙　乾隆四年刻	拾肆
越南地輿圖說	清 盛慶紱纂輯	求忠堂家藏版	六卷　二十二冊	一	綿連紙　光緒九年刻	拾肆
歷代史論	明 張溥撰　孫執升評點	舊松山房版	八卷　二十七冊	一	硃批白紙夾板　光緒年刻	拾肆

書名	撰者	刊行	卷冊	册数	紙・刻	價
歷代史論	明張溥撰 孫執升評點	蒼松山房版	二十二卷	二	光緒　年刻	拾肆
聖賢羣輔錄	晉陶潛著	漢陽葉氏刊	一卷附帝統紀一卷叙略一卷	一	白紙 硃批 同治年刻	拾肆
東林十八高賢傳	東林寺	毘耶室梓行	一冊		竹紙	拾肆
壽者傳	清陳懋仁撰	漢陽葉氏刊	一冊		白紙 同治年刻	拾肆
孫徵君年譜	清魏蓮陸合編	稽善堂刊	二冊		粉紙 光緒丁亥年刻	拾肆
黔書	清田雯編 次 太湖李重鐫	黔蘦使者	上下二冊	一	夾板 貴州綿紙 嘉慶戊辰年刻	拾肆
節本泰西新史攬要	清周慶雲節錄	夢坡室刊	二八卷冊	一	粉紙 光緒年刻	拾肆
帝王表	清齊召南編	小瑯環仙館刊	四冊附帝王廟謚年譜	一	綿連紙 光緒年刻	拾肆
蒙古遊牧記	清張穆撰	壽陽祁氏刊	十六卷八冊	一	竹紙 同治六年刻	拾肆
劍俠傳	明徐渭畫像	王齡刊	四卷二冊	一	綿連紙 咸豐年刻	拾肆

書名	著者	版本	卷冊	部數	紙／刊刻年	價
古今賢女傳	息園外史	精印圖畫	八冊	一	綿連紙	拾肆
文廟祀典圖攷	清龐鐘璐編輯	家藏版	五十二卷 十二冊	二	粉紙 道光年刻 四益字藏書	拾肆
聖廟祀典圖攷	清顧沅輯	賜硯堂家藏版	六卷 附聖蹟圖二卷 二冊	一	白紙	拾肆
大清光緒時憲書	清欽天監編	官殿版	十六卷 八冊 二十一二二三二十四五二二二年 六十二本各一本共計二十七冊	一	白紙	拾肆
三希堂法帖釋文			八十六卷 十六冊	一	竹紙 乾隆年刻	拾肆
增註千姓聯珠	清潘釴佩著 楊宗楷增註	家藏版	四卷 四冊	一	綿連紙 道光七年刻	拾肆
廿一史約編	清鄭元慶逃	江左書林藏版	八卷 八冊	一	竹紙 嘉慶十五年刻	拾肆
廿二史言行略	清過元攷輯	家藏版	四十二卷 十六冊	二	竹紙 乾隆五十一年刻	拾伍
廿一史彈詞注	明楊慎編著	視履堂藏版	十一卷 八冊	一	白紙 道光辛卯年刊	拾伍
國朝諡法攷	清趙鉣纂	世美堂藏版	一冊	一	毛邊紙 道光辛卯年刊	拾伍

二十八

書名	著者	版本	卷冊	數	刊年・用紙	價
西藏圖考	清黃沛翹輯	家藏版	八卷四冊	一	光緒丁酉年刻 毛邊紙	拾伍
三通攷輯要	清湯潛菴編輯	阿書集成局鈆印本	六十冊	二	光緒二十五年 綿連紙	拾伍
康對山先生武功縣志	清孫景烈評註	孫氏刻本	二卷三冊	一	乾隆二十六年刊 綿連紙	拾伍
瀛環志略	清徐繼畬輯著	總理衙門藏版	六十卷十冊	一	同治丙寅年重訂 綿連紙	拾伍
光緒二十年奉天全省府廳州縣地輿圖志	清王志修編輯	王氏校刊	一冊	一	光緒二十年刊 綿連紙	拾伍
大清同治四年歲次乙丑時憲書		硃墨寫本	一冊	一	開化榜紙	拾伍
船山公年譜	清王之春輯	家藏版	二冊前後編	一	綿連紙	拾伍
秦邊紀略		牛斠圃藏書本	二卷六冊	一	綿連紙	拾伍
景定建康志	宋馬光祖撰	仿宋本重刊金陵孫忠愍祠藏版	五十二卷三十冊	四	嘉慶七年刊 毛邊紙	拾伍
胡刻資治通鑑校字記	清熊羅宿著	精刻版本	二卷四冊	一	綿連紙	拾伍

史部

書名	著者	版本	卷	冊	部	附註	價
紀元通攷	清蔡維庚撰	鍾秀山房藏版	十二卷	四冊	一	道光八年刻 毛邊紙	拾伍
紀元編		粵雅堂叢書本	三卷	三冊	一	夾板 竹紙	拾伍
欽定古今儲貳金鑑	清乾隆帝欽定	官版	六卷	二冊	一	綿連紙	拾伍
古品節錄	清松筠撰	直隸重鐫	六卷	六冊	一	道光二年重鐫 綿連紙 一布套	拾伍
襲端毅公奏疏	清姚鼐孳著	聽彝書屋重校刊		五冊	一	光緒癸未年刊 綿連紙	拾伍
三遷志 輯	明王特選等纂	剿本	十二卷	四冊	一	毛邊紙	拾伍
水經志	漢桑欽撰 後魏酈道元註	明萬曆乙卯年刻版	十六卷	十六冊	一	竹紙	拾伍
宋蔡忠惠公別紀補遺	明宋珏增補	遜敏齋精刻本	二卷	二冊	一	綿連紙	拾伍
齊乘	明于欽纂	明刊本	六卷	六冊	一	竹紙 夾板	拾伍
四言史徵	清葛震編輯 曹垕註釋	家藏版	十二卷	二冊	一	康熙年刻 竹紙	拾伍

二十九

書名	著者	版本	卷冊	部數	年代／紙張	價
明名臣言行錄	清徐開仁編輯	家藏版	九十五卷 二十冊	四	康熙年刻／竹紙	拾陸
廿一史彈詞註	明楊慎編著	視履堂藏版	八十一卷	一	乾隆年刻／連史紙	拾陸
選義林遜國全書	清劉懃子著	紫華菴藏版	五十六卷	一	康熙年刻／毛邊紙	拾陸
淨土聖賢錄	清彭希涑述	杭城金士培藏版	九卷 三冊	一	乾隆年刻／竹紙	拾陸
繹史	清馬驌撰	家藏版	一百六十卷 二十四冊	四	康熙九年刊／毛邊紙	拾陸
山東考古錄	清顧炎武著	山東書局重刊本	七冊	一	光緒九年刊／毛邊紙	拾陸
明史例案	劉承幹纂	嘉業堂刊	九卷 四冊	一	光緒八年刊／毛邊紙	拾陸
魯山縣志	清武億等纂	董氏刊本	二十六卷 六冊	一	嘉慶元年／白紙	拾陸
陽信縣志	清王允深纂定	民國勞之常重印活字版	八卷 八冊	一	洋白毛邊紙	拾陸
合肥李勤恪公政書	清李瀚章撰 李經畬等編輯	影印原板	十冊	一	綿連紙	拾陸

史部

三十一

書名	著者	版本	卷	冊	部	用紙	定價
歷代循良能吏列傳彙鈔	清喬用遷鈔	有恆齋藏版		四冊	一	道光甲辰年刊 綿連紙	拾陸
廣名將傳	明黃道周註斷	海山仙館叢書本	二十卷		一	綿連紙	拾陸
史通通釋	唐劉知幾撰 清浦起龍釋	家藏版	二十卷	六冊	一	綿連紙	拾陸
史鑑節要便讀	清鮑東里編輯	家藏版 重刊本	六卷	二冊	一	綿連紙 火板	拾陸
皇明北虜考	明鄭曉撰	明嘉靖年刊本		一冊	一	綿紙	拾陸
繪像列仙傳	清還初道人輯	掃葉山房版	四卷	四冊	一	光緒丁亥年刊 綿連紙	拾陸
漢書地理志校本	清汪遠孫校	振綺堂汪氏刊藏	二卷	二冊	一	道光戊申年刊 綿連紙	拾陸
史微	清張采田撰	多伽羅香館叢書本	八卷	四冊	一	屏守齋重刊 綿連紙	拾陸
欽定八旗氏族年譜	清張采田撰	抄寫本		一冊	一	榜紙	拾陸
淳化閣帖釋文	清朱家標釋	綱錦堂版	二十卷	冊	一	毛邊紙	拾陸

書名	著者	版本	卷冊	冊數	紙	價
禁扁	元王士點纂次	重刊楝亭藏元本	四冊	一	竹紙	拾柒
齊名紀數	清王承烈輯	環山樓藏版 嘉慶癸酉年刻	十二卷	一	毛邊紙	拾柒
唐才子傳	元辛文房撰	蘇州文學山房仿聚珍版印	十卷	一	綿連紙	拾柒
史拾	明陳子龍等	明寫刻木	十八冊	四	共四種 竹紙	拾柒
姓氏尋源 附辨誤八冊	清張澍纂	精刻本 裳華書屋藏版	共二十六冊	四	太史連紙	拾柒
史記前後漢書鈔	清高塘鈔	乾隆五十三年刊本	六冊	一	竹紙	拾柒
四庫簡明目錄標注	清邵懿辰著	仁和邵氏半巖廬所著書之四 仿宋體字刊本	二十卷	一	毛邊紙	拾柒
宋李明仲營造法式	宋李誡奉聖旨編修	石影印宋鈔本小本	三十四卷	一	綿連紙 民國八年印	拾柒
溫州經籍志	館纂	浙江公立圖書館校刊	三十六卷	一	毛邊紙 民國十年刊	拾柒
華嶽全集	明張維新輯	明萬曆丙申年刻	十二卷	二	明綿紙夾板	拾柒

三十一

書名	編著者	版本	卷冊	冊數	紙張	定價
文獻通考合纂	清沈南湖纂	家藏版	二十四卷	一	竹紙	拾柒
周季編略	清黃式三纂	浙江書局刊本	九卷	一	綿連紙	拾柒
康熙政要	清章梫恭纂	紛印本	二十四卷	一	有光洋紙	拾柒
歸方評點史記合筆	明歸有光 清方苞評點	望三益齋刊本	六卷	一	綿連紙	拾捌
南疆繹史	署川溫氏原本 古高易氏勘定	仿宋膠泥版印法	三十六卷	六	綿連紙	拾捌
西湖志	清傳玉露等本 敕撰	官版初印兩浙 鹽釋道庫藏版	四十八卷	四	毛邊紙	拾捌
約章成案匯覽	北洋洋務局纂輯	上海點石齋承印	甲篇十卷十冊 乙篇四十二卷四十二冊	二	洋粉連紙	拾捌
東觀漢紀	漢明帝創修	武英殿聚珍版	二十四卷	一	毛邊紙	拾捌
高士傳續編	清張允掄著	新城縣署刊本	六冊	一	洋粉連紙 光緒二十二年刊	拾捌
廉吏傳		上海涵芬樓影印清殿版	七百十一冊		綿連紙	拾捌
二十四史						二十一

史 部

書名	著者	版本	卷冊	部	刊刻・紙	價
南遊記	清孫文定公撰	守意龕藏版 珠批點鈔本	一冊		絹連紙	拾捌
韻史	清許題花編	十年讀書之廬重刊	上下二卷 一冊	一	咸豐年刻 絹連紙	拾捌
廿一史彈詞	明楊慎編著	關中書院藏版	八十卷 十一冊	一	道光年刻 絹連紙	拾捌
廿一史彈詞	明楊慎編著	關中書院藏版	八十卷 十冊	二	太史連紙 道光年刻	拾捌
實學考	清晏茂琦纂輯	家藏版	四卷 四冊	一	竹紙	拾捌
清秘述聞	清法式善編	家藏版	二八卷 冊	一	毛邊紙刻 詩龕藏	拾捌
廣東陽江直隸廳輿地圖說	清汪拱震繪		一冊	一	開化紙 光緒年繪	拾捌
皇朝諡法表	清鮑康輯	家藏版	一五卷 冊	一	綿連紙 同治三年刊	拾捌
欽定天祿琳琅書目	清于敏中等奉敕編校	殿版	三十卷 十三冊	一	綿連紙	拾捌
滇繋	清師範纂	雲南通志局刊本	四十冊	四	光緒丁亥年刊 貴州絹紙夾版	拾玖

三十二　一

書名	著者	版本	卷冊	部數	紙張刊刻	價
南巡盛典	清高宗等輯	殿版	一百二十卷 四十八冊	四	白紙	拾玖
盛京路程		抄寫本繪圖	二冊	一	白紙	拾玖
衛藏識圖	清馬少雲撰	家藏版	二卷 四冊	一	粉紙 乾隆年刻	拾柒
南嶽集	宋陳田夫撰	長沙葉德輝影宋版刊	三卷 三冊	一	粉紙 光緒年刻	拾玖
太平寰宇記	宋樂史撰	金陵書局刊	二百卷 三十六冊	四	夾版毛邊紙 光緒八年刊	拾玖
綱鑑易知錄	清吳乘權等輯	敦仁堂藏版	四十八冊	八	南粉連紙 乾隆辛未年刊	拾玖
至聖編年世紀	清李灼等輯	亦政堂藏版	二十四冊	二	貫邊紙	貳拾
韻史	清許瀠卷手編 朱玉岑續編	枕漱居藏版	二卷 共三冊	一	毛邊紙	貳拾
三遷志	明史鶚撰	明嘉靖刻本	六卷 四冊	一	白綿紙	貳拾
正續文獻通考識大編	宋馬端臨著 明王圻續 方若珽編 清談潤輯	三香閣方氏家藏版	二十四卷 十冊	二	康熙年刻 竹紙	貳拾

書名	撰者	版本	卷數	冊數	部數	刊刻・紙	價
聖廟祀典圖考	清顧沅敬輯	家藏版	五卷 附圖一卷	六冊	一	道光年刻 粉紙	貳拾
盤山志	清釋智朴纂修	家藏版	十卷 補道四	四冊	一	康熙年刻 連史紙	貳拾
貳臣傳	清國史館原本	排字本	四十卷 貳臣傳十二卷	貳拾四冊	一	光緒二十一年刻 毛邊紙	貳拾
逆臣傳	牛松居士	寫本刊	十六卷	八冊	一	毛太紙	貳拾
衛藏通志	清袁鈞纂修	浙西村舍用 寫本	十六卷	十冊	一	光緒二十一年刻 毛邊紙 夾板	貳拾
鐵琴銅劍樓藏書目錄	清瞿鏞輯	瞿氏刊于罟里 家塾	二十四卷	十二冊	一	屈艸堂藏 毛邊紙	貳拾
經遜疏讀	明熊廷弼撰	湖北通志局 重刊本	十卷	十冊	一	綿連紙	貳拾
燉煌縣志	清蘇履吉撰	木縣衙藏版	七卷	四冊	一	道光十一年刊 連史紙	貳拾
顧端文公年譜	明顧樞編	家藏版 精刻本	二卷	二冊	一	明崇禎二年刊 毛邊紙	貳拾
欽定天祿琳琅書目	清于敏中等奉勅纂校	長沙王氏重刊	正續共三十卷	十冊	一	光緒甲申年刻 綿連紙	貳拾
峋嶁鑒撮	清曠敏本纂	家藏版	四卷	四冊	一	嘉慶年刻 影雕楊氏藏板 白竹紙夾板	貳拾

書名	撰者	版本	卷冊	部	刊刻・紙	價
愛日精廬藏書志	清張金吾輯	靈芬閣徐氏集字版印	三十六卷 續志四卷 十四冊	一	光緒十三年刻 竹紙	貳拾
蘭閨寶錄	清惲珠輯	紅香館藏版	八卷 六冊	一	道光年刻 粉紙	貳拾
歷代名賢齒譜	清易宗湉輯	賜書堂藏版	十九卷 八冊	一	雍正年刊 夾竹紙板	貳拾
讀史紀略	清蕭淪纂輯	澹靜軒藏版	四卷 四冊	一	乾隆年刻 竹紙	貳拾
明史例案	劉承幹纂	劉氏嘉業堂刊	九卷 四冊	一	竹紙	貳拾
歷代名儒傳	馮朱軾蔡世遠編 李滿植分纂全訂	本衙藏版	八卷 二冊	一	雍正四年刻 竹紙	貳拾
甘棠小志	清董醇著	家藏版	四卷 四冊	一	咸豐年刊 連史紙	貳壹
韻史	朱玉岑續編	枕漱居藏版	一卷 上下二冊	一	毛邊紙	貳壹
棗強縣志補正	清方宗誠纂	家藏版	五卷 二冊	一	同治年刊 連史紙	貳壹
滄來自記年譜	清于滄水撰	劉文奎家藏版	一冊	一	白紙寫刻本	貳壹

書名	著者	版本	卷冊	部數	紙	價
歐游雜錄	清徐建寅著	家藏版	上下二冊　卷一	一	光緒年刊連史紙夾板	貳壹
疑年錄	清錢大昕編	家藏版	四冊卷二	一	竹紙	貳壹
藏書記要	孫從記	潘氏鈔刊本	一冊		嘉慶年刊皮紙	貳壹
朱子年譜	宋李果齋原輯	明精鈔本	五冊卷二	一	竹紙	貳壹
經世環應編	明錢禮登輯	明刊本	十八冊卷八	二	竹紙	貳壹
為政忠告	元張養浩著	郭關石寫碧鮮齋影鈔本	上下二冊卷八	一	道光年影刊白紙	貳壹
太谷縣志	清管粵琇等　牟敏纂修	官版	八冊卷八	一	乾隆年刊綿連紙	貳壹
文獻通攷紀要	清齊召南編	家藏版	上下二冊	一	毛邊紙	貳壹
歷代帝王表	清齊召南編	小瑯環仙館藏版	三冊卷三	一	道光四年刊白紙	貳壹
張楊園先生年譜	清姚夏輯	家藏版	四卷附錄一冊		白紙	貳壹

書名	著者	版本	卷冊	部數	紙/刊	架位
元至順鎮江志	冒廣生刊	陳慶年校勘記二卷	二十一卷 共二十八冊	一	連史紙	貳壹
欽定蒙古源流	清陸錫熊奉敕進	重刊殿本	八卷 四冊	一	乾隆年刊 絹連紙	貳壹
揚州北湖小志	清焦循著	家藏版	六卷 四冊	一	嘉慶年刊 樹皮紙藏 白紙	貳壹
列仙傳	清澄初道人輯	任茲堂刊	二卷 四冊	一	道光年刊 白紙	貳壹
經世要略	明萬廷言編輯	明萬曆精刻本	十二卷 二冊	一	竹紙	貳壹
直齋書錄解題	宋陳振孫撰	江蘇書局刊	二十二卷 六冊	一	光緒九年刊 綿連紙	貳壹
史記論文	清吳見思評點	尺木堂藏版	一百三十卷 二十冊	二	康熙年刊 二夾版 竹紙	貳壹
遼金二史紀事本末	清李有棠編纂	李移鄂樓刊	前四十卷 又五十二卷 共八十二編 八十冊	二	光緒年刊 夾板白紙	貳壹
廿一史約編	清鄭芷畦述	善成堂藏版	八編 共八冊	一	竹紙	貳壹
甲子會紀	明辟懋族編輯	精鈔本 明嘉靖版	五卷 四冊	一	竹紙	貳壹

書名	著者	版本·刊刻	卷·册	紙張·刻印	號
四庫湖北先正遺書題要／四庫湖北先正遺書存目	清盧靖輯刊	盧氏家藏版 初印本	四卷附記 共八扎 一册	綿連紙 夾板	貳壹
念一史彈詞註	明楊慎纂	家藏版	上下二卷 一册	竹紙 乾隆年刻	貳壹
黃忠端公年譜	清莊起儔編	家藏版	四卷附遺 二册 一	白紙 連史紙 光緒年印	貳壹
歷代四裔紀元統表	清李鳳苞彙編	仿江南製造局 原本石印	四卷 四册 一	連史紙 道光年刻	貳壹
太祖高皇帝聖訓	清太祖	殿版	四〇卷 四册 一	開化紙	貳壹
國朝柔遠記	清彭玉麟定 王之春編	廣雅書局刊	二十卷 二册 一	竹紙 光緒十七年刻	貳壹
戚少保年譜耆編	閩戚祚國彙纂	仙遊崇勳祠藏 版	十二卷 二册 一	夾板 毛邊紙 民國十四年印	貳壹
回疆通志	清和寧撰	鉛印本	十二卷 二册 一	夾板 連史紙	貳壹
守汴日志	清李光墬撰	梁為淀重校刊 上海同文書局	四卷 一册	綿連紙 康熙戊子年刻	貳貳
碧血錄	清莊仲方著論 夏燮卹檜圖	石印原刻本	五册 一 三十五一	綿連紙 光緒八年刻	貳貳

431

432

書名	著者	版本	卷冊	函數	紙	刊年	等第
鳳臺祇謁筆記	清惲愉等撰	趙熙和校刊本	二冊	一	竹紙	同治庚午年刊	貳叁
咸淳臨安志	宋潛說友撰	清錢唐汪振綺堂仿宋本重雕精刻本	一百卷	四	毛邊紙	道光庚寅年刊	貳叁
欽定古今儲貳金鑑	清乾隆帝欽定	官版	六卷	一	毛邊紙		貳叁
司馬溫公年譜	清顧棟高編輯	求恕齋重刊	六卷十五冊	一	毛邊紙		貳叁
王荊公年譜	清朱孔彰撰	長州朱氏刊本	三十冊	一	竹紙	光緒丁酉年刊	貳叁
中興將帥別傳	清劉開纂	南林劉氏刊	十三冊	一	綿連紙	光緒十年刊	貳叁
廣列女傳	清吳榮光撰	俞樾重刊	二十冊	一	毛太紙		貳叁
歷代名人年譜	清國史館原本	天祿開藏版	十冊	一	毛太紙		貳叁
滿洲名臣傳	清國史館原本	京都琉璃廠榮錦書坊檢字	四十八卷四十八冊	六			貳叁
漢名臣傳	清阿桂家藏版		三十二卷三十二冊	四	毛太紙		貳叁
阿文成公年譜	清那彥成纂	家藏版	三十六卷十六冊	二	綿連紙		貳叁
幸魯盛典	清金居敬等奉敕纂修	殿版 開化紙	四十卷三十六冊	一		康熙二十四年刊	貳叁

書名	撰輯者	版本	卷冊	部數	用紙刊年	等級
昭代名人尺牘小傳	清吳修采輯	石印版	二十四卷	一	連史紙	貳叁
逸周書	晉孔晁註	明刻本	十卷 四冊	一	竹紙	貳叁
名賢畫像傳	清王會典輯	國華齋一社石印	上下二冊	一	道光油光紙印 夾板	貳叁
吳郡名賢圖像贊	清顧湘舟輯	長洲顧氏家藏版	二十卷 八冊	一	道光年刊 綿連紙	貳叁
練川名人畫像	清程祖慶編次	程氏仿澱竹册刊	四卷附象二卷續編三卷 八冊	一	道光年刻 綿連紙	貳叁
資治通鑑綱目發明	清尹起莘撰	陳世修等集刻本	五十九卷 六册	一	毛邊紙	貳叁
闕里誌	明陳鎬纂輯	明精刻本	二十四卷 十二册	一	清開化紙印	貳叁
闕里文獻攷	清孔繼汾述	家藏版	一百卷 八册	二	乾隆年剏 毛邊紙	貳叁
高僧傳 一二三集	梁釋慧皎選唐釋道宣撰宋釋贊寧等撰	金陵刻經處刊江北刻經處刊本 精刊	共八十五卷 二十二册	四	光緒十三十四年刊 毛邊紙	貳肆
晚笑堂畫傳	清上官周畫	家藏版	二册	一	乾隆癸亥年刊 綿連紙	貳肆

書名	著者	版本・印行	卷冊	部數	刊年・紙張	價
八瓊室金石補正	劉承幹編	吳興劉氏希古樓刊	共一百三十六卷 六十四冊	八	毛邊紙 夾板	貳肆
左文襄公奏疏	清左宗棠撰	上海圖書集成局印	一百十九卷 二十冊	一	光緒庚寅年印 綿連紙	貳肆
劍俠傳	撰名闕　明徐渭繪像	王齡重刊精刻本	四卷 二冊	一	咸豐七年刻 綿連紙	貳肆
吳可讀奏議	清吳可讀撰	精寫本	一冊	一	雙綿連紙	貳肆
郎園讀書志	葉德輝撰	上海澹園鉛印 版印	十六卷 十六冊	二	民國十七年印 綿連紙	貳肆
持靜齋藏書記要	清莫友芝輯	文學山房聚珍 版印	上下二冊	一	同治年刊 連史紙	貳肆
名賢畫像傳	清王念典輯	國華鑄一社印	上下二冊	一	油光紙	貳肆
曾文正聖哲畫像記	清曾國藩撰	國華鑄一社印	上下二冊	一	連畫像傳共一夾紙版 油光紙	貳肆
讀史紀略	清蔣湘帆輯	澹靜齋重刊	四卷 四冊	一	道光二十年刊 竹紙	貳肆
聖賢像贊	明冠洋子著	曲阜會文堂藏版	四冊	一	光緒四年重刊 毛邊紙	貳肆

三十七一

書名	著者・版本	卷	冊	函	紙・刊年	價
學古堂藏書目	清黃捐藏／家藏版	四	一	一	羅田周氏藏／竹紙	貳肆
龍游縣志	余紹宋撰／京城印書局鉛印	四十一	十六	二	龍門紙	貳肆
聖教史紀	美國教士謝衛樓撰／通州公理教會藏版	五	四	一	西一千八百九十 年刻／綿連紙	貳肆
龍門四書人物備考	清辟方山先生原本　陳明卿先生增定／三樂齋刊	十二	六	一	乾隆五年刻／竹紙	貳肆
鑑撮（附讀史論略）	清曠敏本編／巾箱本	五	五		嘉慶年刻／毛邊紙	貳肆
莫愁湖志	清馬士圖輯著／松筠齋　家藏版	六	二		宣統年刻／連史紙	貳肆
四庫全書表文箋釋	清林鶴年纂／求恕齋刊	四	四		白毛邊紙	貳肆
熙朝紀政	清王慶雲敬述／上海書局鉛印	八	四		光緒年印／粉連紙	貳肆
懲懷主人自訂年譜	清張廷玉撰／張紹文重校刊　家藏版	六	二		毛邊紙	貳肆
明李文正公年譜	清法式善纂輯／家藏版	七	二		嘉慶年刻／毛邊紙	貳肆

書名	著者	版本	卷冊	部數	刊印年・紙	價
新疆禮俗志 附小正	王樹枏纂	陶廬叢書聚珍 仿宋印書局印	一 附新疆小正一卷 一冊	一	龍門紙	貳肆
晚咲堂竹莊畫傳	清上官周書	家藏版	上下二冊	一	乾隆年刻	貳肆
楹書偶錄 附讀編	清楊紹和纂	海源閣版	五卷 續編四卷 共十二冊	二	連史紙	貳肆
續山東考古錄	清葉圭綬述	家藏版	三十二卷	六	咸豐元年刻 綿連史紙	貳肆
讀史紀略	清蕭澐纂輯	楊氏澐靜齋刊	四卷	一	同治年刻 白竹紙	貳肆
海岱史略	清王毓超編	家藏版	一百四十卷 二十四冊	四	嘉慶二十三年刻 毛邊紙	貳肆
古文舊書攷 附訪餘錄	日本島田翰著	藻玉堂印	四卷 附訪餘錄一卷	一	白毛邊紙	貳肆
詳刑要覽	清吳訥編纂	求放心齋藏版	二卷	一	道光年刻 毛邊紙	貳肆
廿一史彈詞註	明楊慎編著	樹玉堂藏版	八卷 十一冊	一	雍正年版 夾竹版紙	貳肆
聖賢像贊	明冠洋子撰	明崇禎版	四卷 四冊	一	白紙	貳肆

三十八

書名	撰輯者	版本	卷册	夾	刊年	紙	價
李文正公年譜	清法式善纂輯	家藏版	七卷二册	一	嘉慶年重刊	竹紙	貳肆
萬世玉衡錄	清蔣伊編輯	御覽進呈本	四卷四册	一	乾隆二年刻	竹紙	貳肆
百美新詠	清袁闌編輯	集腋軒藏版	四卷四册	一	乾隆年刻	綿連紙	貳肆
金石圖說	清褚峻摹圖劉世珩編補	劉世珩刊印	甲乙共四卷四册	一	光緒年刻	官紙精印	貳伍
籌濟編	清楊景仁輯	家藏版	三十二卷八册	二	道光年刻	綿連紙	貳伍
孔門弟子傳略	明夏洪基編輯	明刻版	上下二册	一		竹紙	貳伍
歷代帝王統系	明夏洪基纂	明刻版	上下二册	一		竹紙	貳伍
歷代甲子編年	明夏洪基纂訂	明刻版	上下二册	一	以上三種共一夾	竹板紙	貳伍
疑年錄彙編	張惟驤增輯	小雙寂盦刊	十六卷附人表一八册	一	民國十四年刻	白毛邊紙	貳伍
大事記解題	宋呂祖謙撰	武英殿聚珍版校訂宋本	十二卷通釋三卷附二册	二	乾隆五十一年刊	白紙	貳伍

大清太宗文皇帝聖訓	大清太祖高皇帝聖訓	濟寧直隸州續志 附濟寧縣志	西周史徵	關帝事蹟徵信編	讀史漫錄	西湖志	毓秀堂畫傳	龔氏家譜	明狀元圖考 附圖朝三元題詠
天聰朝	天命朝	清唐煦等纂修	李泰芬學	清周廣業崔應榴纂輯	清于慎行著	清傅王露等總修	清張熙陛書	清龔守正撰	顧鼎臣纂編 孫祖訓緝圖 黃應澄繪圖
殿版開化紙	殿版開化紙	鉛印本	家藏版	京都甕城關帝廟藏版	存素齋藏版	浙江書局重刊	石印本	家藏版	漢陽葉氏藏版 福源書室重刊
六卷二册	四卷一册	三十四卷四册 共濟寧縣志四卷十六册	五十七卷六册	三十卷補遺選一卷六册	二十卷十二册	四十八卷二十册	四册	上下二册	三元題詠二卷 共八册
		二	一	一	一	二	一		一
乾隆四年刻	乾隆四年刻	民國十五年印 龍門紙	民國十六年鉛印 夾板連史紙	光緒八年刻 夾綿板連史紙	道光年刻 夾綿板連史紙	光緒四年刻 二連板夾史紙	連史紙	綿連紙	咸豐六年刻 綿連紙
柒	柒	貳伍	貳伍	貳伍	貳伍	貳伍	貳伍	貳伍	貳伍

三十九

一

書名	朝代/著者	版本	卷冊	數	刊刻	價
大清世祖章皇帝聖訓	順治朝	開化紙殿版	六卷二冊	以上共一種函一	乾隆四年刻	柒
大清聖祖仁皇帝聖訓	康熙朝	開化紙殿版	六十卷二十三冊	五	乾隆六年刻	柒
大清世宗憲皇帝聖訓	雍正朝	開化紙殿版	三十六卷十六冊	四	乾隆五年刻	柒
大清高宗純皇帝聖訓	乾隆朝	開化紙殿版	三百卷一百零一冊	三十	嘉慶十二年刻	柒
大清仁宗睿皇帝聖訓	嘉慶朝	殿版	一百十卷一百十一冊	十	道光四年刻	捌
大清宣宗成皇帝聖訓	道光朝	殿版	一百三十卷一百三十冊	二十	咸豐六年刻	玖
大清文宗顯皇帝聖訓	咸豐朝	殿版	一百十卷一百冊	二十	同治年刻	玖
大清穆宗毅皇帝聖訓	同治朝	殿版	一百六十卷一百六十冊	三十	光緒五年刻	拾
名山勝概記	明何振卿纂輯 明	版	四十八卷三十二冊	四	竹紙	貳伍
京口三山志	渦周伯義輯局	版	志廿六卷全山志廿卷北固山續志八卷焦山志十四卷	三	光緒年刻毛邊紙	貳伍

書名	著者	版本	卷冊	部數	刻印・紙	價
白鹿書院志	清毛德琦原訂 周兆蘭重修	書院自刊版	十九卷 八冊	一	同治十年補刊 毛邊紙	貳伍
三不朽圖贊	清張陶菴纂	鈔印 阿羅版	一卷 一冊	一	民國七年印 連史紙	貳伍
錢遵王讀書敏求記校証	清管庭芬原輯 章鈺補輯	長洲章氏刊	四卷附佚文等 六冊	一	民國丙寅年刊 白毛邊紙	貳伍
海國圖志	清魏源撰	急當務齋刊	一百卷 二十四冊	二	光緒六年刻 白紙 夾板	貳伍
通鑑釋文辯誤	元胡三省輯著	明刻本	十二卷 四冊	一	竹紙	貳伍
明鑑	清胡敬等纂	官版	二十四卷 十二冊	一	白紙	貳伍
明末紀事補遺	南沙三餘氏纂	家藏版	十卷 八冊	一	嘉慶年刻 竹紙	貳伍
西域墩談	椿園七十一著	抄寫本	四冊	一	同治年刻 竹紙	貳伍
天祿閣外史	明黃愚著	明嘉靖版	八卷 二冊		竹紙	貳伍
萊州府志	清嚴有禧纂修	官版	十六卷 八冊		乾隆年刻 白紙	貳伍

四十一

書名	編輯	版本	卷冊		紙刊	編號
百孝圖說	清俞葆真編輯 河間俞氏著		二冊	一	同治年刻綿連紙	貳陸
姑蘇名賢小紀	明文震孟論次	明萬曆版本 精刻	上下二冊	一	竹紙夾版	貳陸
台州金石錄	清黃瑞編輯	吳興嘉業堂刊	十三卷闕訪四卷 八卷台頓五	一	竹紙	貳陸
闕里述聞	清鄭曉如敬述	西湖華文堂刊	八卷十四冊	一	夾綿版連紙同治年刻	貳陸
懿行編	清李澄編輯 徐惺鑒定	家藏版	四冊八卷	一	竹紙康熙年刻	貳陸
補藝文志	清倪燦撰	廣雅書局刊	共八冊五卷	一	夾精版榜紙印毛邊紙	貳陸
通鑑總類	清沈愚輯	讀我書齋刊 重刊元本	二十冊二十卷	一	夾版連史紙光緒年刻	貳陸
井田圖攷	清朱克己訂定	山東書局刊	上下二冊	一	夾綿版連紙同治五年刻	貳陸
讀史節要	清汪承鑣輯	家藏版	六十二卷十二冊	一	夾綿版連紙同治五年刻	貳陸
御撰資治通鑑綱目	勅編次 清張廷玉等奉勅編次	殿版開化紙	四十冊二十卷	一	乾隆十一年刊有硃印玉軸	貳陸

史部

書名	著者	版本	卷冊	部數	印本	定價
左文襄公年譜	清羅正鈞纂	湘陰左氏校刊本	十卷 二冊	一	光緒年刊	貳陸
蓬萊縣志	清蔡永華等修	版藏縣署	十四卷 八冊	一	道光年刊 夾版毛邊紙	貳陸
元朝秘史		葉氏觀古堂藏版 影抄元足本刊	十二卷 續六卷 二冊	一	竹紙 光緒年刊	貳陸
豫章九家年譜	清楊希閔輯	海東書局藏版	九種共十二冊	一	連史紙 光緒年刊	貳陸
胡刻大清一統輿圖	清胡林翼纂輯	湖北撫署景垣樓藏版	南北共二十三冊	二	綿連紙 光緒年刊	貳陸
平定關隴紀略	清易孔昭纂輯	蘭州署藏版	十二卷 三冊	二	白紙 同治二年刊	貳陸
陋巷志	明呂兆祥重修	明嘉靖版	八卷 四冊	一	明白毛邊紙	貳陸
節婦傳	清楊錫紱著	家藏版	十六卷 四冊	一	竹紙 乾隆年刊 鶴侶氏藏偉人藏	貳陸
平叛記	清毛霦編	家藏版	上下 二冊	一	毛邊紙 康熙年刊	貳陸
資治通鑑	宋司馬光奉敕編集 元胡三省音註	明刻本	二百九十四卷 附釋文辨誤十二卷 共一百冊	十	綿連紙 十夾板	貳陸

四十一

書名	著者	版本	卷冊	套	紙張/刊刻	價
續資治通鑑	清畢沅編纂	德裕堂藏版	二百二十卷 八十冊	八	毛邊紙 嘉慶年刻	貳陸
尚史	清李鍌青著	悅道樓藏版 寫刻本	七十卷 二十八冊	四	開化紙 乾隆年刻	貳陸
歸方史記	明歸有光著 方苞評點 清	家藏版	一百二十四卷 三冊	一	綿連紙	貳陸
紀效新書	明戚繼光著	京都寶林堂梓	十五卷 八冊	一	竹紙	貳陸
練兵實紀 附雜記	明戚繼光著	四庫全書本京都寶林堂梓	十五卷 六冊	一	竹紙	貳陸
繹史	清馬驌著	家藏版	一百六十卷 五十冊	六	竹紙	貳柒
西清古鑑	清梁詩正等奉勅纂輯	殿版 大開本	四十卷 十六冊	一	開化紙	貳柒
金石圖說	清褚峻輯	貴池劉世珩宣校刊本	四冊	一	白綿紙 光緒甲午年刊成	貳柒
夢坡室獲古叢篇	清周夢坡輯	影印本 大開本	十二冊	一	綿連紙	貳柒
李明仲營造法式	宋李誡奉旨編修	民國宋啟鈐佐影鈔宋紹興本按栞寧本格式校刊	八冊	一	大開本 白紙	貳柒

書名	著者	版本	卷冊	部	紙張・刊印	定價
流沙墜簡	羅振玉排纂	上虞羅氏宸翰樓印	三冊	一	日本厚皮紙夾版	貳柒
大選京外各官類例　急選京外各官類例		紅格精鈔	二冊	一	光緒三十三年訂　毛邊紙	貳柒
粵海關乾隆元年至十年撫部院准部轉關案卷		鈔本	一冊	一	毛邊紙	貳柒
武聖關壯繆遺蹟圖誌		活字版精印本	一冊	一	龍門紙	貳柒
歷代名臣言行錄	清朱桓輯	蔚齋藏版	二十四卷　三十二冊	二	嘉慶丁巳新鐫　綿連紙夾版	貳柒
二十史朔閏表　附四曆回曆	陳垣纂	勵耘書屋本	一冊	一	民國十四年印　綿連紙	貳柒
書目答問　附類軒語	清張之洞輯	家藏寫刻本	分二冊	一	光緒年刊　連史紙	貳柒
歷代疆域表　附沿革表	清段長基編輯	味古山房藏版	共六卷　十冊	一	嘉慶年刊　白紙	貳柒
先聖生卒年月日攷	清孔廣牧敬述	廣雅書局刊	一附三公年表　二冊	一	光緒十五年刊　毛邊紙	貳柒
夏侍郎年譜	清夏僧復撰	聚珍仿宋印書局印	一冊	一	民國九年印　綿連紙	貳柒

史部　四十二

書名	著者	版本	卷册		紙版刊刻	價
錢敏肅公奏疏	清錢鼎銘著	存素堂藏版	七卷 四册	一	光緒年刊 夾縺連紙版	貳柒
元史譯文証補	清洪鈞撰	家藏版	四卷 四册	一	光緒年刊 夾竹紙版	貳柒
四洪年譜	清洪汝奎編輯	晦木齋刊	四卷 四册	一	宣統元年刻 夾縺版連紙	貳柒
尚友錄	清廖用賢編纂 張伯琮補輯	天祿齋藏	十二卷 二十二册	一	光緒元年刻 竹紙夾版	貳柒
丙丁龜鑑正續合刻	宋柴望輯		二卷 七册	一	竹紙	貳柒
魏鄭公諫錄	唐王方慶集 王先恭校注	長沙王氏藏板	五卷 二册	一	光緒年刊 綿連紙	貳柒
魏鄭公諫續錄	元翟思忠撰	長沙王氏藏版	一卷 二册	一	光緒年刊 綿連紙	貳柒
魏文貞公故事拾遺	清王先恭集	長沙王氏藏版	三卷附年譜一 二册	一	光緒年刊 綿連紙連上二種共一夾板	貳柒
安南志略	清黎崱編	樂善堂藏版	二十卷 四册	一	毛邊紙 扮印	貳柒
疇人傳	清阮元撰 海鹽常惺齋張氏重校刊袖珍本		四十六卷 附續傳六卷 共十二册	一	光緒年刻 連史紙夾板	貳柒

447

書名	著者	版本	卷冊	部數	刻印·用紙	編號
通鑑綱目韻言	清柯曉崗著	問心堂藏板	上下二冊	一	康熙年刻 毛邊紙	貳捌
國朝先正事略	清李元度纂	循陔艸堂刊	六十卷 三十二冊	四	同治年刻 竹紙	貳捌
道齊正軌	鄧鳴鶴纂述	家藏板	二十卷 八冊	一	道光二十三年刻 竹紙	貳捌
曾文定公年譜	楊希閔編	三餘書屋叢書	一冊	一	竹紙	貳捌
李忠定公年譜	清黃宅中輯	家藏板	二冊	一	光緒年刻 白紙	貳捌
栗恭勤公年譜	清張壬林編輯	家藏板	十五卷 上下二冊	一	光緒年刻 白紙	貳捌
史記內編	漢司馬遷著 明鄧元錫評選	明崇禎板	二十四冊	四	竹紙	貳玖
黃巖西橋王氏譜	清王舟瑤纂	聚珍板印	十二卷 附家集二十卷 共十二冊	一	白竹紙 夾板	貳玖
前後漢紀 附校記	漢荀悅撰	嶺南學海堂刊本	六十二卷 十四冊	一	綿連紙 光緒丙子年刊	貳玖
平定準噶爾方略	清傅恒等奉勅纂修	殿版 開化紙	一百七十一卷 一百冊	二	前編正編續編 黃宮綾書皮 木夾板	叁拾

書名	著者	版本	卷冊	箱／函	紙張・年代	價
慉案		塘寫本 開化榜紙	一冊	一	乾隆四十年至 道光二十四年	叁拾
弘毅公衍慶錄	清額宜都巴圖魯曾孫愛必達纂	家藏版	四十二卷	一	绵连紙	叁拾
聖教史略	清葡若瑟譯	鈆印本	十八冊	一	油光紙	叁拾
新史合編道講	清弘薑等奉	土山灣印書館	二十冊	共廿	同治八年 一千九百十三年 洋印紙	叁拾
廿四史	清 勅校刻 藏板	嶺南莊古堂	三千二百八十六卷 共八百五十冊	四函	光緒年刻 红木箱 绵连紙	
九通	唐杜佑等撰	浙江書局刊	九種共一千冊	一百零九箱 六函	光緒丙午年刻 毛透紙	
史荟附讀史論略	清楊銘柱纂	家藏板	論略二卷 共四冊	一	光緒丙申年刻 竹紙	小箱
慶典章程		官刻版	五冊	一	光緒年刻 竹紙	小箱
廿四史三表	清段長基編	紅杏山房藏板	三表共廿四冊	一箱	光緒元年刻 白紙	
歷代輿地圖	清楊守敬纂輯	觀海堂刊	共四十二冊	一箱	光緒丙午年刻 連史紙	

書名	著者	版本	卷冊	函箱	印紙
順天府志	清張之洞等纂	官板	一百三十卷 共六十四冊	八函 二箱	光緒丙申年刻 毛邊紙
西清古鑑	清梁詩正等奉勅纂	遜宋書館仁日 本銅鑄	四十卷 二十四冊	一箱	東洋綿紙
古玉圖譜	宋張達道等奉勅編纂	清初余文儀撫宋刻本五彩設色套版	三十二卷	一箱	綿夾連紙
五種紀事本末	清高士奇等撰	江西書局刻版	五百零八卷 一百三十六冊	一箱	同治癸酉年刊 綿連紙
萬壽盛典	奉勅纂修	初印開化紙版	一百二十卷 四十冊	四函 一箱	
大清一統志	清馬齊等奉勅撰	初印本紙版	五百卷 六十冊	一箱	光緒壬寅年印 毛邊紙
欽定大清會典	清崑岡等奉勅纂修	上海寶善齋石印本	一百卷 一冊	一箱	光緒戊申年印 綿連紙
欽定大清會典事例	清李鴻章等奉勅纂修	上海商務印書館石印本	一千二百二十卷 二木箱	合前裝	光緒戊申年印 綿連紙
影宋百衲本史記		涵芬樓借溧陽陶氏本影印初印本	一百三十卷 二十四冊	一箱	綿連紙
西藏記			二卷 四冊	一	白紙

四十五

叁壹

書名	編纂	版本	卷冊	函套	紙張・刻印	等第
石渠寶笈	清紀昀等奉勅纂	涵芬樓印	四十四卷 五十冊	六	連史紙	叁壹
欽定古今儲貳金鑑	清乾隆帝勅纂	四庫全書本內府精抄 闕化紙	共三冊	一匣	毛邊紙 樟木匣	叁壹
宋陳少陽先生盡忠錄	明汪廷訥編	環翠堂版精刻本 明萬歷戊戌年刻	二十二卷 二十四冊	版 四夾	毛邊紙 樟木板	叁壹
入鏡陽秋	敕纂	抄寫精本	二十二卷 續二卷 八冊	一箱	連史紙	叁壹
欽定四庫全書總目	清紀昀等奉敕纂	廣東書局重刊	二百卷 一百二十冊	一箱	白綿紙 同治七年刻	叁壹
史纂左編	明唐順之編輯 胡宗憲校刊	明嘉靖年刻本	一百四十二卷 一百冊	一箱	賞紙	叁壹
新元史	柯劭忞撰	復耕堂初刻本	二百五十七卷 六十冊	二箱	毛邊紙	叁壹
欽定日下舊聞攷	清英廉等奉勅編纂	武英殿版初印	一百六十卷 二十四冊	二匣	綿連紙 嘉慶甲子刻	叁壹
歷代帝王統系	傅去爭删訂	于時亭藏版 半修堂	四卷 四冊	二匣	雪雅堂藏版 綿連紙	叁壹
通鑑學要	清姚培謙 張景星同錄	飛鴻堂藏版	共三十七卷 二十冊	二匣	乾隆辛巳年刻 綿連紙	叁壹

四十六 一

書名	著者	版本	卷冊	紙張裝訂	函號
赤城論諫錄	明謝鐸等編 內台州叢書續編	四庫全書本	二十卷	毛邊紙	叁壹
元廣東遺民錄	清溪漁隱輯	家藏版	上下二冊 二卷	綿連紙	叁壹
理學張抱初先生年譜	明張信民門人馮奮庸編	明刻本	一冊	夾連紙	叁壹
皇朝道學名臣言行錄		宋版	卷八十三二十三 四冊	金菊子藏本 共計二百零七頁	叁壹
眞文忠公續文章正宗	宋眞德秀撰	宋版	二十卷 十一冊	孫壯伯恒藏本 麻沙紙 共計十四頁	叁拾
太祖皇帝大破明師於薩爾滸山之戰書事文		滿漢文開化紙版	一冊	一匣	叁壹
欽定元王惲承華事略補圖	清徐郙等奉敕補	殿版	六大冊 二卷	一紅木夾板 綿連紙	叁壹
陳氏中西回史日曆	陳垣撰	國立北京大學研究所國學門叢書	二十卷 五冊	朱墨兩色鉛印 洋平面粉連紙	叁壹
古品節錄	清松筠撰	本衙藏版	六卷 六冊	嘉慶四年新鐫 延清書屋藏本	叁壹
元也里可溫考 開封一賜樂業教考	陳垣撰	鉛印本	一冊	毛邊紙	叁壹

書名	撰者・版本	部數		紙	價
譚　黔	清陳明遠撰　鉛印大字本	一	冊	綿連紙	叁壹
先文勤公自訂年譜	清王凱泰撰　家藏版	一	冊	毛邊紙	叁壹
鄰蘇老人年譜	清楊守敬自述　石印本	一	冊	綿連紙	叁壹
王文敏公奏疏稿	清王懿榮撰　江甯印刷廠排印	一	冊	綿連紙	叁壹
永嘉郡記	宋鄭緝之撰　清孫詒讓校集　石印本	一	冊	綿連紙	叁壹
容菴弟子記	民國袁世凱傳記　沈祖憲等編纂　鈆印本	一	冊	洋紙	叁壹

以上共計陸百肆拾伍種

四十七

455

書名	著者註	版本	卷冊數	函數	備考	編列號數
字學匯海	清龔光甸等版	京都秀文齋刻	四冊 一		光緒己丑出版 連史紙	壹
錢遵王讀書敏求記校註	清管庭芬等輯	長州章氏刊	九卷 六冊 一		民國丙寅出版 連史紙	壹
十家語錄摘要	清謝闌生輯	家藏版	三卷 四冊 一		竹紙	壹
輋書疑辨	清萬斯同纂	供石亭版	十二卷 四冊 一		嘉慶丙子年刻 竹紙	壹
漢書日記	明劉直齋著	家藏版	六卷附補編一卷 冊 一		雍正年刻 夾連紙板	壹
傳子	晉傅玄撰	長沙葉氏刊	三卷 二冊 一		光緒壬寅刊 連史紙	壹
小學	清彭定求纂	家藏版	上下兩冊 附孝傳 一		道光年刻 白毛邊紙	壹
太史華句	明凌迪知輯	明版	八卷 五冊 一		明萬曆年刻 明綿紙	壹
孫子十家註	孫武子著	浙江書局刊	十三卷 六冊 一		光緒三年刻 毛太紙	壹

四十八

書名	著者	版本	卷册	（定價·元）	出版年·用紙	（定價·角）
桐城吳氏點勘十子	清吳汝綸點勘	衍星社鉛印	十二册	一	宣統二年刊　油光紙	貳
集說全眞提要	清黃伯祿輯	上海慈母堂鉛印	六册	一	光緒丙午年印　油光紙	貳
十竹齋書畫譜	明胡曰從摹		八册	一	光緒己卯年刻　夾版	貳
月令粹編	清秦嘉謨著	蔡氏刊本	二十四册	一	嘉慶十七年刊　毛太紙	貳
讀書雜誌	清王念孫著	金陵書局刊	二十四册	四	同治庚午年刻　毛邊紙計十種	貳
本草綱目	清李時珍編輯	合肥張氏味古齋重校刊	共七十六卷　四十八册	八	光緒己酉年刻　連史紙	貳
子史精華	清雍正帝勅定　張廷玉等奉旨纂修	江蘇江寧王景桓刊	一百六十卷　四十八册	六	白綿紙	貳
古今僞書攷	清姚際恒著	浙江書局版	上下兩卷	一	光緒十八年刊　毛太紙	貳
植物名實圖考	清吳其濬著	山西濬文書局藏版	共六十卷　計四十册	四	光緒年刻　四夾板　白綿紙	貳
奇器圖說	清王徵譯稿	家藏本	四册	一	嘉慶年刻　夾連紙	貳

書名	著者	版本	卷册	部	紙	等第
通雅	明方以智撰	立敬館版	五十二卷 二十册	二	連史紙	貳
賞奇軒四種合編		文德堂版	四册	一	連史紙	貳
方氏墨譜	明方建元編	明版	六卷 八册	一	萬曆年刻白綿紙	貳
輟耕錄	明陶宗儀撰	武進陶氏景元本刊	三十卷 十册	一	乾隆辛巳年刻毛邊紙	貳
廣博物志	清董斯張著	高輝堂藏版	五十卷 四十册	二	光緒九年刻毛邊紙	貳
封神演義	明鍾惺批評	掃葉山房刊	二十卷 十九册	八	毛邊紙	貳
三元秘授	桐城張氏著	百忍堂藏版	六集 六册	一	毛太紙	叁
續紅樓夢		抱甕軒版	三十卷 二十册	二	崇毛卿氏藏 嘉慶己未刻 白毛太紙	叁
桐陰清話	清倪雲癯著	家藏版	八卷 四册	一	同治甲戌重刻白紙	叁
東周列國志	清蔡元放批評	書成山房刻琭套版	十二册	二	咸豐四年刻竹紙	叁

子部

四十九　一

書名	著者	版本	卷冊	數	紙張・附記	等級
鑑撮	清贋敏本編	家藏版	四卷附諟史論略一卷　五冊	一	白綿紙	叁
事類統編	清黃葆眞增輯	家藏版	九十三卷　三十六冊	六	長沙龍氏重校藏版　夾連紙	叁
南省公餘錄	清梁章鉅撰	家藏版	四卷　二冊	一	夾連紙	叁
唐子潛書	清唐甄著	石印本	二卷　一冊	一	上海大經綸書局　有光紙	叁
戊戌履霜錄	退盧居士	退盧刊本	八卷　三冊	一	豫章叢書本附　堅冰志光宣戊各一卷白毛太紙	叁
記事珠	清張以誰選	木版	十卷　十冊	二	上海掃葉山房校　毛邊紙刻光緒壬午年	叁
增補類腋	清趙克宜增輯	角山樓版	六十七卷　二十冊	一	竹紙夾板	叁
汪子中詮	明汪應蛟撰	明萬曆刊本	六卷　六冊	一	白紙夾板	叁
古今類傳	清黃穀士輯	家藏版	四卷　四冊	一	竹紙　光緒二十三年刊	叁
老子翼	明焦竑輯	漸西村舍刻版	八卷　四冊	一	毛邊紙	叁

子部

書名	著者	版本	冊卷	數	紙張	備註	價
老子衍	李惺樵	家藏版	一册	一	綿連紙	自然室雜述之一	叁
晝禪堂隨筆		抄寫本	二册 四卷	一	白毛邊紙		叁
呻吟語節錄	明 呂坤著	家藏版	四册 六卷	一	綿連紙		叁
西廂記		此宜闊增訂本	六册 六卷	一	硃批 綿連紙	清同治八年左戲等刊於武林	叁
溫公家範	清 朱軾校正	家藏版	二册 十卷	一	毛太紙		叁
舊聞隨筆	清 姚仲實著	家藏版	一册 四卷	一	竹紙		叁
正脈疏音義		抄本	一册	一	毛邊紙		叁
心經註解	松溪道人無垢 註	元版	一册	一	竹紙	完熟氏藏	叁
竹葉堂雜記	清 姚元之著	家藏版	二册 八卷	一	毛太紙 夾板	光緒年刻	叁
名理探	傅汎際譯義	北京公教大學 輔仁社影印	三册 五卷	一	洋平綿紙	民國十五年印	叁

五十一

書名	撰者	版本	卷冊		價	紙/刻	
宗鏡錄	宋慧日永明妙圓正修智覺禪師延壽集 清字之綱等奉敕刊		一百卷	二十四冊	四	雍正十二年刻 綿連紙	肆
媿林漫錄	清羅式玨撰	江蘇書局刊本	二冊		一	光緒庚寅年刊 綿連紙	肆
集古十種	日本人作	精刻本	三卷		一	東洋綿紙	肆
明季稗史	明文秉等撰	留雲居士排字本	十六冊		二	共十六種 綿連紙	肆
書影	清櫟下老人撰	因樹屋刊本	十卷		一	竹紙	肆
壹是紀始	清祝亭著	家藏版	二十二卷	六冊	一	光緒辛卯年刻 竹紙 京都文奎堂藏版	肆
續同書	清福申輯	家藏版	二十四卷	六冊	一	綿連紙	肆
宋瑣語 附晉宋書故		家藏版	四冊		一	竹紙	肆
崇正合編	唐彝倫編	周宅鎬翻刻版	五冊		一	毛太紙	肆
陽明集要三編	清施四明評輯	黔南重刊本	十二冊		一	貴州綿紙 夾板	肆

子部

書名	著者	版本	卷冊	部數	紙張・印刷	類
夷堅志	宋洪邁撰	重刊宋本	六十卷 二十冊	一	毛太紙	肆
味餘書室隨筆	清嘉慶帝撰	殿版	四卷 二冊	一	綿連紙 同治六年刻	肆
正學編	清潘世恩輯	家藏版	二卷 八冊	一	竹紙 嘉慶年刻	肆
金川瑣記	清李心衡著	官版	四卷 六冊	一	連史紙 無套 光緒十三年印	肆
文選類雋	清何嶧青編	積山書局石印	一十四卷	一	油光紙 夾板	肆
七克	清麗迪我譔	京都始胎大堂藏版	四卷 七冊	一	油光紙 夾板	肆
洗冤錄集註	清王又槐增輯	翰墨園版	五卷 六冊	一	夾版 油光紙 道光二十四年刻	肆
思辨錄疑義	清劉蓉撰	思賢講舍校刊	一冊	二	毛太紙	肆
李文清公日記	清李文圍撰	影印本	十六卷 二冊	二	綿連紙	肆
國朝尚友錄輯	清李佩芳等編	南洋七日報館印	八冊		粉連紙 光緒年印	肆

五十一

書名	著者・版本	卷冊	部	刊年・用紙	類
文料大成	清冷香子編 名德堂版	四十卷 十四冊	一	光緒年刻 毛太紙	肆
詩句題解	慎記莊石印	四卷 四冊		光緒年刻 粉紙	肆
四書典林	清江永撰 鴻寶齋石印	三十卷 附四書 計古人典林十二冊		光緒年印 白綿紙	肆
三畏格言	清計文卿輯 寄觀閣藏版	一卷 一冊		光緒丁酉年刻 東昌紙	肆
責忘約言	清王滌心著 慎修堂藏版	四卷 四冊	一	咸豐五年刻 連史紙 夾板	肆
復性書	抄本	一卷 一冊		竹紙 硃墨字	肆
篆文金剛經	清田伏侯寫 家藏版	一冊		單宣紙 辛酉年刻	肆
金剛經	汪大燮寫 家藏本	一冊		民國十七年石印 計兩部	肆
驪術・奇談	清寓若曙編 掃葉山房石印	四卷 四冊	一	連史紙	肆
篆文老子	清田伏侯寫 家藏版	一冊		單宣紙	肆

子部

項目	孔子家語	述學	元和姓纂	人譜類記	呂子節錄	古格言	格言聯璧	呂祖直解金剛經	武經七書彙解	宋元以來畫人姓氏錄
著者	魏王肅註	清汪中撰	唐林寶撰	明劉宗周撰	明呂坤著	清梁章鉅輯	清金蘭生著	清王聯璧書	清朱鹿岡輯	清魯駿編輯
版本	上海同文書局影印內府藏本	家藏版	金陵書局刊	陝甘督署重印	甘肅藩署版	張祿卿督刊	仁濟善堂版	龍雲齋版	索綽絡氏家塾藏版	家藏版
卷	十五卷	二卷	十卷	上下兩卷	四卷	十二卷			十八卷	三十六卷
冊	一冊	二冊	四冊	二冊	二冊	四冊	二冊	一冊	八冊	二十冊
	一	一	一	二	一	一	一	一	二	二
紙	綿連紙	綿連紙	竹紙一夾板	連史紙	連史紙夾板	白綿紙一夾板	毛邊紙	綿連紙	連史紙	綿連紙
刻印			光緒六年刻古歡洪氏校藏	宣統己酉刻	宣統己酉刻		光緒十六年重刊	民國十五年重刊		
等	肆	肆	伍	伍	伍	伍	伍	伍	伍	伍

五十二
一

書名	著者・版本	卷冊	部數	用紙・刊記	價
人鏡類纂	清程之禎輯　江夏程氏藏版	四十六卷　十六冊	二	黃毛太紙　同治癸酉年刊	伍
兔瓜錄	明戚長恤著　家藏版	六十四卷　冊	一	黃毛邊紙	伍
列子	周列禦寇撰　景翻宋刊本	八卷　二冊	一	綿連紙　夾板	伍
池北偶談	清王士禎撰　文粹堂藏版	二十六卷　八冊	一	毛邊紙	伍
妙法蓮華經指掌疏		七卷　十二冊	一	毛邊紙	伍
金壺精萃	清郝在田輯　松竹齋版	四卷　二冊	一	粉紙　一夾版　名書家寫　光緒丙子年刻	伍
何博士備論	宋何去非撰　留香室開雕版	上下二冊	一	高麗紙	伍
聽訟彙案	孝緒撰　日本東陽津版　日本稽古精舍版	三卷　三冊	一	高麗紙　一夾版	伍
菜根譚	明洪應明著　家藏版	上下二冊	一	夾板　綿連紙　道光乙未重刊	伍
菜根譚	明洪應明著　家藏版	一冊	一	毛太紙	伍

書名	著者	版本	卷冊	部數	紙張／刻印	價
孫子參同	梅國禎撰	家藏版	六卷 上中下三冊	一	毛邊紙	伍
呂語集粹	清尹會一輯	家藏版	四卷 一冊	一	毛邊紙 劉綱藏書	伍
訂譌雜錄	清胡廷佩述	崴笈書屋刊	十卷 四冊	一	毛邊紙	伍
庸行編	清史措臣原輯 東允中述	家藏版	八卷 四冊	一	同治甲戌年刻 白紙	伍
劉海峰文	清劉大魁著	家藏版	十卷附詩六 六冊	四	大版夾連紙 同治年刻	伍
史姓韻編	清汪煥曾述	聚珍版印 金陵書局	六十四卷 二十四冊	一	油光紙 民國八年印	伍
金剛經旁解	湯蟄召	石印本	一冊	一	白綿紙 道光十年刻	伍
小兒語	漁隱開翁撰	寶琴齋刊	一冊	一	白綿紙 道光十年刻	伍
辨學集	清曾和瑙撰	家藏版	八卷 八冊	一	毛邊紙 光緒甲申刻 共五種	伍
續心影集	清李士龢編輯	甘肅蘭州郡署開雕	四冊	一	綿連紙 光緒丙子年刻	伍

五十三

書名	撰者	版本	卷冊	紙／刊年	價
七經樓文集	清蔣湘撰	家藏版	六卷六冊	道光二十七年刊綿連紙	伍
味餘書室隨筆	清嘉慶帝撰	殿版	二卷二冊	開化紙	伍
燕京歲時記	清富察敦崇禮臣氏編	京都文德齋刻本	一冊	光緒丙午年刻綿連紙	伍
張文襄幕府紀聞	清漢陽詔易者撰	活字版大字本	二冊	宣統庚戌年刻綿連紙	伍
老學菴筆記	宋陸游撰	上海掃葉山房石印本	二卷二冊	宣統三年印綿連紙	伍
滿清官場百怪錄	雲間顏公著	上海掃葉山房印	四卷四冊	民國二年印綿連紙	伍
螢雪叢說	明子俞子撰	明刻本	二卷二冊	白紙	伍
文心雕龍	北齊劉勰撰	粵省翰墨園藏版	十卷四冊	道光十三年刊硃批綿連紙	伍
韓子迂評		元何□校 明萬曆己卯門無□刻	二十卷十二冊	明綿紙	伍
小窗別紀	明吳從先評輯	明刻本	四卷四冊	竹紙	伍

子
部二

書名	著者・版本	卷冊	部數	紙張（刊年等）	等級
小窗自紀	明吳從先著　明刻本	四卷四冊	一	竹紙	伍
儒門法語	清彭定求編　彭氏刻本	二冊	一	乾隆三十五年刊　竹紙	伍
榮根談	明洪應明著　重刻增訂本	上下二冊	一	乾隆三十三年刊　竹紙	伍
古言	明鄭曉撰　明嘉靖年刊本	四卷二冊	一	明白綿紙	伍
鴻苞節錄	清屠隆纂著　寶硯齋藏版	十卷十冊	一	咸豐七年刻　綿連紙	陸
小窗清紀	明吳從先評輯　明刻本	四冊	一	竹紙	陸
小窗艷紀	明吳從先批選　明刻本	十四卷八冊	一	竹紙	陸
小窗清紀	明吳從先評輯　明刻本	六冊	一	竹紙　夾板	陸
小窗別紀	明吳從先評選　明刻本	八冊	一	夾板　竹紙	陸
芥子園畫傳	鹿柴先生　李笠翁鑒定本	五卷五冊	一	竹紙　夾版	陸

五十四

本表為直行書目（自右至左），今轉為橫排列出。

書名	著者	刊印·版本	卷冊	部數	紙張·刊年·收藏	價
聖祖仁皇帝庭訓格言	清康熙帝製	抄本	一冊	一	礬綿連紙	陸
丹鉛餘錄	明楊用修撰	明嘉靖丁酉年刊	四卷三冊	一	白紙　平壽高翰生藏	陸
名家批點荀子	唐楊倞註		二十卷六冊	一	竹紙　四句齋藏	陸
聊齋誌異	清蒲松齡著	廣順但氏刊硃批	十六卷十冊	一	粉紙夾板　道光壬寅年刻	陸
第一才子書	聖嘆外書　毛宗崗評批	翠玉山房刊硃批	六十卷	二	連史紙　光緒七年刻	陸
經策通纂	清吳澄夫輯	點石齋石印	二種共五十六卷八十冊	六	六夾板連史紙　光緒十四年印	陸
警睡編	清華燦菶纂	家藏版	四卷四冊	一	一夾板連史紙　光緒六年印	陸
太平廣記	唐李昉等奉勅撰	三讓睦記藏版	五百卷四十八冊	〔手寫註〕	毛太紙　道光丙午年刻	陸
續太平廣記	清陸壽名集	雲外樓藏版	八卷八冊	一	毛太紙　道光三年刻	陸
千百年眼	明張和仲纂	四明王氏刊于版　日本江戶　銅版	十二卷二十二冊	一	連史紙　光緒年刻　駱體漢紙藏	陸

471

書名	著者	版本	卷冊	部數	紙張・備註	價
十竹齋書畫譜	明胡日從摹古	掃葉山房藏版	八冊	一	南粉連紙 光緒己卯年重刻	陸
繡像紅樓夢	清曹雪芹著	京都聚珍堂印	一百二十卷 二十四冊	一	縐連紙 夾板	陸
清代軼聞	裘毓麟著	上海中華書局 鉛印本	十四冊	一	洋紙 民國四年印	陸
墨餘錄	清毛對山著	文元堂版	十六卷 六冊	一	毛太紙	柒
鏡花緣	清李汝珍著	點石齋印	共六冊	一	光緒十四年印 粉紙 夾板	柒
商子	明楊慎評釋 顧鄒初	朝爽閣版	一冊		竹紙	柒
玉茗堂還魂記	湯顯祖撰	暖紅室重刊	上下二冊	一	夾連紙	柒
呻吟語	明呂坤著	明萬曆版	八卷 六冊	一	白毛邊紙	柒
御定萬年曆			上下二冊	一	連史紙	柒
帝王經世圖譜	宋唐仲友撰	武英殿聚珍版	十六卷 六冊	一	毛邊紙 一夾板	柒

書名	編著者	版本	卷冊	部數	紙張	價
課子隨筆節鈔	清張又渠輯家藏版		六卷續編一卷 一冊	一	毛邊紙	捌
玉谿生詩詳註	唐李商隱著 清馮孟亭編訂	德聚堂藏版	三卷 四冊	一	迪莊藏 白紙 夾板	捌
樊南文集詳註	唐李商隱著 清馮孟亭編訂	德聚堂版	六卷 四冊	一	白紙 迪莊藏	捌
古意新情	日本西師意	李茂棠印刻	一冊	一	雙綿連紙	捌
日涉編	明陳堦編輯	明萬曆辛亥年刻本	十二卷 十二冊	一	明綿紙	捌
性理大方全書	明李廷機校正	金陵李洪宇梓行	七十卷 十八冊	二	篇首有明永樂皇帝御製序文竹紙 古錦套黃絹書皮	捌
老子	田潛篆	影印本	一冊	一	迪史紙	捌
教家編	清梁顯祖纂	閑道堂藏版	二卷 二冊	一	毛邊紙	捌
子史精華	清張廷玉等奉勅撰	仿殿版	一百六十卷 四十八冊	六	連史紙 夾板	捌
畜德錄	清席啟圖纂輯	上海掃葉山房石印本	二十卷 六冊	一	綿連紙	捌

子部

五十六 一

473

書名	著者	版本	卷冊	部數	備註	
酌中志餘		野史氏家藏版	二卷 二冊	一	綿連紙 夾板	捌
淮南子	漢高誘註	浙江書局 武進莊氏本校刊	二十一卷 六冊	一	竹紙 光緒二年刊	捌
宋豔	清徐士鑾輯	蝶園藏版	十二卷 六冊	一	毛邊紙 光緒辛卯年刊	捌
唐開元小說六種	清葉德輝輯	葉氏觀古堂刊	二冊	一	竹紙 宣統三年刊	捌
制義叢話	清梁章鉅撰	知足知不足齋本	二十四卷 八冊	一	綿連紙 光緒辛巳年刊	捌
理學辨似	清潘昭撰	虞山潘氏叢書本	一冊	一	綿連紙 民國五年印	捌
菿漢微言	清章炳麟述	鉛印本	一冊	一	綿連紙	捌
誠子庸言	清龔啟智撰	鉛印本	二冊	一	皮紙	捌
格古論要	曹昭著	抄寫本	四冊	一	毛邊紙 黃氏萬卷樓藏	捌
雪菴清史	明樂純著	明萬曆年刻本	四五冊卷	一	竹紙	捌

書名	著者	版本	卷/冊	部	紙・裝・年	號
學仕遺規	清陳宏謀輯	福州正誼書院藏版	正集各四卷 補集十冊	一	綿連紙 夾板	捌
天祿閣外史	漢黃憲著	明刻本	八卷 四冊	一	竹紙	捌
北堂書鈔	隋虞世南撰	南海孔氏鋟本	一百六十卷 二十冊	四	綿連紙 光緒戊子年印	捌
楞嚴自知錄	清王辮印錄	家藏版	二冊	一	綿連紙 夾板 康熙戊辰年刻	捌
古玉圖考	清吳大澂輯	上海同文書局影印大本	二冊	一	連史紙	捌
聖諭廣訓 附直解	清康熙帝御製	官版大本	三冊	一	綿連紙	捌
羣書治要	唐魏徵奉勅撰	日本版	五十卷 五十冊	四	日本皮紙	捌
星軺指掌	清聯芳 清慶常 同譯	同文館聚珍版	四冊	一	綿連紙 光緒二年刊	捌
塗記	清繆蓮仙輯	如此草堂版	四卷 四冊	一	毛邊紙 道光年刻	玖
兩般秋雨盫隨筆	清梁紹壬纂	振綺堂刊	八卷 八冊	一	粉紙 道光十七年刻	玖

五十七

書名	著者	版本	卷册		紙・刻	
蜀碧	清彭馨泉編述	天祿閣版	四卷 二册	一	嘉慶年刻 白紙	玖
小志	清王徵君撰	家藏版	十二卷 六册	一	道光年刻 白紙	玖
漢書·蒙拾	清杭世駿鈔撮	家藏版	三卷 三册	一	屈儀藏 夾竹板紙	玖
補世說新語	宋劉義慶撰	茂清書屋版	二十卷 十二册	一	毛太紙	玖
探本錄	雲澹人著	家藏版	三十三卷 六册	一	咸豐元年刻 毛邊紙	玖
玉海蹟記		浙江書局版	上下 二册	一	竹紙	玖
歷代名媛圖說		申昌書畫室出版	二册	一	光緒五年印 一粉紙夾板紅木	玖
董解西廂	顧渚山樵點定刊	夢鳳樓暖紅室	四卷 二册	一	綿連紙	玖
酉陽雜俎	唐段成式撰	崇文書局版	二十卷 續集十卷 共六册	一	光緒三年刻 粉紙夾板	玖
涑水紀聞	宋司馬光撰	崇文書局刊	六卷 四册	一	光緒三年刻 粉紙夾板	玖

子部

書名	著者	版本	卷冊	函	紙／刻	等
世說新語	宋劉義慶撰	崇文書局刊	六卷 四冊	一	光緒三年刻	玖
第九才子	樵雲山人編	同文堂版	四卷 四冊	一	毛太紙	玖
夢溪筆談	宋沈括撰	番禺陶氏愛廬校刊	二十六卷 補筆談三 共補筆談四 三冊	一	光緒三十二年刻 綿連紙夾板	玖
龍文鞭影		侗卿居版	二卷 二冊	一	輝發敬軒藏 道光板	玖
玉海	宋王應麟編	成都王氏用元刻本校補重刊	二百卷 二十冊	十	川板連紙夾板	玖
香祖筆記	清王士正著	申報館印	十二卷 二冊		竹紙鉛印 光緒十年刻	玖
小學紺珠	宋王應麟著	家藏版	十卷 六冊	一	粉紙	玖
豆棚閒話	艾納居士原本	致和堂版	十二卷 四冊	一	同治十二年刻	玖
孔子集語	清孫星衍撰	陽湖孫氏本寫刊	十七卷 六冊	一	光緒年刻 竹紙	玖
小知錄	清陸鳳藻箐	琴雅堂版	十二卷 十冊	一	嘉慶年刻 白毛邊紙夾板	玖

粉紙以上共十三種一夾板

五十八

書名	著者	版本	卷冊		紙・刊年	價
四書反身錄	清李容著	三韓劉氏版	四卷 八冊	一	竹紙	玖
王陽明出身靖亂錄	明墨憨齋編	弘毅館刊	三卷 三冊	一	高麗紙 朝崗氏藏	玖
海島算經	晉劉徽撰	武英殿聚珍版	一 全冊	一	竹紙 乾隆年版	玖
禪林寶訓	釋淨善重集	般若堂刻	一卷 四冊	一	竹紙	玖
法華擊節	明釋德清述	明萬曆版	一 冊	一	竹紙	玖
世說新語補	宋劉義慶撰	葛氏嘯園版	八卷 二十冊	一	連史紙	玖
世說‧新語	宋劉義慶撰	紛欣閣版	六卷 六冊	一	白紙	玖
趙註孫子	明趙靈舟註 亦西齋藏版		四卷 五冊	一	竹紙 道光年刻	玖
約書	清謝子玉著 家藏版		四卷 十二冊	一	一竹夾紙版 同治年刻	玖
百孝圖	清俞葆真編輯 家藏版		二卷 四冊	一	粉紙 同治年刻	玖

子
部

書名	撰者	版本	卷冊	部數	紙・刻年	價
選註孫子	夏壽田選註	硃絲格石印大字	二冊	一	綿連紙	玖
人譜	明劉宗周著	崇文書局刊	人譜類記六卷 計共三冊	一	連史紙 光緒三年刻	玖
三國演義	清毛宗崗評	澹雅書局刊	五十一卷 二十冊	一	竹紙	玖
庭訓格言	清康熙帝製	殿版	一冊	一	綿連紙	玖
牡丹亭		清暉閣原版 暖紅室重刊	二十冊	一	連史紙	玖
二如亭羣芳譜	明王象晉纂輯	明天啟年刻本	二十冊	二	毛邊紙	拾
蔡氏九儒書	清蔡發撰	三餘書屋藏版	八卷 六冊	一	綿連紙 同治戊辰春鐫	拾
蔡氏九儒書 附蔡氏通譜蔡福州外紀	清蔡發撰	三餘書屋藏版	八卷六冊 又十卷一冊 又全八卷一冊	一	綿連紙 同治戊辰春鐫 康熙六十年刻	拾
南華經解	清宣穎著	家藏版	三冊	一	綿連紙 康熙六十年刻	拾
名句文身表異錄	明王志堅輯	明寫版本	二十四冊	一	竹紙 崇禎庚辰年刻	拾

五十九

書名	撰者	版本	卷冊	部數	紙・刊刻	價
農政全書	明徐光啟原本	曙海樓藏版	六十卷 十六冊	二	道光癸卯重刊 綿連紙 夾棉版	拾
博古圖	明程士莊撰	萬曆戊子年黃德時版	三十卷 十六冊	一	白毛太紙	拾
聖門十六子書	清鴻巽嶠校刊	昌平書院藏版	十二冊	二	道光壬辰年刻 毛邊紙	拾
神仙鑑	清黃掌綸先生 評訂	華藏圖版	二十二卷 二十四冊	四	康熙年刻 毛邊紙	拾壹
蕩寇志	清俞仲華著	家藏版	二十冊	二	粉紙版	拾
五種遺規	清陳宏謀輯	金陵書局刊	共十冊	一	同治紙年刻 夾竹版	拾
封氏聞見記	唐封演著	雅雨堂版	二十卷 十冊	一	迪莊紙藏 夾竹板紙	拾
輟耕錄	陶南邨著	福瀛書局刻 許恒遠堂藏版	三十卷 十三冊	一	光緒年刻 竹紙	拾
擇識錄	清方今吾氏輯	官版	九卷 四冊	一	乾隆五十八年刻 綿連紙	拾
聖諭像解	清粱延年編輯	江蘇撫署恩壽 印	二十冊	一	光緒年刻 夾棉版連紙	拾

子部

書名	著者	版本	卷冊	部數	紙張・刊刻	價
錢錄	清紀昀等奉勅撰	殿版	十六卷 四冊	一	乾隆五十二年刻 粉紙夾版	拾
文昌雜錄	清龐元英著	雅雨堂版	六卷 二冊	一	乾隆年刻 竹紙	拾
太平清話	清陳繼儒撰	東洋版	二卷 二冊	一	東洋綿紙	拾壹
課子隨筆鈔	清張又渠輯	家藏版	六卷 六冊	一	綿連紙	拾壹
欣賞編 附繪妙一册	明沈津編集	明刻本	八卷 八冊	一	明綿紙	拾壹
南華經箋註	明釋性通註	清乾隆己巳年刻本	八冊	一	竹紙	拾壹
述記	清任文田撰	映雪草堂藏版	四冊	一	毛邊紙	拾壹
漢學商兌	清方東樹述	浙江書局刊本	三卷 四冊	一	光緒庚子年刊 綿連紙	拾壹
朝野雜記	宋李心傳撰	井研袁氏刊本	四十卷 十二冊	一	光緒癸巳年刊 綿連紙	拾壹
蠶桑崖際	清王約時記	滂喜齋刊	一卷 六冊	一	光緒年刻 竹紙	拾壹

六十一

書名	著者	版本	卷冊	部	紙張・刊刻	價
經咒　觀世音菩薩大悲陀羅尼經	伽梵達摩譯		一冊	一	白紙　咸豐元年刻	拾壹
東塾讀書記	清陳澧撰	家藏版	五卷二十五冊	一	竹紙	拾壹
經餘必讀	清胡承諾著	三餘草堂版	四卷附年譜一六冊	一	毛邊紙珠點　嘉慶年刻	拾壹
讀書記	清雷曉峯輯	成裕堂刊	八卷四冊	一	毛邊紙　光緒年刻	拾壹
謝華啟秀	明楊慎編	阮敬嬌藏版	五卷附廣啟秀七卷共六冊	一	綿連紙	拾壹
記事珠	清張贊虞輯	聚元堂板	十卷十冊	二	毛太紙	拾壹
刪定荀子	清方苞刪定	平湖屈氏藏本	一冊	一	綿連紙	拾壹
刪定管子	清方苞刪定	平湖屈氏藏本	二冊	一	綿連紙一夾板	拾壹
列子	漢劉向校	閱過五校刊	上下二冊	一	綿連紙珠點	拾壹
北學編	清魏蓮陸集	蓮池書院刊	四卷附補遺三共一冊	一	毛邊紙　同治七年刻	拾壹

書名	撰者	版本	卷冊	部數	紙・刊年	價
儒門法語輯要	清彭定求原編 馮定釗輯要	山東書局重刊本	一冊	一	內附儒門法語夾板	拾貳
歸元鏡	釋智達拈頌	乾隆甲辰年刊本	二卷二冊	一	綿連紙	拾貳
緯義攟	清喬松年撰	強恕堂藏版本	十四卷八冊	一	綿連紙 光緒三年刻	拾貳
新義錄	清孫璧文輯	漱石山房藏版 光緒丙戌年增本	一百四十卷	一	光緒壬午年刊	拾貳
竹葉亭雜記	清姚元之著	家藏版	八卷四冊	一	竹紙 光緒年刻	拾叁
小滄浪筆談	清阮元記	浙江節院刊	四卷四冊	一	竹紙 嘉慶年刻	拾叁
人範	清蔣大始輯	家藏版	四卷六冊	一	粉紙	拾叁
水滸圖贊	明杜堇撰	羊城廣百宋齋藏本	二冊	一	綿連紙	拾叁
五種遺規	清陳宏謀編輯	金陵書局重修本	十冊	一	毛邊紙 同治戊辰年印	拾壹
冊府元龜	宋王欽若等奉勅撰 清丁序賢重校本		一千卷 一百六十冊	二三十	綿連紙 乾隆甲戌年刊	拾貳

子·部

六十二一

書名	著者	版本	卷／冊	函	用紙	價
漢雋	明林鉄輯	明芸帘版	十四卷 一冊	一	毛太紙	拾叁
述記	清任兆麟述 字版	忠敏堂家藏大	四冊	一	毛邊紙 夾板	拾叁
世說新語	宋劉義慶撰	明凌濛初訂版	七卷附補遺 五冊	一	竹紙	拾叁
浪跡叢談	清梁章鉅撰	家藏版	十一卷附續談六卷三談八卷 共冊	一	竹紙	拾叁
學統	清熊賜履編	家藏版	五十三卷 十六冊	一	綿連紙 夾板	拾叁
知古錄	清恒秫撰	避熱窩家藏版	三冊	一	綿連紙 夾板	拾叁
古格言	清梁章鉅輯	任位俊等重刊	四十二卷	一	毛邊紙	拾叁
龍舒淨土文	王日休撰	衍法寺重刊	二十二卷	一	毛邊紙	拾叁
封神演義	明鍾惺評釋	集成圖書公司鉛印	十卷	一	油光紙 光緒三十四年印	拾叁
說岳全傳	清錢彩編次	大文堂版	二十卷	一	毛邊紙	拾叁

書名	著者	版本	卷冊	部	刻年・紙張	價
急就篇	宋王應麟補註	福山王氏刊置 天壤閣家塾	四卷二冊	一	光緒六年刻 毛邊紙	拾肆
古今學變	日本伊藤長胤著	皇都書林 林權兵衛出版	三卷三冊	一	高麗紙 夾板	拾肆
折獄龜鑑	宋鄭克原書	山陽李氏閑妙 香室所集刻	八卷二冊	一	道光十五年刻 夾板綿連紙	拾肆
庭訓格言	清聖祖仁皇帝製	殿版	一冊	一	綿連紙	拾肆
湘煙錄	清閔子京凌駿甫同輯	凌氏鳳笙閣版	十六卷六冊	一	嘉慶年刻 竹紙	拾肆
年將軍兵法	清年羹堯著	豹樹樓刊	四卷四冊	一	綿連紙	拾肆
莊子雪	清陸樹芝輯註	粵東儒雅堂版	三卷六冊	一	毛邊紙	拾肆
知聖道齋讀書跋尾	明彭元瑞撰	明刻本	二卷二冊	一	竹紙 大字	拾肆
疑耀	明李贄閣甫著	明萬曆年刊本	七卷六冊	一	先覺先生獨志堂 竹物紙	拾肆
儒行集傳	明黃道周輯	家藏版	二卷二冊	一	毛邊紙	拾肆

子部

書名	著撰	版本	冊／卷	函	紙・刊年	類
北東園筆錄全集	清梁恭辰撰述	不愧屋漏齋主人重刊本	八冊／四編廿四卷	一	光緒二十年刊 綿連紙	拾肆
蘇黃題跋	宋蘇軾著 黃庭堅	又實齋藏版	五卷 四冊	一	乾隆五十年鑴 綿連紙	拾肆
程氏家塾讀書分年日程	元程端禮姚	廣東文英閣刊	三卷 二冊	一	光緒十八年刊 毛邊紙	拾肆
十竹齋書畫譜	明胡曰從摹古	張學瞱重刊	八冊	一	綿連紙	拾肆
海上名家畫稿		慎思草堂刊	二冊	一	萃珍書屋藏本 光緒年刻 粉紙	拾肆
菜根談	明洪應明著	岫雲寺監院冰琳刊	二冊	一	乾隆三十三年刻 竹紙	拾肆
墨子後語	清孫詒讓撰	家藏版	一冊	一	夾板 竹紙	拾肆
於越先賢像傳贊	王齡撰 任渭長畫版	王氏敬和堂藏	二冊	一	咸豐年刻 沈敦和 綿連紙	拾肆
七十二候箋	清錢吉生畫	文美齋藏版 華文書局印	二冊	一	光緒年印 連史紙	拾肆
井眉居雜著	清姚前機撰	家藏版	一冊	一	白紙	拾肆

子部　六十四　一

書名	著者	版本	卷	冊	部	用紙・備考	價
醉墨軒畫稿	清胡鄒伯稿	石印本	四卷	四冊	一	綿連紙 宣統元年印	拾肆
庭聞錄	清劉健述	家藏袖珍本	六卷	四冊	一	綿連紙	拾肆
農桑輯要	元司農司撰	仿聚珍版刻本	七卷	三冊	一	綿連紙	拾肆
文中子中說	隋王通撰 晉阮逸註	明精刻本 敬忍堂版	十卷	四冊	一	竹紙 閔微草堂藏本	拾肆
義門讀書記	清何焯撰	家藏版	十二卷	十二冊	二	竹紙	拾肆
寄園寄所寄	清趙吉士著	姑蘇文秀堂藏版	十二卷	十二冊	一	竹紙	拾肆
小豆棚	清曾衍東著	上海申報館仿聚珍版印 石印	十六卷	六冊	一	竹紙 光緒丙戌年印	拾肆
京塵雜錄	清楊掌生著	上海同文書局 石印	四卷	二冊	一	綿連紙	拾肆
鏡花緣	清李汝珍撰	翠筠山房刻版	十六卷	十六冊	二	竹紙 光緒戊子年刊	拾肆
花月痕全書	清眠鶴道人撰	閩雙笏廬藏版	十六卷	十六冊	一	綿連紙 火板	拾肆

490

子部

書名	著者	版本	卷冊	部	紙張・刊印	價
西湖佳話	清墨浪子搜輯	精繪設色全圖／版本金陵王衙藏	十六卷 八冊	一	竹紙	拾肆
益智圖	清童叶庚著	京都琉璃廠遵／林書室藏版	二冊	一	綿連紙	拾肆
蘇沈良方	宋蘇軾集／沈适輯	武強賀氏仿知／不足齋本校印	十四卷 四冊	一	光緒丁酉年印／綿連紙	拾肆
漢溪書法通解	清戈守智纂	金閶賀氏仿知／寫刻本家藏版	八卷 六冊	一	綿連紙	拾伍
增補繪像山海經廣註	清吳任臣註	金閶書業堂藏	十八卷 六冊	一	乾隆五十一年刊／毛邊紙	拾伍
羣芳列傳	清馬大魁譔	精刻套／餐秀閣藏版印	四十卷 四冊	一 錦套	道光二年刻／綿連紙	拾伍
增像全圖三國演義	清羅本撰	石印精本	六十卷 二十冊	二	綿連紙	拾伍
聊齋志異新評	清蒲松齡撰	廣順但氏刊／硃批評點本	十六卷 十冊	二	道光壬寅年刊／綿連紙	拾伍
後聊齋志異圖說	清王韜撰	上海鴻文書局石印	十二卷 八冊	一	光緒辛卯年印／綿連紙	拾伍
繪圖增像五才子書	清施耐菴撰／金人瑞評釋	上海廣百宋齋校印大字本	十冊	一	有光洋紙／光緒辛卯年印	拾伍

六十五

491

書名	著者	版本	卷冊	部數	紙張	價
對山印稿	清楊對山印存	石藏楊氏遺厚堂	八卷	一	道光年刻 富古香藏 粉紙夾板	拾伍
賢媛圖說		延古齋版	一冊	一	光緒丙午年刻 粉紙夾板	拾伍
楹聯叢話	清梁章鉅輯	桂林署齋刊	十四卷 附續話六冊 共二四卷	一	道光年刻 粉連紙	拾伍
文中子中說	隋王通撰 阮逸註	敬忍居刊	二十卷	一	粉紙大字	拾伍
景宋本中說	隋王通撰 阮逸註	貴陽陳氏審定 宋本	十卷	一	光緒年刻 竹紙	拾伍
方氏墨海	明方瑞生輯	涉園景印原刻本	書圖三六卷 共計七六冊	一	綿連紙 藍字	拾伍
息齋藏書	著	家藏版	十二卷	一	康熙年刻 竹紙	拾伍
譚史志奇	陽直中菴子輯著	五知堂家藏版	八卷 四冊	一	毛太紙	拾伍
畫譜采新	清姚彥臣輯	審經堂石印	二冊	一	光緒乙酉年刻 顏景字藏 粉紙	拾伍
茶經茶錄等十二種			四冊	一	竹紙	拾伍

書名	著者	版本	卷冊	部數	刊刻・用紙	價
宣和譜牙牌彙集	浪槐河上漁人杏園輯博昌散人雲庵氏重訂	家藏版	二冊	一	撰連紙 光緒年刻	拾伍
聰訓齋語	清張英著	家藏版	四卷六冊 附澄懷主人年譜六卷共四冊	一	毛邊紙 光緒六年刻	拾伍
澗泉日記	宋韓淲撰	武英殿聚珍原本	三卷三冊	一	粉紙 乾隆年刻	拾伍
讀書做人譜	清龍曉岸輯	張奐承手鈔本	二冊	一	竹紙 同治十一年寫	拾伍
礴花做法		抄寫本	一冊	一	東昌紙	拾伍
呻吟語	明呂坤著	松茂堂藏版	六卷六冊	一	綿連紙 同治年刻	拾伍
文子	清孫鏘詝評 朱弁等註	家藏本	十二卷六冊	一	竹紙	拾伍
莊子·集解	清王先謙集解	思賢書局版	八卷三冊	一	連史紙 宣統年刻	拾伍
先正格言	瓣香書室輯	家藏版	十卷四冊	一	毛邊紙 計二部 道光年刻	拾伍
迪吉錄	清顧茂猷編輯	刊於福州西江別墅	八卷八冊	一	綿連紙 夾板 光緒丙戌年刻	拾伍

六十六

書名	著者	版本	卷冊	函	紙張・刊刻	價
紅樓夢圖詠	清改七薌繪	淮浦居士精刊本	四冊	一	光緒十年刊 綿連紙	拾伍
日知錄	清顧炎武撰	黃氏西爽草廬重刊定本	三十二卷十六冊	二	道光十四年刊 毛邊紙	拾伍
談徵	外方山人輯	上苑堂藏版	五冊	一	道光三年鐫 毛邊紙	拾伍
級齋畫賸		陳氏得古歡室精刻本	四冊	一	光緒內子年刊 綿連紙	拾伍
賞奇軒四種合編			一冊	一	粉紙	拾伍
硫砲先生梅譜	清洪硫砲寫	京華印書局版	一冊	一	連史紙	拾伍
管子纂詁	日本安井衡纂 江戶書林玉山堂版		二十四卷十二冊	一	慶應元乙丑年刻 夾板高麗綿紙	拾伍
管子纂詁	唐房玄齡註	明刻本	二十四卷十二冊	二	陸芳洲原陳氏藏 竹紙	拾伍
六壬圖像		抄寫本五彩精繪	共二十四冊	四	紅格雙東昌紙	拾伍
管子義正	清洪頤煊撰	徐積餘校刊	八卷二冊	一	光緒年刊 毛邊紙	拾伍

子部

書名	編著	版本	冊卷	部數	紙刻	價
子史粹言	清丁晏述	頤志齋版	上下二冊	一	竹紙 道光年刻	拾伍
花陣綺言	楚江仙隱石公纂輯 吳門翰史茂生評選	明刻本	上下二冊	一	竹紙	拾伍
畫學簡明	清鄭紀常著	麥幻居版	四題句等七卷 共附十冊卷	一	綿連紙 同治年刻	拾伍
菊譜	清穆谷瑛寫	中華書局印行	二冊	一	述史紙石印	拾伍
人壽金鑑	清程得齡輯	崇文書局刊	二十二卷六冊	一	白紙 光緒元年刻	拾伍
字義	清陳安卿撰	味道腴軒刊	上下二冊	一	毛邊紙 夾板 光緒乙未年刻	拾伍
對類	明吳勉學攷註	明版	二十卷十二冊		竹紙	拾伍
大慈恩寺三藏法師傳	唐釋慧立本釋	明崇禎版	一五卷冊		竹紙	拾伍
妙法蓮華經		明版	二八卷冊		竹紙	拾伍
金剛經	隋天竺闍那崛多共達摩笈多譯 添品	白雲觀藏版	一冊		白紙 光緒年刻	拾伍

六十七

書名	編者・著者	版本	卷册	部	刊刻・用紙	價
方言	漢揚雄記 晉郭璞註	思賢講舍版	十三卷二冊	一	光緒年刻 白紙	拾伍
陰騭文圖說	清黄正元纂輯	晉文齋藏版	四卷四冊 續	一	道光年刻 白紙夾竹紙版	拾伍
慾海慈航	清黄正元纂輯	晉文齋藏版	一冊	一	道光年刻 竹紙	拾伍
性天眞境	清黄正元註釋	晉文齋藏版	附戒士子格文 功過共三冊	一	道光年刻 竹紙 三種共一夾板以上	拾伍
西廂記		程士任自莘刊 于成裕堂 袖珍本	十二冊零	二	雍正年刻 白紙	拾伍
文林畫譜	玫芳軒主人寫	日本版	十七卷 十七冊	二	明治年刻 白紙	拾伍
五經類典襄括	同文書局主人 編輯	同文書局石 印袖珍本	六十四卷 六冊	一	光緒十年石印 連史紙	拾伍
朝市叢載	清楊靜亭原輯 李紅若纂輯	文光樓藏版	八卷 八冊	一	光緒年刻 毛太紙	拾伍
先哲叢談	日本谷壯太郎 輯	江島喜兵衛版 袖珍	四卷 四冊	一	明治十七年印 白紙	拾伍
四本堂座右編	清韓山子輯	家藏版	二集共四十八卷 八冊	一	康熙年刻 竹紙	拾伍

書名	著者	版本	卷冊	數	用紙	價
墨法輯要	明沈繼孫撰	涉園影印文津閣舊鈔本	一冊	一	綿連紙	拾陸
天工開物志	明宋應星撰	涉園據日本明和年所刊以古今圖書集成本校訂付印	三卷三冊	一	綿連紙	拾陸
弟子箴言	清胡達源撰	蒲圻但氏刊本	十六卷四冊	一	毛邊紙 光緒乙未年刊	拾陸
管子	管仲	士禮居黃丕烈撫宋刻本	二十四卷六冊	一	綿連紙 嘉慶丙寅年刻	拾陸
天中記	明陳耀文纂	明萬曆己丑年刊本	六十卷十六冊	六	白竹紙	拾陸
彙苑詳註	明鄒善長撰	明萬曆乙未年刊本	三十六卷十四冊	二	竹紙	拾陸
二如亭羣芳譜	明王象晉纂輯	明崇禎二年刊本	二十八冊	二	綿連紙	拾陸
潛確居類書	明陳仁錫纂輯	明刻本	八十冊	四	毛邊紙夾板	拾陸
申江勝景圖	清黃逢甲編	上海點石齋石印本	二卷二冊	一	綿連紙 光緒十年印	拾陸
感應編印譜	清汪學成撰	家藏版	一冊		綿連紙	拾陸

書名	撰著者	版本	卷／冊數	部數	印紙・刊年	編號
聊齋誌異	清蒲松齡撰	羊城青雲樓藏版	十六卷・二冊		同治己巳年刻　綿連紙	拾陸
〃		硃批評點版	十六冊		綿連紙	拾陸
事類賦	宋吳淑撰	依宋崇正書院本校刊	三十二卷・八冊	一	民國十五年　洋白毛邊紙	拾陸
廣事類賦	清華希閔著	崇德堂藏本	十四冊		民國十五年　綿連紙	拾陸
骨董瑣記	清鄧之誠輯	明齋叢書本　鉛印	八冊		道光辛巳年刻　綿連紙一部　毛邊紙共二部	拾柒
古今秘苑	十二桐樓主人	袖珍本　原刻版	六冊		竹紙	拾柒
癡說	清紀陰田著	懷清堂藏版	八卷・四冊	一	開化紙	拾柒
真德秀政經心經	宋真德秀撰	清武英殿影宋刊本	二冊		白綿紙	拾柒
海瓊白真人語錄	道士謝顯道編	抄寫本	二冊	一	竹紙	拾柒
愚齋語錄	清熊孝昌著	敬業山房藏版	三卷・三冊	一	康熙年刻　竹紙	拾柒
孫子選註	夏壽田奉命選註	硃格石印本	一冊		綿連紙	拾柒
居仁日覽	內史監進本石印		一冊		民國四年印　綿連紙	拾柒

六十九　一

書名	著者	版本	卷冊	部數	紙張年代	價
老子	田溍寫篆	文楷齋版	一冊	一	竹紙	拾柒
蘿摩亭札記	清徐溝橋抄撮	家藏版	八卷四冊	一	粉紙 同治年刻	拾柒
郎潛紀聞	清陳康祺著	家藏版	二十四卷四冊	一	連史紙 光緒年刻	拾柒
明季遺聞	清鄒漪輯	家藏版	四卷四冊	一	夾綿紙板 順治年刻	拾柒
芥子園畫傳三集	王司直等摹古	芥子園刊	四冊	一	白紙	拾柒
芥子園畫傳四集	丁皋著	芥子園刊	五冊	一	綿紙 嘉慶年刻	拾柒
芥子園畫傳	王安節摹古	芥子園刊	五卷四冊	一	粉紙 康熙年刻	拾柒
西清箚記	清胡敬輯	進呈本	畫像考二卷國朝院畫錄二卷共四冊 四卷附南薰殿圖	一	綿連紙 嘉慶年刻	拾柒
聖諭像解	清梁延年輯	廣州復初堂重刊古香閣藏版	二十冊	一	綿連紙	拾柒
畫傳合編	王安節等摹古刊	金圓書業堂重刊	四冊	一	粉紙 乾隆年刻	拾柒

書名	著者	版本	卷冊	部數	紙張・刊刻	價
讀書叢錄	清洪頤煊錄	家藏版 廣東省城富文齋刊	二十四卷 六冊	一	道光二年刊 毛邊紙	拾柒
畫家三昧	清王竹禪繪	安禪堂刊	六冊	一	夾板 綿連紙	拾柒
畜德典錄	清席啟圖纂輯	湘潭縣懺心寺藏版	二十卷 十二冊	一	毛太紙 同治丁卯年宜刊	拾柒
問奇典註	唐英增釋	古柏堂本	十六卷 五冊	一	綿連紙	拾柒
莊子	莊周	明世德堂本	十卷 四冊	一	明綿紙	拾柒
恩福堂筆記	清英和撰	家藏版	二卷 一冊	一	道光年刻 竹紙	拾捌
晳是編	清屈成霖編輯	家藏版	十二卷 四冊	一	光緒年刻 夾板 竹紙	拾捌
太上感應篇	清惠棟箋註 羅椒先生引經	家藏版	一冊	一	乾隆年刻 夾板 綿連紙	拾捌
讀書錄	明薛瑄撰	明嘉靖訓本	二十卷 六冊	一	竹紙 夾板	拾捌
約書	清謝階樹撰	家藏版	十二卷 四冊	一	道光年刻 竹紙	拾捌

子部

書名	著者	版本	卷冊	部	紙	價
原富	英斯密亞丹原本 清嚴幾道譯述	南洋公學譯書院印	十一卷 八冊	一	光緒年印 夾竹私紙	拾捌
點石齋畫報		上海點石齋石印	六十冊	十	綿連紙	拾捌
歐陽文忠公全集	宋歐陽修撰	乾隆丙寅年重刊 孝思堂藏版	一百六十八卷 二十四冊	四	毛邊紙	拾捌
藝文類聚	唐歐陽詢等撰	華陽宏達堂重刊明萬曆本	一百卷 三十二冊	四	毛邊紙	拾捌
老子道德真經 莊子南華真經 列子沖虛真經	李 莊 列 注	明精刻本	十六冊	二	綿連紙	拾捌
閱微草堂筆記	清紀昀撰	河間紀氏原本 北京盛氏藏版 硃批評點	二十四卷 十二冊	一	綿連紙	拾捌
金科輯要	桂官武昌侯	北京金科流通處鉛印大字本	十八冊	二	毛邊紙	拾捌
荊川稗編	明唐順之撰	明萬曆辛巳年刊本	一百廿卷 八十冊	八	明綿紙 夾版	拾捌
遯世編	明錢一本品定 吳亮論贊	明刻本	六冊	一	竹紙	拾捌
陰騭文圖說	清桂 撰	京都琉璃廠有耀齋刻字鋪藏版	四卷 四冊	一	嘉慶辛酉年刊 竹紙	拾捌

七十一

書名	著者	版本	卷・冊	函	紙・刊年	定價
方言疏証	清戴震疏証	漢青錢重刊 微波榭本	十三卷 四冊	一	光緒年刻 竹紙	拾捌
唱道眞言	青華道父祖師 蛋製	盧靜室藏版	五卷 二冊	一	道光年刻 粉紙	拾捌
尚直理編	釋空谷景隆述	批點本 抄寫本	一冊	一	培經堂主人印 夢生庭主人藏 毛邊紙	拾捌
世說新語	宋劉義慶撰	思賢講舍刊	六卷 三冊	一	光緒年刻 硃點 毛邊紙	拾捌
月令粹編	清秦嘉謨輯	琳琅仙館刊	二十四卷 六冊	一	嘉慶年刻 夾竹板紙	拾捌
上諭成語		鈔寫本附滿文 翻譯	六冊	一	宣紙大字	拾捌
權衡一書	清王植輯	崇雅堂藏版	二十四卷 二十四冊	四	竹紙	拾捌
世說新語補	宋劉義慶撰 梁劉孝標註	葛氏嘯園藏版	二十卷 六冊	一	粉紙	拾玖
原人內篇	清陳劍潭著	王漢超刊	六卷 二冊	一	民國十二年刻 竹紙	拾玖
記纂淵海	宋潘自牧纂輯	明萬曆己卯年刊本	一百卷 四十八冊	六	明綿紙	貳拾

子部二

書名	著者	藏版/刊本	卷冊	數	備註	價
鴻書	明劉仲達纂輯	明萬曆辛亥年精刻本	一百零八卷 五十六冊	八	竹紙	貳拾
三寶太監西洋記通俗演義	明羅懋登撰	明萬曆丁酉年刊本	二十卷 二十冊	二	光緒五年重刊 白紙	貳拾
返性圖		思過齋藏版	十卷 十冊	一	竹紙	貳拾
論衡	漢王充撰 清顧汝連校本	顧築居藏版	三十卷 八冊	一	竹紙	貳拾
百子全丹	明郭偉選註 明刻本		十二卷 十冊	一	竹紙	貳拾
五經類編	清周世樟編輯	聚錦堂藏版	二十八卷 十六冊	一	乾隆丁未年刻 竹紙	貳拾
第六才子書 附醉心篇	金聖嘆原本	文盛堂藏版	八卷 附醉心篇三卷 共十二冊	二	箕華堂 竹紙	貳拾
胎產秘書		家藏版	三卷 二冊	一	綿連紙	貳拾
胎產新書	清吳煜校訂	成娛堂刊	二十卷 六冊	一	連史紙 夾板 光緒年刻	貳拾
儒林外史	清吳敬梓撰	齊省堂藏版	十六卷 二十冊	一	同治年刻 竹紙夾版 此書計有兩部	貳拾

七十二

書名	撰者	版本	卷・冊	部	紙・刊年	價
管子評註	唐房玄齡註　明朱養和輯	聚文堂藏版	二十四卷	二	嘉慶甲子年刊　綿連紙	貳拾
管子　丁此聘訂閱	葛鼎　丁此聘訂閱	家藏版　寫刻本	二十四卷	一	毛邊紙	貳拾
蘇黃題跋　附尺牘小詞	明黃嘉惠校	明刻本	共十六卷　八冊	一	竹紙　夾板	貳拾
古雋考略		明精刻本	六冊	一	夾連紙	貳拾
佛祖統系道影		釋守一宜刻本	四卷　四冊	一	綿連紙	貳拾
關學編	明馮從吾撰　清李元春續編	傳經堂藏版	二卷　四冊	一	乾隆丙子刊　白毛邊紙	貳拾
課子隨筆節鈔	清張又渠輯　徐桐節鈔	殿版	六卷　四冊	一	同治十年刊　白毛邊紙	貳拾
日知薈說	清乾隆帝御製	殿版	四卷　四冊	一	乾隆丙辰刊　開化紙	貳拾
唐類函	明俞安期彙纂	明萬曆精刻本	二百卷　二十冊	八	大字　毛邊紙	貳拾
小嬛嬛仙館類書十二種　訂	小嬛嬛仙館增訂	牽玉閣彙刻	十二種共廿二卷　共十二種八冊	一	同治六年刻　白紙	貳拾

子部

書名	撰者	版本	卷・冊	部	刊印・用紙	價
古學彙纂	明周時雍輯	明崇禎本	十六卷 十六冊	二	民國八年印 油光紙	貳拾
儒林外史	清吳敬梓著	育文書局石印	六冊	一	乾隆壬子年刻 編連紙	貳拾
耳食錄	清樂官譜著	夢花樓藏版	十二卷 六冊	一	同治年刻 連史紙	貳拾
燕子箋記	雪韻堂批點	寄傲山房藏版	四冊	一	光緒十三年印 竹紙	貳拾
古事比	清方中德輯著	點石齋石印	五十二卷 六十二冊	一	乾隆年刻 白紙	貳壹
七修類彙	清郎仁寶著	耕烟草堂刊	十一卷 續集七卷 五卷 十六冊	二	嘉慶年刊 連史紙	貳壹
異談可信錄	清郅暄輯	碧山樓藏版	十二卷 二十三冊	二	光緒二十年印 竹紙	貳壹
駢雅訓纂	清朱謀瑋纂	積山書局石印	八卷 十六冊	二	光緒二十年印 連史紙	貳壹
息影偶錄	清張延輯	南潯書尾藏版	八十卷 八冊	一	嘉慶年刊 連史紙	貳壹
三國演義	聖嘆外書 毛宗崗評	點石齋石印	六十卷 七十二冊	一	光緒八年石印 夾板連史紙	貳壹

書名	編著者	版本	卷册	部數	紙張	定價
百家摘奇	明劉孟雷輯	明萬曆版 寫刻本	四卷 四册	一	竹紙	貳壹
金壺字攷	古柎適之原編 石齋增訂	貼安堂藏版	初集四卷 附補共四十二册 註	一	夾板毛邊紙 乾隆年刻	貳壹
知本提綱	清楊厚著 鄭世鐸註	崇本齋版精刻本	二十四卷 十册	一	夾連紙 乾隆年刻	貳壹
月令粹編	清秦嘉謨纂輯	琳瑯仙館刊	八册	一	毛邊紙 嘉慶年刻	貳壹
少室山房筆叢 附詩藪篇	明胡應麟撰	廣雅書局刊	共詩藪十二卷 共四十八卷 十六册	二	白紙	貳壹
書言故事大全	明胡繼宗集	明精刻本	十二卷 十二册	二	開化紙	貳壹
人倫道德綱要	清李熙編纂	珠絲格 精寫本	一册	一	竹紙	貳壹
問奇典註	唐英增釋	抄寫本	上下二册	一	竹紙 乾隆年刻	貳壹
陔餘叢攷	清趙翼著	渦貽堂藏版	四十三卷 十四册	一	竹板紙 康熙年刻	貳壹
學海津梁	清崔學右編輯	文起堂刊	二册	一	毛邊紙 康熙年刻	貳壹

子部

書名	著者	版本	卷・冊	部	用紙・附註	價
歲華紀麗	唐韓鄂撰	明毛氏汲古閣本	四卷 二冊	一	竹紙	貳壹
請益錄	釋性一閱	明精寫刻本	二卷 二冊	一	竹紙 繡佛夷子藏	貳壹
存古約言	明呂維祺著	明崇禎版	六卷 二冊	一	竹紙	貳壹
韓子	秦韓非著 硃批點	明萬曆精刻本	二十卷 六冊	一	明白綿紙 清紀昀藏書印	貳壹
諸子拔萃	明李雲翔評選 硃批評點	明天啟精刻	八卷 十六冊	二	竹紙	貳壹
莊子因	清林雲銘選	輔仁堂藏版	六卷 六冊	一	康熙年刻 竹紙	貳壹
楹聯叢話	清梁章鉅輯	環碧軒藏版	十二卷 續編四卷 巧對續編八卷 共八冊	一	白毛邊紙 夾板	貳壹
穀貽彙編	北齊顏之推著 明陶希臯輯	明刻本	十四卷 十冊	一	道光年刻 竹紙	貳壹
四存編	明顏元著	家藏版	共十一卷 二冊	一	康熙年刻 毛邊紙	貳壹
夢迹圖	清紹葛民記	石印精印寫本	一冊	一	綿連紙	貳貳

七十四　一

書名	著者・版本	卷冊	部數	紙・刻	價
尺牘青蓮	明何偉然纂　明刻本	十二卷	一	竹紙	貳貳
海內奇觀	明楊爾曾撰　明萬曆版精刻圖繪本	十卷	一	周復揚藏　竹紙	貳貳
補過齋日記	楊增新著　家藏版	十九卷附註陰符經一卷	二	民國辛酉刻　連史紙	貳貳
墨子閒詁	清孫詒讓撰　家藏版	十五卷附錄一卷目錄一卷後語二卷共八冊	一	光緒年刻　連史紙	貳貳
古籌算考釋	清勞乃宣撰　完縣官舍刊	六卷	一	光緒十二年刻　白紙	貳貳
歷代名人畫譜	明顧炳然摹本　鴻文齋石印	四冊	一	光緒年刻　縮連紙	貳貳
七十二候牋	清錢吉生畫　華文書局印	上下二冊	一	白紙	貳貳
銅人鍼灸經	宋王惟一奉旨編修　宜刊宋本　硃印	四卷五冊	一	綿連紙	貳貳
聖諭像解	梁延年解　味經堂重刊本	二十卷	一	夾綿版連紙　咸豐年刻	貳貳
鴻雪因緣	清麟慶著　凝香室板	三集共六冊	一	夾版連紙　道光年刻	貳貳

子部

書名	著者	版本	卷冊	部數	刊刻・用紙	價
故事黃眉	明鄧百拙生彙編	明萬曆版	十三卷	一	毛太紙	貳貳
白眉故事	許以忠集	聖錦堂刊	十卷四冊	一	康熙年刻 竹紙	貳貳
聖諭像解	清梁延年解	味經堂重刊本	二十卷	一	咸豐年刻 夾綿連紙板	貳貳
聖諭廣訓	清聖祖製	殿版	滿漢各二卷四冊	一	開化紙	貳貳
野記	明祝允明撰	元和祝氏藏版	二卷四冊	一	同治甲戌年刻 太史紙	貳貳
志異新編	滿福慶著	家藏版	二卷四冊	一	乾隆年刻 粉紙	貳貳
近世一百名家畫集	振青書畫社輯	珂羅版影印	四冊	一	連印紙	貳貳
八面鋒	永嘉先生著	湖海樓刊	十三卷	一	嘉慶年刻 粉紙	貳貳
清異錄	宋陶轂撰 陳氏庸閒齋重刊		上下二卷四冊		光緒年刻	貳貳
表異錄	王志堅輯		共六十卷 二冊		光緒年刻	貳貳
歷代名媛圖記	清汪道昆輯	點石齋照相縮印本	二卷二冊	一	光緒五年印 連史紙	貳貳

七十五 一

書名	著者／評訂	版本	卷冊	部	紙張／裝	價
第一才子書	聖嘆外書 毛宋崗評	經綸堂藏版	五十一卷 二十一冊	二	竹紙 二夾板	貳貳
右台仙館筆記	清俞樾著 家藏版		六十二冊	一	夾板 綿連紙	貳貳
御製大雲輪請雨經	清乾隆帝製	精刻本	二冊		綿連紙	貳貳
聖諭廣訓直解		仿殿版	二冊	一	宣紙	貳貳
蒙齋筆談	宋鄭景望撰	明刻本	上下二卷 一冊	一	竹紙	貳貳
萬全玉匣記		紫雯道人重印	一冊	一	油光紙	貳貳
金壺精萃	清田石齋原著 祝任田編訂	寫刻精印本	二四冊	一	綿連紙 光緒年刻	貳貳
金剛經	孫仲樂改袖珍	寫刻本	上下二冊	一	榜紙 黃氏藏本 乾隆年刻	貳貳
昌道言	清胡蟄英著 胡雙桂軒藏版		五卷 二冊	一	綿紙 道光年刻	貳貳
養性閒筆語錄摘要	清鄧逢光撰 廣雅徐謙刊本		四冊	一	夾板	貳貳

子部

書名	著者	版本	冊／卷	部	紙張・刊年	價
莊子	清王闓運註	王氏刊本	二冊	一	原毛邊紙	貳貳
投壺新格	宋司馬光撰	舊抄本	一冊		毛邊紙	貳
人生必讀書	清唐彪輯著	華陽張廷憲等重刊本	十二冊	一	光緒二十年重刊　毛邊紙	貳
擇執錄	清王家啟編次	家藏版	三十二卷　八冊	一	雍正壬子年刊　竹紙	貳
陸子學譜	清李紱編	無恕軒藏版	二十卷　十二冊	一	夾板　竹紙	貳
增訂太上感應篇圖說	鐵珊增訂	鐵珊重刊	十二卷　二冊	二	同治十三年刻　綿連紙	貳貳
閱微草堂筆記	清紀昀撰	紀樹馥重刊廣州財政司藏版	二十四卷　十二冊	二	道光十五年刻　南粉連紙	貳貳
聖諭像解	梁延年解	湖南寶善堂重鐫本	二十卷　二十冊	一	光緒丁亥年刻　杭連紙	貳貳
意林語要	明馬總編	明嘉靖己丑年抄本	五冊	一	清阮元鑒藏版　竹紙	貳貳
巾經纂	清宋宗元著	家藏版	七十六卷　二十冊	一	乾隆辛未年刊　竹紙	貳

書名	著者	版本	卷冊		紙	價
百尺樓叢畫	清王耀如繪	石印著色	八卷八冊	一	綿連紙	貳貳
惠迪錄	大原氏著錄	家藏版	六卷二冊	一	毛邊紙	貳貳
古事苑	明鄧志謨撰	明萬曆丁巳年刻本	二十三卷六冊	一	竹紙	貳貳
莊子旁註	清吳承漸輯註	璥水春波漁舍藏版	五卷五冊	一	毛邊紙	貳貳
心賞編	明王象晉撰	明萬曆刻本	二冊	一	竹紙	貳貳
佛說四十二章經解 附佛遺教經解	明釋智旭撰	京都廣慧寺重校梓	共二冊	一	竹紙	貳貳
近思錄發明	清施璜纂註	桐城李寄鴻堂藏版	十四卷六冊	一	竹紙	貳貳
壽親養老新書	明鄧銶撰	明本重刊	四卷四冊	一	同治九年刊夾板綿連紙	貳貳
辟塵珠	明胡文煥選輯	明萬曆年寫刻本	一冊	一	竹紙	貳貳
南華經註	宋林巘齋口義 明王鳳洲等評點	精刻本五色批點	十六冊	一	綿連紙	貳貳

書名	撰者	版本	卷册		紙	價
文房四攷圖說	清唐秉鈞撰	家藏精刻本	八卷	八册 一	連史紙	貳貳
道原精萃	清倪懷綸等輯	聚珍版		八册 一	洋宜紙	貳貳
榮根譚	明洪應明撰	胡氏精刻本		二册 一	毛邊紙夾板	貳貳
藤陰雜記	清戴璐撰	英興會館藏版		二册 一	毛邊紙	貳貳
紅樓夢偶說	品三廬月草舍居士撰	寶硯山房校刊		二十二册 一	毛邊紙	貳貳
滿文御製避暑山莊圖詠		殿版		一册 一	開化榜紙	貳貳
鴻雪因緣圖記	清麟慶撰	琹雲陰堂藏版		二册 一	白綿紙	貳貳
秦淮八豔圖詠	清張景祁撰	寫刻本		一册 一	白綿紙	貳貳
庸書	清宋育仁撰	家藏版	四卷	四册 一	綿連紙	貳貳
規家日盆編	清姚體傑撰	明刻本		二册 一	竹紙夾板	貳貳

書名	著者	版本	卷冊	部數	紙張·刻印	價
太玄經	晉范望解贊	明郝梁刊 明嘉靖精刻本	十卷附太玄音論	一	明綿連紙 趙彦良藏	貳貳
芥子園畫傳 第一集	王安節摹古	芥子園精刻本	五卷四冊		康熙年刻 綿連紙	貳貳
芥子園畫傳 第二集	王安節等摹古	金閶書業堂刊	四卷五冊		乾隆年刻 綿連紙	貳貳
芥子園畫傳 第三集	王安節等摹古	金閶書業堂刊	四卷四冊		螺裝 乾隆年刻 綿連紙	貳貳
芥子園畫傳 第四集	丁皋著	抱青閣藏 芥子園本	四卷四冊	一	嘉慶年刻 共以上四集一夾板	貳貳
當代名畫大觀	王念慈主編	碧梧山莊影印	六冊	一	連史紙	貳貳
讀畫軒印存	清王俊集印	琴圃藏版本	上下二冊	一	光緒年刻 綿連紙	貳貳
太上感應篇	清惠棟箋註	翰院分書精刻本	一冊		同治年刊本 綿連紙	貳貳
伊江筆錄	清吳熊光撰	廣雅書局刊本	上下卷一冊		毛邊紙	貳貳
肇言瀝液	清梁顯祖彙編	精刻版本 家藏	八卷四冊		毛邊紙	貳貳

二樹紫籐花館印選	雲台二十八將圖	瑜伽燄口	困學紀聞	士林彙訓	賞左錄	梁氏印譜四種 附鑄書八要	列子	長春眞人西遊記	尊鄉贅筆
清周彥威選	清張士保畫		宋王應麟撰	清關槐述		清梁登庸學篆	周列禦寇	李志常述	清董含著
硃墨套印	金陵張志琚刻	版 京都龍泉寺藏	清河義門校本 桐華書塾刻	端溪書院 梓精刻本	舊抄本	朱墨套印精刻	明嘉靖年精刻 本	道藏輯要本 胃集三	精寫刻本
一冊	一冊	一冊	二十冊	八冊	上下二卷 二冊	六冊	八卷 六冊	二冊	三卷 四冊
一	一		一	一	一	一	一	一	一
綿連紙	道光丙午年刊 綿連紙	道光乙未年 榜紙	毛邊紙	綿連紙	白綿紙	乾隆壬午年刊 綿連紙	明奉國將軍朱氏 藏書 明綿紙	竹紙	竹紙
貳貳	貳貳	貳貳	貳貳	貳貳	貳貳	貳貳	貳貳	貳貳	貳貳

子部 七十九

書名	著者／刊者	版本	卷・冊	部	刊年・用紙	分類
農圃瑣談	清 楊景仁等撰 桂林唐九		二冊	一	光緒六年刊 綿連紙	貳貳
農雅	清 倪倬撰 龍薄霖輯 如堂刊	我我書屋藏版	六卷 二冊	一	嘉慶甲戌年刊 竹紙	貳貳
桐陰論畫（附桐陰畫訣 續桐陰論畫）	清 秦祖永著	家藏版精刻本 硃批評點	十五卷 五冊	一	同治三年刊 綿連紙	貳貳
穀玉類編	清 汪兆舒輯	錢唐金晏文曜氏刊	十四卷 四冊	二	乾隆戊寅年刊 毛邊紙	貳貳
說郛	明 陶宗儀纂	涵芬樓據明鈔本鉛本	一百卷	一	毛邊紙	貳叁
鄭氏應讖五代紀	清 江日昇撰	氏家抄稿本	十五卷 十冊	四	龍門紙	貳叁
聖諭像解		承宣堂仿殿版	十二卷 二冊	二	康熙二十年刻 綿連紙	貳叁
楚騷綺語	明 張之象輯	精刻本 明萬曆丙子年	六卷 六冊	一	白紙	貳叁
大悲心懺		硃墨套印 精刻本	二冊	一	綿連紙	貳叁
第七才子書	清 高則誠	初刊袖珍本	十六卷 二冊	二	雍正乙卯年刊本 綿連紙	貳貳

書名	著者	版本	卷／冊	函	紙・刊刻	編號
墨娥小錄		學圃山農重校版明吳穎書刊本精刻小箱本	六冊	一	綿連紙　乾隆丁亥年鐫	貳貳
乾坤大音	清劉闊萬輯	范氏家藏版	八冊	一	竹紙　同治十三年刻	貳貳
四機成竹		鈔寫本	四冊	一	竹紙	貳
夏商合傳	清鍾惺伯編輯	稽古堂刊	共十冊　八卷	一	竹紙　嘉慶年刻	貳
日下舊聞錄		安和軒藏版	四卷　二冊	一	夾板竹紙　咸豐年刻	貳參
強學錄類編	清夏錫疇著	仕學齋藏版	四卷　四冊	一	綿連紙　道光十三年刻	貳參
居業錄粹語	明胡居仁撰　清正鼎校正	清張伯行刊本	四卷　六冊	一	綿連紙　道光丙申年刻	貳參
明齋小識	清諸聯輯著	奎韻樓藏版	十二卷　四冊	一	竹紙　道光甲午年刊	貳參
辨惑編	元謝應芳撰	四庫全書本守山閣叢書子部	四卷　二冊	一	竹紙	貳參
士林彝訓	清關槐逃	廣東院署藏版	八卷　二冊	一	竹紙	貳參

書名	著者	版本	卷冊	套	紙張／刊年	價
津門雜記	清張燾輯	家藏版	三卷 三冊	一	綿連紙 光緒十年刊	貳叄
聖學總論	清陸有吉等述	古田凝道齋存版	四冊	一	竹紙	貳肆
古今類傳	清蕭毅士等輯	家藏版	四卷 四冊	一	竹紙	貳肆
樗繭譜	清鄭珍纂 莫友芝註	獨山莫氏刊本	二冊	一	貴州綿紙 道光十七年刻	貳肆
翻譯名義集選		精刻本	二冊	一	毛邊紙	貳肆
文萃十三種	清張道絡評	人鏡軒藏版	四十五卷 二十冊	二	竹紙 嘉慶辛未年刻	貳肆
札逐	清孫詒讓撰	家藏版	十二冊	一	綿連紙 光緒二十年刊	貳肆
金谿順齋先生策海	明張順齋撰 明人沈季文編次	王如金校刊 明刻本	二十二卷 十二冊	一	白紙	貳肆
兩晉清談	清沈㷊之輯	盍簪堂藏版 巾箱本精刻版	十二卷 六冊	一	綿連紙 嘉慶庚申年鐫	貳肆
繹志	明胡承諾譔	三餘草堂藏版	十九卷 八冊	一	毛邊紙 光緒辛卯年刻	貳肆

書名	著者	版本・刊印	卷冊	部數	刊年・紙	價
書林餘話	清葉德輝述	葉啟勳登印鉛印	上下二卷 二冊	一	綿連紙	貳肆
中州道學編	清耿介輯	嵩陽書院藏版	二卷 二冊	一	綿連紙	貳肆
西域聞見錄	清七十一著	復四山房家藏版 袖珍本	八卷 四冊	一	乾隆四十二年刻 綿連紙	貳肆
四書古人典林	清江永原編	同文書局石印	十八卷 古人典林冊共四冊 袖珍本精印	一	光緒年印 綿連紙	貳肆
子平眞詮	清沈孝瞻著	報恩草堂刊版	一冊	一	光緒年刻 綿連紙	貳肆
知古錄	清恒希纂輯	家藏版	三卷 三冊	一	同治二年刻 竹紙	貳伍
新世說	清易宗夔撰述	家藏版	八卷 四冊	一	民國十一年刻 連史紙	貳伍
重刊宋本棠陰比事	宋桂萬榮撰	聚珍仿宋刊	一冊	一	述史紙	貳伍
孔叢子	宋宋咸註	海昌陳氏重刊 宋嘉祐本	七卷 四冊	一	光緒年刻 沈史紙	貳伍
養性聞筆語錄摘要	清鄧厚菴著		四冊	一	連史紙	貳伍

子部

書名	編著／版本	卷冊	部	紙張	價
食憲·鴻秘	清年希堯輯 家藏版	上下二冊	一	夾竹紙板 雍正年刻	貳伍
十竹齋書畫譜	明胡正言輯 十竹齋本	十六卷十六冊	一	綿連紙	貳伍
顏氏家訓	北齊顏之推撰 章經濟堂刊	七卷四冊	一	竹紙	貳伍
慎言	明何浚川著 明嘉靖版	二十三冊	一	夾竹紙板	貳伍
鬼谷子	明吳勉學校 明精刻本	一冊	一	竹紙	貳伍
金剛經	釋鳩摩羅什譯 大謙註· 定慧講堂版 明刻本	二冊		竹紙	貳伍
易言	杞憂生著 中華印務總局刊	上下二卷二冊	一	光緒年刻 毛邊紙	貳伍
呂祖太極生生數	金桂抄錄	上下二冊	一	道光年寫 夾紅格紙板	貳伍
劉·雪湖梅譜	清王思任編輯 墨妙山房藏版	上下二冊	一	白紙	貳伍
首楞嚴直指	釋般刺密譯 傅弘烈刻	五十卷十冊	一	毛邊紙	貳伍

八十二

書名	著者	版本	卷	冊	數量	紙/刻	價
墨子	清畢沅校註	靈巖山館藏版	十五卷	六冊	一	乾隆年刻 張石州藏 竹紙	貳伍
紅樓夢圖詠	清改七薌畫	淮浦居士刊 精印本	四卷	四冊	一	光緒年刻 綿連紙	貳伍
荀子	唐楊倞註	安雅堂重刊 嘉善謝氏藏版	二十卷	八冊	一	乾隆年刻 綿連紙	貳伍
聊齋志異圖詠		廣百宋齋本 同文書局石印	十六卷	四冊	一	連史紙 火板	貳伍
東周列國志	清蔡元放評點	上海書局石印	二十七卷	八冊	一	連史紙 火板	貳伍
水滸傳畫譜	日本重信畫	精印本 益章		上下二冊	一	東洋綿紙	貳伍
十鐘山房印舉		精印本 益章		一冊	一	匡齋藏古之一 綿連紙	貳伍
百華詩箋譜	清張龢菴繪 五色套印	文美齋刻版	二卷	一冊	一	光緒丙午年刻 綿連紙	貳伍
詩賦題典雅	清邱大猷編 次荓註	家藏版	五卷	五冊	一	竹紙	貳伍
七巧六畫圖	清毛應觀著	家藏版		一冊	一	竹紙	貳伍

子部

書名	著者	版本	卷冊	部	刊年（紙）	價
傳經表 通經表	清畢沅撰	華陽宏達堂刻本	二冊	一	光緒五年刊（毛邊紙）	貳伍
自鏡編	清楊其烮編輯	家藏版刻本 精刻本	四冊	一	嘉慶庚申年刊（毛邊紙）	貳伍
敷度衍	清方中通衍	方氏通刊	二十四卷 八冊	一	毛邊紙 光緒四年刊	貳伍
國朝漢學師承記	清江藩纂	聚珍版印	八冊	一	毛邊紙 光緒二年印	貳伍
老子故	馬其昶述	抱潤軒周氏刊	上下二冊	一	夾板	貳伍
太上道德經淺註	佑帝君註	文齋藏版	上下二冊	一	綿連紙	貳伍
老子元翼（附考異附錄）	明焦竑原輯 清郭乾泗重較	清蘇伍梓本	上下二卷 四冊	一	竹紙	貳伍
呂子節錄（附補遺）	明呂坤著 清陳宏謀評輯	江西書局刻本	六冊 四冊	一	光緒丁亥年刊（綿連紙）	貳伍
補過齋讀老子日記	楊增新撰	家藏版	六冊	一	綿連紙	貳伍
補過齋讀陰符經日記	楊增新撰	家藏版	一冊	一	綿連紙	貳伍

書名	著者	版本	卷冊	部	紙・刻年	價
補過齋日記 附陰符經	楊增新新撰	家藏版	二十九卷 二十九冊	二	綿連紙	貳伍
理學宗傳	清孫奇逢輯	浙江書局刻本	二十六卷 十二冊	一	光緒庚辰年刻 竹紙	貳陸
聖諭像解		湖南寶善堂重刊本	二十卷 十二冊	一	光緒丁亥年刻 杭連紙	貳陸
世說新語補	宋劉義慶撰 明何良俊增訂重刊 明王世貞刪	清黃汝琳補訂重刊 茂清書屋版	二十卷 八冊	一	乾隆壬午年刊 竹紙	貳陸
羣書備考	明袁黃著	明崇禎壬午年刻本	四卷 八冊	一	竹紙	貳陸
隨園隨筆	清袁枚著	小倉山房藏版	二十八卷 六冊	一	嘉慶戊辰年刻 竹紙	貳陸
九章算術細草圖說 附海島經細草圖	魏劉徽註	語鴻堂藏版	九冊	一	嘉慶庚辰年刻 竹紙	貳陸
三教搜神大全		葉德輝仿元版刊	七卷 二冊	一	宣統元年刊 連史紙	貳陸
易知編	李廷遴編輯	蘇州織造署藏版	上下二冊	一	嘉慶年刻 夾毛板邊紙	貳陸
讀書雜釋	清徐鼒纂	福寧郡齋藏版	十四卷 四冊	一	咸豐年刻 夾綿連紙	貳陸

子部

書名	著者	刊刻／版本	卷冊	部	紙・刻	編號
山海經	晉郭璞傳	清郝懿行箋疏刊 阮氏琅嬛仙館刊	十八卷 圖讚一冊	一	毛邊紙 夾板 嘉慶年刻	貳陸
止止堂集	明戚武毅公著	家藏版	三卷 四冊	一	綿連紙 夾板 光緒年刻	貳陸
呻吟語	明呂坤著	羅氏重刊于成都書寄廬	六卷 四冊	一	白竹紙 光緒年刻	貳陸
寄園寄所寄	清趙吉士著		二十卷 十六冊	二	竹紙 道光年刻	貳陸
方輿類聚	清酈申輯	芸香堂刊	十六卷 十六冊	一	綿連紙 道光年刻	貳陸
莊子正義	清陳壽昌輯	怡顏齋刊	八冊	一	綿連紙 光緒十九年刻	貳陸
讀書雜志	清王念孫撰	家藏版	八十二卷 二十四冊	四	綿連紙	貳陸
古今釋疑	清方中履著	漢清閣藏版	十八卷 十二冊	二	綿連紙	貳陸
諸佛世尊如來菩薩尊者名稱歌曲		明永樂十二年刊本 大開本	八冊	一	明綿紙大開本	貳柒
道德寶章	宋道士白玉蟾註 元趙松雪書	京都白雲觀藏版	八十四冊	一	宣紙	貳柒

書名	著者	版本	卷冊	部	紙張	價
聖學格物通	明湛若水編	明嘉靖七年刊大開本	一百四卷 二十四冊	四	明白宣紙	貳柒
二程全書	宋程頤撰	河南嵩邑兩程故里影堂藏版	六十七卷 二十六冊	一	清同治丙寅年刻河南綿紙	貳柒
欽定授時通考	清蔣溥等奉勅纂修	江西書局刊	七十八卷 二十四冊	二	乾隆七年刻白竹紙	貳柒
增廣詩句題解彙編	清姚培謙集	慎記莊石印 袖珍本	四卷	一	光緒年印白竹紙	貳柒
類脈		綠蔭堂藏 袖珍本	共五十四卷 二十四冊	四	迻史刻白紙	貳柒
大學續衍精義	明劉洪謨續衍	明刻本	八卷 十四冊	一	乾隆年刻白紙	貳柒
竹窗隨筆	明釋袾宏著	明萬曆版精刻本	共六冊	一	白紙	貳柒
文史通義	清章學誠著	粵東菁華閣刻本	十一卷	一	光緒癸巳年刻毛邊紙	貳柒
困學紀聞	宋王應麟著	閩氏刊本	二十卷 六冊	一	竹紙	貳柒
唐一切經音義	清莊炘等校正	曹籀重刻	二十五冊	一	毛邊紙夾版	貳柒

書名	著者	版本	卷・册	函	刊年・紙	價
御製數理精蘊	清康熙帝製　精刻	江寧藩署藏版　精刻本	五十三卷　四十册	六	光緒八年刊　綿連紙	貳柒
分類字錦	勅纂　清張廷玉奉	殿版	六十四卷　六十四册	八	毛邊紙	貳捌
景宋本備急灸方（重刻鍼灸擇日編集）	宋聞人耆年撰	室藏版　精刻景宋本	四卷　共二册	一	開化紙	貳捌
居業錄	明胡居仁撰	明萬曆刻版	四卷　四册	一	竹紙	貳捌
淨土津梁	釋了慰解		十五卷　共九册	一	乾隆年刻　竹紙	貳捌
邵子全書	宋邵雍撰	宋陸游評　明萬曆精刻本	二十四卷　二十四册	一	夾板　竹紙	貳捌
太平御覽	宋李昉等奉勅撰	清鮑崇城校　宋版校本	一千卷　一百二十册	十二	嘉慶十七年刊成　夾板綿連紙	貳捌
呂氏春秋	明凌稚隆批校	宋版刻本	二十六卷　二十六册	一	貴陽趙氏藏　綿連紙	貳捌
朱子語類	宋朱熹撰	應元書院藏版	一百四十卷　四十册	四	同治壬申年刊成　毛邊紙	貳玖
增定漢魏六朝別解	明葉紹泰纂	明崇禎版	六十二卷　二十四册	二	竹紙	貳玖

八十五　一

感應篇註釋全解	盾鼻餘瀋	四字類賦	課子隨筆	五種遺規	容齋隨筆	列子	奉天錄	鬼谷子	封氏聞見記
	柳葆元易策謙錄刊	清張師戴撰輯	清張師戴編輯	清陳宏謀編輯	宋洪邁撰	唐盧重元解	唐趙元一撰	梁陶宏景註	唐封演撰
	家藏版	樂役園藏版	漂陽華聚書牡印	金陵書局重刊	明崇禎重刻本	石研齋版	享掃精舍刊	石研齋板	江都秦氏刊
三三 卷 册	一 册	二十七 卷 册	四十 卷 册	共五十七 卷種 册	五筆共七十四卷 九 册	八 四 卷 册	二 四 卷 册	二 三 卷 册	二十 卷 册
一	一	一	一	二	一	一	一	一	一
乾隆年刻 竹紙	光緒七年刻 竹紙	道光年刻 毛邊紙	民國十一年刻 毛邊紙	同治年刊 竹紙	嘉慶八年刻 夾板 竹紙	嘉慶八年刻 夷山王氏藏 綿紙	道光年刻 夷山王氏藏 綿紙	嘉慶十年刻 夷山王氏藏 綿紙	乾隆年刻 夷山王氏藏 綿紙
貳玖	貳玖	貳玖	貳玖	貳玖	貳玖	貳玖	貳玖	貳玖	貳玖

陰隲文圖說	陰隲文像註	陰隲文像註	兼明書	夢溪筆談 附補筆談續筆談	子品金函	文品薴函	史品赤函	斌品烏函	詩品會函	書品同函
桊桂圖註家藏版	清趙如升輯著 蔡輝齋刊	唐邱光庭撰 橫川吳氏刊	宋沈适著 明刻版	明陳仁錫選 明刻版	明陳仁錫選 明刻版	明陳仁錫選 明刻版	明陳仁錫選 明刻版	明陳仁錫選 明刻版	明陳仁錫選 明刻版
四卷 一冊	四卷 四冊	五卷 一冊	四卷 四冊	共附補說八一冊 二十六卷	四卷 四冊	三卷 三冊	四卷 四冊	二卷 二冊	二卷 二冊	二卷 二冊
一				一			一 以上三種共一函			八十六
嘉慶五年刻 竹紙	竹紙	嘉慶年刻 飛滿閣藏 毛邊紙	竹紙	竹紙	竹紙	竹紙		竹紙	竹紙	竹紙
貳玖	貳玖	貳玖	貳玖	貳玖	貳玖	貳玖	貳玖	貳玖	貳玖	貳玖

書名	撰者	版本	卷冊	函	紙張	刊刻	編號
啟品有函	明陳仁錫選	明刻版	二卷 二冊	一	竹紙		貳玖
逸品繹函	明陳仁錫選	明刻版	一卷 二冊	一	竹紙 以上五種共一函		貳玖
鴻苞集	明東海居隆著	明刻版	四十八卷 二十四冊	四	竹紙		貳玖
智品	明樊王衡評 品於倫增編	明刻版	十三卷 十八冊	二	竹紙		貳玖
勸善書	明仁孝皇后撰	明永樂版 寫刻本	二十六卷 十冊	二	竹紙		貳玖
九九消夏錄	清俞樾撰	家藏版	二十四卷 十二冊		竹紙		貳玖
七巧書譜	清嚴竹舟作	聽月山房仿刊	上下 二冊		連史紙	光緒十八年刻	貳玖
佛祖統承道景	趙宗寫訂	劉開旭鐫 段祺瑞影印	四卷 四冊	一	綿連紙	民國十年印	貳玖
式古編	清莊瑤輯 周尚德堂刊		二卷 四冊	一		民國十一年刻	貳玖
禪林寶訓筆說	釋智祥註		一二冊		竹紙	乾隆年刻	貳玖

子部

書名	著者	版本	卷冊	部數	紙張・備註	價
建國詅眞	徐樹鈞撰	影印原寫本	四冊	一	綿連紙	貳玖
新刻古今事物考	明王三聘輯	明刻本	八卷四冊	一	竹紙	貳玖
萬綠金剛經集註	清增德集註	家藏版	一冊	一	綿連紙	貳玖
性理奧	明丁進纂	明刻本	十卷四冊	一	竹紙	貳玖
智襄補	清馮夢龍纂輯	斐齋藏版	二十八卷六冊	一	竹紙	貳玖
事物記原補遺		舊精鈔本	二冊	一	竹紙	貳玖
酌雅齋丹黃消夏錄	清福增格撰	精寫刻本 酌雅齋藏本	二冊	一	綿連紙 乾隆辛巳年刻	貳玖
說類	明郭茂槐纂輯	明刻本	六十二卷二十冊	二	竹紙	貳玖
式古編	清莊瑤輯	留有餘齋藏版	五卷二冊	一	毛邊紙 道光戊戌年刊	叁拾
課子隨筆	清張師藏輯	留有餘齋仔版	十卷四冊	一	毛邊紙 道光癸卯年重梓	叁拾

八十七 一

書名	著者	版本	卷冊	紙張・刊年	價
玉堂薈記	清楊士聰撰	吳興劉氏刊業堂刊	四卷一冊	毛邊紙	叁拾
老解老	蔡廷幹撰	仿宋精刊本	一冊	綿連紙 民國十一年刊	叁拾
列子	周列禦寇	浙江書局據明世德堂木校刻	八卷十冊 一	毛邊紙 光緒二年刊	叁拾
志學編	清余寅正編次	務本堂藏版	上下二卷一冊	毛邊紙 光緒元年重刊	叁拾
盾墨	清溫毅纂	家藏版	四卷一冊	毛邊紙	叁拾
印正稿	明張信民著	門人馮懋庸訂本	六卷一冊	白毛太紙 光緒二十年刊	叁拾
羅近溪先生語要	清陶望齡輯	江寧府城重刊	一冊	毛邊紙 民國十七年印	叁拾
中國戲劇之組織	齊如山著	北華印刷局印	一冊	平粉連紙	叁拾
曼衍心漏	彊籃子著	家藏版	三卷一冊	述史紙	叁拾
閑邪錄	清姚端恪公原纂 蔣正校補輯	三鑑堂藏版	二十卷十冊	白紙 乾隆年刻	叁拾

子部

書名	著撰者	版本・刊印	卷冊	數	用紙	箱
增刪卜易	野鶴老人著	文成堂刊	四卷六冊	一	竹紙	叁拾
禪門佛・事全部	玉崑嵐撰集	永鎰齋刊	二卷一冊	一	粉連紙	叁拾
真教自証	耶穌會 晁德莅撰	鉛印本	一冊		油光紙	叁拾
輕世全書	極西陽瑪諾譯	宜刊本	四卷一冊	以上二種共一夾版		叁拾
韻語省心編	清王金鼎增輯	抄寫本	二冊		藍格白紙	小箱
心鏡編	清譚文光輯	家藏本	二十卷二十冊	硃點	乾隆年刻 竹紙	小箱
文學研究法	姚孟振編	東城印字館 鉛印	一冊		油光紙	小箱
熙朝人鑑	清張之萬撰	家藏版	上下二集 共八卷八冊	一	光緒年刻 毛邊紙	小箱
拾餘四種	清劉沅撰	家藏版	十三卷二冊	一	竹紙	小箱
金湯・借箸	明周鑑毫輯著 史可法手書序文	明精抄本 硃圈點	十冊	木	竹紙	八十八 一匣

八十八 一

書名	撰著者	版本	卷冊	函匣	紙・裝	刻年	等級
宗鏡錄	宋釋延壽集	清雍正帝重刊 殿版 開化紙初印	一百卷 二十冊	四夾板	黃綾書皮精裝		
維摩詰所說經	姚秦三藏法師鳩摩羅什奉詔譯	滿內府精寫本 開化紙 御硃批圈註本	正義一百卷 三冊	一夾版 一木匣	黃綾書皮精裝		
初潭集	明李卓吾撰	明精刻本 硃批點	三十卷 八冊	一木匣			
一切經音義 附檀一切經音義	唐釋慧琳等撰	藏版 獅谷白蓮社 日本楅桒維東	正義一百卷 縮義五十五冊	一箱	日本皮紙 綿連紙	日本元文三年刊	壹
古今事文類聚	元朱祝穆編	元朝精刻本	共九十六冊	十六紅箱 兩木箱	毛邊紙	乾隆年刻 樟木夾板	
事物異名錄	清厲荃原輯 閩槐堂增纂	粵東刊本	四十二卷 十冊	一	白綿紙		
管子韓非子合刻		明呂嚴等全刻 精刻本	共四十四卷 二十冊	二夾版 一木匣	明白綿紙		叁壹
曾文正公手書日記	清曾國藩手撰	上海中國圖書公司照原本影印	四十冊	一箱	綿連紙		
耕織全圖	清康熙帝御製	大本 上下	二冊	一	白紙	康熙三十五年刻	叁壹
編珠	隋杜公瞻撰	官刻本	續二 四卷二冊		綿連紙	康熙三十七年刻	叁壹

書名	著者	版本・印刷	卷冊	印行	紙張
刑案匯覽	清鮑春芸叅定	圖書集成局	六十卷		連史紙
御定駢字類編	祝慶祺編次	仿袖珍本印　鉛印	四十冊　一箱	光緒丁亥年印	
	清雍正帝定	石印　上海同文書局	二百四十卷　四十八冊　一箱	民國十年印	綿連紙
忍字輯略	清朱錫珍原輯	慕玄父重刊　鉛印本	五卷		綿連紙
磨盾餘談	清張炳著	活字板大字　精印本	一冊		毛邊紙
舊聞隨筆	清姚永樸撰	鉛印本	四冊		毛邊紙
主制羣徵（贈言附）	清湯若望著	明新安程榮校刊本	上下二冊		毛邊紙
法言	漢楊雄著	用四庫全書本鉛印　新會陳氏校刊	十冊		毛邊紙
靈言蠡勺	西人畢方濟撰	鉛印　新會陳氏校刊	上下二卷二冊		毛邊紙
救世新教教綱教法		鉛印本	一冊		毛邊紙
人格	唐文治著	鉛印本	一冊		毛邊紙

（各條下均鈐「叁」「壹」印記）

書名	著者	版本	冊數	紙張・刊年	價
勸學篇	清張之洞撰	雨湖書院刊 大字本	一冊	綿連紙 光緒戊戌年刊	叁 壹
覺世真經註解		樂善齋鋟本	一冊	綿連紙 道光癸未年刊	叁 壹
癯翁叢抄 原本	清李庚長手抄	鉛印本	上下二卷 二冊	毛邊紙	叁 壹
正修上達 原本		松防書屋藏版	一冊	綿連紙 光緒庚辰年刊	叁 壹
呂祖直解金剛經 光佛直解	圓通文尼自在佛直解版	北京龍雲齋藏版	一冊	綿連紙 民國十年重刊	叁 壹
養真集	養真子著	鉛印本	上下二卷 二冊	洋紙	叁 壹
人道大義錄	清夏彝武撰	大字印	一冊	洋紙	叁 壹
四十二章經講錄	太虛法師講	活字版 大字印	六卷 二冊	毛邊紙	叁 壹
康熙幾暇格物編	清康熙帝御撰	海棠仙館原本 寫本石印	上下 二冊	洋紙	叁 壹
己亥談時	清宋伯魯撰	鉛印大字	二冊	洋紙	叁 壹

玄機直講	大悲神咒	教諭語	柏堂師友言行記	庸吏庸言	續理窟	理窟	西行日記	護法論	鐸書
楊學淵輯	唐釋伽梵達磨譯	清謝金鑾撰	清方宗誠撰	清劉衡存稿	清李杕著	清李杕著	清池仲祐撰	宋張商英撰	明韓霖撰
長沙積善小補堂校刊	上海成文厚書局石印本附圖像	田刻坊藏版	福建省城吳玉鉛印本	蓬萊慕玄父校刊本印	家藏版	本書館鉛印大字	上海土山灣印書館活版大字本	上海土山灣印書館鉛印大字本	商務印書館鉛印大字本	明初重刻元本清撫刻	新會陳氏校刊鉛印
三卷	一冊	一冊	四冊	二冊	二冊	二九冊	上下二卷一冊	一冊	一冊
民國辛酉年刊	光緒甲申年印	綿連紙	洋白毛邊紙	綿連紙	潔白洋紙	洋紙	洋紙	毛邊紙	毛邊紙
叁壹	叁壹	叁壹	叁壹	叁壹	叁壹	叁壹	叁壹	叁壹	叁壹

玉海	西山讀書記	高上玉皇本行集經	藏文藥師尊經	學務平議	大意尊聞	說教	大學古本質言	俗言	又問
宋王應麟撰	宋真德秀撰	清張照奉敕書	大隆善護國寺任持喇嘛等度造	清孫詒讓撰	清方東樹著	清彭光譽撰	清劉沅著	清劉沅著	清劉沅著
精刻宋蝴蝶裝本版	精刻宋蝴蝶裝本版	乾隆二年刻本		瑞安廣明印刷局石印本	家藏版	進呈本文光齋刻版	竹陰書屋重鐫本	豫誠堂藏版	樂善堂藏版
卷一百十一	一	上中下三卷	一	一	三	一	一	一	一
一冊	冊	三冊	冊	冊	卷冊	冊	冊	冊	冊
共計四十四頁	共計三十八頁麻沙紙金菊子李寅藏本	刻絲夾版	清康熙庚午年造	綿連紙	毛邊紙	綿連紙	光緒庚辰年刻白紙	咸豐四年刻白紙	光緒丙戌年重刊白紙
叁壹	叁壹	叁壹	叁拾	叁壹	叁壹	叁壹	叁壹	叁壹	叁壹

以上共計捌百伍拾玖種

545

杜詩鏡銓	唐宋八大家文鈔	柔橋文鈔十六卷	藝文珠璣類編	遜學齋文鈔	抱潤軒文集	純甫古文鈔	古文奇賞	分類尺牘	留葊盦尺牘
清楊倫編輯	明茅坤評選	清王子莊著	章伯棠訂集	清孫琴西著	馬其昶撰	清戴柟撰	陳明卿選評	清王蘗仙輯	清嚴士竹蓀
望三益齋版	金閶龔太初刊版	上海圖光書局印	抄本	家藏版	家藏版	家藏版	虎林堂策欄梓行	珍藝書局鉛印	木版
二十二卷 十二冊	共一百五十八卷 計四十四冊	十六卷 八冊	十六冊	三十二卷 十二冊	二十二卷 四冊	二十六卷 二冊	二十八卷 十二冊	三十卷 六冊	二四冊
一	八	二	二	二	一	二	二	一	〇
同治十一年重刻 毛太紙	白蘭岩家藏本 集賢堂藏本 毛太紙 八夾板	玩芳草堂叢書之一 油光紙	白棉紙	同治十二年刻 毛邊紙	單宣紙	夾連紙 同治庚午年刊	郎衙藏版 竹紙	光緒年版 洋毛太紙	毛太紙
貳	貳	貳	貳	貳	貳	貳	貳	貳	參

547

書名	著者	版本	卷冊	部數	紙張・備考	
恩誦堂集	清李倘迪著	家藏版	十二卷附文二卷 二冊	一	稻連紙	叁
芸香館遺詩	清女史那遜蘭保蓮友撰	家藏版	二卷 一冊	一	白棉紙 無套	叁
徐文定公集	清李秋輯 刊	江南主敎姚雅	六卷 四冊	一	油光紙 鉛印	叁
遼東三家詩抄	袁金鎧等集		四種共十四卷 七冊	一	連史紙 奉天會館存版	叁
多歲堂詩集	清成書撰 家藏版		三種七卷 四冊	一	竹紙	叁
多歲堂古詩存	清成書選評 家藏版		八卷 四冊	一	道光年刻 竹紙	叁
口鐸日鈔	李九標筆記 梓	上海慈母堂重	八卷 四冊	一	油光紙 夾板	叁
味古齋所見集		紫色版	一冊	一		叁
詩夢鐘聲錄	清榮廷樸臣等集錄	家藏版	一冊	一	光緒年刻 白毛邊紙 無套	叁
二鄉亭詞	清宋琬著	家藏版	二冊	一	乾隆年刻 白竹紙 無套	叁

書名	著者	版本	卷冊	部	刊印・用紙	價
約園志	清徐樹銘輯	家藏版	三冊	一	白棉紙	叁
王臨川文集	宋王安石撰	大興殷氏刊	六十三卷十冊	二	光緒八年刻　竹紙	肆
司馬文正公集	宋司馬光撰	百祿堂版	八十二卷二十冊	二	乾隆甲子年刻　竹紙	肆
蘇東坡・詩全集	清王施合註	文蔚堂	三十二卷十二冊	二	乾隆年刻	肆
御選唐宋詩醇	清乾隆帝選	浙江書局重刻	四十七卷二十冊	二	毛太紙	肆
宋六十一名家詞		明毛氏汲古閣原本錢塘汪氏重校刊	共八十九卷三十六冊	四	白毛邊紙　翁之潤藏	肆
唐宋文醇	清乾隆帝御選	浙江書局校刊	二十卷五十八冊	二	毛太紙	肆
陶淵明集	晉陶潛撰	胡伯劍仿蘇寫原刻本	十卷三冊	二	光緒三年刻　毛太紙	肆
塾課古文匯選	清溫承惠評選	家藏版	六卷八冊	一	光緒己卯年刊　賞宜紙　綿連紙　嘉慶癸酉年刊	肆
沈氏唐宋八家文讀本	清沈德潛評點	東洋版	八卷八冊	一	明治十一年印　東洋棉紙	肆

九十四　一

書名	著者	版本	卷冊	部數	紙張刊年	價
金忠節文集	明金聲撰	家藏版	八卷四冊	一	毛太紙	肆
續古文辭類纂	清王先謙選	盧受堂王氏刊本	三十四卷八冊	一	毛邊紙 光緒壬午年刊	肆
笠翁一家言全集	清李漁著	芥子園版	二十四冊	二	共四集 雍正八年刻	肆
薛文清公集	明薛瑄撰	家藏版	四冊	一	毛太紙	肆
文章軌範	宋謝枋得選	桐陰書屋校刊本硃批	七卷二冊	一	綿連紙	肆
曝書亭集	清朱彝尊撰	家藏版	八十卷又附笛漁小稿十卷二十冊	二	竹紙	肆
璇璣碎錦	清萬紅友著	似靜齋重刊	上下兩冊	一	綿連紙 光緒戊子年刻	肆
茹經堂文集二編	唐文治著	家藏版	九卷四冊	一	白竹紙	肆
用六集	清刁包著	順積樓藏版	十二卷六冊	一	毛太紙 康熙年刊	肆
衛廬精舍藏稿	清胡直正著	齊思書塾刊	四十一卷十二冊	一	毛太紙 光緒癸卯刊	肆

書名	著者	版本	卷冊	部	紙・印	價
湘綺樓書牘	清王闓運著	廣益書局鉛印	四七卷 一冊	一	民國四年印 油光紙	肆
東坡尺牘	宋蘇軾撰	廣益書局石印	二冊	一	民國元年印 油光紙	肆
皇朝經世文編	清賀長齡編	雙峰書屋重校 刊本	七十二冊	八	光緒丁酉印 綿連紙	肆
皇朝經世文續編	清葛士濬輯	上海掃葉山房重校圖書集成印書局代印	一百二十卷 二十冊	二	綿連紙 同治癸酉年刻 味經軒徐氏藏本	肆
南豐劉先生文集	清劉孚經撰	上海聚珍仿宋印書局印	四附補遺卷 四冊	一	毛邊紙	肆
古今謠諺 附拾遺	明楊慎纂 清史孟蘭增輯	止園藏版	四冊	一	竹紙 同治癸酉年刻	肆
朱文公楚辭集註	宋朱熹集註	聽雨齋本	六卷 八冊	一	綿連紙 八十四家評點硃批本	肆
惜抱先生尺牘	清姚鼐撰	海園閣寫刻本	二卷 八冊	一	綿連紙 咸豐五年刊	肆
文章指南	明歸有光選 清許筱蓮輯	皖江節署校刊	五冊	一	夾板 黃毛太紙 光緒二年刊	伍
鐵橋漫稿	清嚴可均撰	長沙蔣氏重刊 本	四冊	一	綿連紙 光緒乙酉年刊	伍

書名	著者	版本	卷冊	部	紙裝・刊刻	價
秋蟪吟館詩鈔	清金和撰	鉛印本	四卷 八冊	一	東洋毛邊紙	伍
全上古三代秦漢三國六朝文	清嚴可均輯	廣州廣雅書局刊版	七百四十六卷 一百冊	十	連史紙 十夾板 光緒丁亥年刻	伍
朱子全集	宋朱熹著	紫霞洲祠堂藏版 咸豐庚申年印	一百零四卷 四十冊	四	綿連紙 道光乙未年刻	伍
朱子古文	清周大璋編次	寶研齋花宅藏版	六卷 六冊	一	綿連紙 北京文奎齋承刊	伍
陶樓文鈔	清黃彭年撰	硃印 長洲章鈺刊本	十四卷 六冊	一	毛邊紙 夾板 貴州文奎齋承刊	伍
太史升菴遺集	明楊慎撰	明萬曆年刊本	二十六卷 四冊	一	毛邊紙 夾板	伍
定盦文集	清龔自珍撰	吳煦刊本	七卷 三冊	一	綿連紙 同治七年刊	伍
有明名賢遺翰	清謝世伯輯刻	漢泉文淵書局藏版	二卷 四冊	一	綿連紙 咸豐元年刊本	伍
明賢尺牘	清王舍章 程化驤同輯	鄴氏榆園刊	四卷 八冊	一	連史紙夾板 光緒年刻	伍
楊升菴全集	明楊慎著	發拙山房版	八十卷 二十冊	二	毛太紙 二夾版 乾隆乙卯年刻	伍

書名	著者	版本	卷冊	數	刻印紙張	價
五朝古文		江蘇書局刊	唐宋金元明五種 計共六十四冊	八	光緒癸未年刻 大版白毛邊紙 八夾板	伍
宋曾文定公全集	清彭毅齋編訂	七業堂藏版	十七卷 十二冊	一	康熙壬申年刊 又毛邊紙 敬堂堂藏	伍
六朝唐賦	清馬俣驤選註	玉燕巢馬氏 刊	上下兩冊	一	甲戌書春寫 名家書刻藏	伍
擊壤集	宋邵雍撰	家藏版	六卷 十冊	一	夾板 毛太紙	伍
伊川擊壤集	宋邵雍撰	明刻本	二十六卷 二十冊	一	夾板 綿連紙 明竹紙	伍
雲間三子合稿	陳子龍等撰	峭帆樓重校刻本	九卷	一	夾板 綿連紙	伍
歸雲樓題畫詩	清徐世昌撰	進修堂藏版	二卷	一	連史紙	伍
鹿洲初集	清藍鼎元著	家藏版	三十六卷 十三冊	一	夾版 綿連紙	伍
去僞齋集	明呂坤著	開封府署雕版	十卷 十三冊	一	夾版 綿連紙	伍
白沙子全集	明陳獻章著	碧玉樓藏版	十三冊	一	乾隆辛卯重刊本 綿連紙	伍

九十六

553

外制集	皇明宸藻	文章辨體	嵐漪小艸	閩風集	默盦集	從游集	離憂集	頌譚詩話	北海集
明 高拱著	明 太祖等撰	明 吳訥編述	清 翁方綱撰	宋 舒岳祥撰	清 王舟瑤撰	清 陳瑚輯	清 陳瑚輯	清 陳瑚輯	明 馮琦著
高氏重刻本	明刻本	明天順年刊本	南昌使院鋟版	吳興劉氏嘉業堂刊	上海國光書局鈆印本	峭帆樓刻行	峭帆樓刻行	崑山趙氏峭帆樓校刻本	明萬曆年重刻本
二冊	二冊	五十卷 十二本	一冊	十二卷 二冊	十卷 三冊	二卷 二冊	一卷 二冊	四卷 二冊	五十八卷 十六冊
一	一			一					二
康熙己巳年重刊 毛邊紙	明竹紙	明綿紙 漢陽周貞亮收藏	竹紙	毛邊紙	有光洋紙	毛邊紙	毛邊紙	毛邊紙	明毛邊紙
陸	伍	伍	伍	伍	伍	伍	伍	伍	伍

書名	著者	版本	卷冊	部數	紙張・年代	陸
王臨川全集	宋王安石撰	清溧陽繆氏刊本	一百卷 十六冊	二	光緒癸未年刊	陸
涵芬樓古今文鈔	吳曾祺纂錄	商務印書館鉛印	十三類 計一百冊	十	宜統二年初版 連史紙	陸
文苑英華選	官定山輯	光明正大之堂藏版	六十四卷 二十四冊	二	毛邊紙	陸
黛韻樓遺集 陳孝女遺集 合刻	清陳淑宜著	家藏版	五種共十二卷 六冊	一	連史紙	陸
古今翰苑瓊琚	明楊慎選	家藏版	十二卷 十二冊	二	竹紙	陸
歸元鏡	清釋智達撰		上下二冊	一	竹紙 乾隆年版	陸
傳經寶文集	清朱駿聲撰	刘氏求恕齋刊	十二卷附賦一冊	一	竹紙 夾板	陸
徐文長文集	明徐渭著 袁宏道評點	明刻本	三十五卷 十五冊	一	竹紙	陸
明五大家集	明宋濂方孝孺王慎中唐順之歸有光	視古堂藏版	五十卷	五	温陵書林梓行 竹紙張汝瑚評選	陸
弘正四傑詩集	明李夢陽何景明徐禎卿邊貫	長沙張氏淵雨樓醫版	六十九卷 十六冊	一	綿連紙 光緒乙未年刻 張雨珊輯	陸

集部 九十七

書名	著者	版本	卷冊	數	紙張	價
歸震川·大全集	明歸有光撰	上海國學扶輪社石印大字本	五十五卷十二冊	一	綿連紙宣統二年印	陸
留耔盦尺牘叢殘	清嚴士竹稿	家藏·版	四卷四冊	一	咸豐年刻毛太紙	柒
文章軌範	宋謝枋得選	桂林賜谷尉氏家塾藏版	七卷二冊	一	白紙	柒
六朝唐賦	清劉傳庚選註	玉燕書巢馬氏刊	上下二冊	一	夾板綿連紙劉祖懋藏	柒
刈存詩草	清王玉衡著	家藏版	上下二冊	一	竹紙	柒
漁洋文略	清王士禎著	家藏版	十四卷五冊	一	毛邊紙	柒
輯刻唐文粹	清姚鉉纂	杭州許氏榆園刊	一百卷選二十六冊	二	二夾板綿連紙光緒年刻	柒
鮚埼亭集	清全祖望著	借樹山房版	五十卷經史問答三十八卷附外集共三十二冊	二	毛邊紙二夾板	柒
古文苑	宋章樵註	江蘇書局版	二十一冊	一	連史紙夾板光緒年刻	柒
續古文苑	清孫星衍選	江蘇書局版	二十六卷二十冊	一	連史紙夾板光緒年刻	柒

集部	寶綸堂文鈔	柳柳州全集	宋石學士詩集	桃花扇	錯中錯 曲本	古雋	亦園亭全集	笠翁傳奇十種	望溪先生集	文選
	清齊次風譔 家藏版	唐柳宗元撰 清孫琮評 廣益書局 石印本	李振綱校輯 家藏版	雲亭山人編 蘭雪堂重校刊 本		明楊慎編 明精刻本	清孟超然撰 家藏版	清李漁撰 世德堂藏版	清方苞撰 藏鈞衡校刊	梁昭明太子選 金陵書局刊 懷清堂藏版
	八卷 四冊	四卷 四冊	一冊	五卷 五冊	四卷 二冊	八冊	二十冊	二十冊	十八卷補遺二卷年譜二卷計十六冊	六十卷 十冊
	一	一	一	一	一	一	二	一	二	一
	粉紙	綿連紙	夾板	綿連紙 光緒乙未年刊	綿連紙 道光己丑年鐫	夾板 綿連紙 碧琳瑯館藏本	夾板 毛邊紙	毛邊紙 夾板	毛邊紙	綿連紙 夾板 同治八年刊
九十八一	捌	捌	捌	捌	捌	捌	捌	捌	捌	柒

書名	著者	版本	卷冊	部數	版刻・紙張	價
劉誠意伯文集	明劉基著	南舊果育堂藏版	二十卷 十冊	一	粉紙夾板	捌
楚辭	漢劉向集	大字版	十七卷 四冊	一	綿連紙夾板	捌
續文選	明湯公孟撰	希貴堂版	三十二卷 十六冊	二	毛邊紙夾板	捌
古詩源	清沈確士選	步月山房版	十四卷 四冊	一	光緒年刻 毛邊紙夾板	捌
古文翼	清唐介軒定本	黃氏藝文堂刊本	八卷 八冊	一	同治年刻 毛邊紙	捌
授經堂重刊遺集	清洪亮吉撰	授經堂重校刊本	二百二十二卷 八十四冊	六	光緒丁丑年刊 綿連紙	捌
古文辭類纂	清姚鼐撰	問竹軒新刻本	七十五卷 二十六冊	一	同治八年刻 綿連紙夾板	捌
清芬樓遺藁	清任啟運撰	家藏版	二十四卷 二冊	一	光緒戊子年刻 毛邊紙	捌
文章軌範	宋謝枋得輯	桂林賜谷謝氏家塾藏版	七卷 四冊	一	硃批圈點本 綿連紙	捌
文章指南	明歸有光選 許筱蓬蒐輯本	皖江節署校刊本	五冊	一	光緒二年刻 綿連紙	捌

集部　九十九　一

書名	著者	版本	卷數	冊數	部數	刊年	紙張	價
蘇文公詩集	宋蘇軾著	粤東省城翰墨園藏版　硃批	五十二卷	十二冊	二		綿連紙	捌
文章正宗　附壇集十二卷	宋真德秀輯　清紀昀評	清楊氏復刊本　硃批	共四十二卷	三十冊	三		毛邊紙	玖
古詩選	清王士禎選	金陵書局刻本	十二卷	十二冊	一	同治五年刻本	綿連紙	玖
重訂增註知愧軒尺牘	清管斯駿著	上海錦玉山房重校刊　硃批袖珍本	十六卷	十六冊		光緒戊子年刊	綿連紙	玖
選註六朝唐賦	清馬傳庚選註	京都松林齋刊本	二本		一	光緒丙子年刊	綿連紙	玖
唐人萬首絕句選	宋洪邁原本　清王士禎選	初印本	七卷	四冊		雍正壬子年刊	毛邊紙	玖
六朝文絜	清許梿評選	家藏版　袖珍本	四卷	四冊	二	光緒丁丑年刻	綿連紙	玖
癸巳存類稿	清俞正燮撰	求日益齋刻本	十四卷			道光十三年刻	毛邊紙	玖
文選音義	清余蕭客輯著	家藏版	八卷	四冊	一	乾隆二十三年刻	毛邊紙	玖
古詩歸	明鍾惺等選定	明萬曆丁巳年刻	十二卷	四冊	一		竹紙	玖

書名	著者	版本	卷・冊	部	紙張・刊刻	等第
李太白文集	清王琦輯註	聚錦堂藏版	三十六卷 十六冊	一	竹紙 乾隆二十三年刻	玖
杜工部集	唐杜甫撰	五色批 初印本	二十卷 十二冊	二	連史紙	玖
龍川文集	宋陳亮撰	重刊 退補齋藏版 初印本	三十卷 十二冊	一	毛邊紙 同治戊辰年刊	玖
古文觀止	清吳乘權等手錄	金陵李光明莊 梓	十二卷 六冊	一	毛邊紙	玖
方正學文集	明方孝孺著 徐渭評理	明刻本	十一卷 八冊	一	毛邊紙	玖
宋忠憲韓魏王安陽集	清黃邦寧重修	畫錦堂藏版	五十卷 十五冊	一	白毛太紙 乾隆庚寅年刻	玖
三魚堂集	清陸隴其著	掃葉山房版本	十二卷 八冊	一	毛邊紙	玖
三魚堂日記	清陸隴其撰	浙江書局刊 柳樹芳校	十卷 四冊	一	毛邊紙 同治庚午年刊	玖
宋文歸	明鍾惺選	集賢堂版 明寫刻本	二十卷 四十冊	四	毛邊紙	玖
松筠集四種	清松筠著	家藏版 西藏圖	共四卷 四冊	一	粉紙夾板 道光年刻 計兩部	玖

560

書名	著者	版本	冊數	部數	紙張裝訂	價
東萊先生古文關鍵	宋呂祖謙評 江蘇書局刊		二冊	一	光緒年刻 竹紙夾板	玖
文章遊戲全編	清經蓮仙輯 積山書局石印		四編	一	光緒年刻 連史紙	拾
古文淵鑑	清徐乾學等奉旨編注	五色批 殿版	三十二冊	四	康熙年刻 白棉紙	拾
李二曲全集	清李容撰	廣東版	四十六冊	二	共二冊夾板軒藏	拾
四忠文集	清劉季昭重刊	遯荊堂版	共十四種	二	同治十二年刻 二竹紙夾板	拾
御製文初集	清道光帝撰	殿版	五冊	一	光緒年刻 單宣紙 一夾板	拾
古詩源	清沈德潛選	謝文盛堂版	四冊	一	竹紙 毛太紙夾板	拾
茅鹿門先生文集	明茅坤著	明版	三十六卷十二冊	一	竹紙夾板	拾
容城三賢文集	清魏一鰲輯劉	家藏版	共三十二冊	二	竹紙	拾
文天祥集	宋文天祥撰 文燮丹輯	家藏版	九十六卷冊	一	夾連紙夾板	拾

集部

一百一

書名	撰著	版本	卷冊	部數	刊年／紙	價
梅村家藏稿	清吳偉業著	董氏誦芬室刊	五十八卷附補 八冊	一	宣統三年刻 綿連紙	拾
吳氏一家稿	清吳錫麒等著	家藏版	十六種計共十六冊	二	咸豐五年刻 連史紙	拾
陸子文集	宋陸象山著	太儒家廟版	三十六卷 十冊	一	同治年刊 毛太紙	拾
白香山詩集	唐白居易撰 清汪西亭編訂	一隅草堂版	四種共十冊	一	竹紙	拾
御製文餘集	清道光帝撰	殿版	二冊	一	綿連紙	拾
文選補遺	宋陳東山輯	郟環館版	四十卷 十二冊	二	毛邊紙	拾
文選	梁昭明太子選 唐李善注	海錄甄版	六十卷 六十冊	一	道光二十五年刊 毛邊紙	拾
元氏長慶集	唐元稹著 明馬元調校刻本	明萬曆甲辰年	十附補遺六卷 六冊	二	竹紙	拾壹
白氏長慶集	唐白居易撰 明馬元調校刻本	明萬曆甲辰年	七十一卷 二十六冊	四	竹紙	拾壹
笠翁一家言全集	清李漁撰	芥子園藏版	二十六卷 二十冊	二	竹紙	拾壹

書名	著者	版本	卷冊	數	紙/刻	價
古文淵鑑	清徐乾學等奉旨編注	浙江書局刊	六十四卷三十二冊	一	同治年刻竹紙一夾板隱鶴樓藏版	拾壹
陸子全書	清陸隴其著	武林薇署刊	八種共十二冊	一	粉紙夾板同治年刻	拾壹
李義山詩集	唐李商隱撰馮浩朱鶴齡箋註	廣州倅署刊	三卷四冊	二	綿連紙五色批點同治年刻	拾壹
古樂苑	明梅鼎祚編	明刻本	五十二卷十八冊附古樂苑衍錄四卷二冊	四	明白棉紙	拾貳
三昧集箋註	清王士禎選本吳煊等輯註	翰墨園重刊聽雨齋本硃批圈點	三卷六冊	一	南粉連紙	拾貳
明名人尺牘小品	清王元勳等輯	抱芳閣刊本	四卷四冊	一	綿連紙光緒辛巳年刻	拾貳
斯文精粹	清尹穉善輯	家藏版	十二卷二冊	二	毛太紙	拾貳
安吳四種	清包世臣著	重校本	三十六卷十六冊	二	毛邊紙光緒十四年印	拾貳
板橋集	清鄭燮撰	玉書樓藏版	六卷二冊	一	毛太紙	拾貳
戴氏遺書（文集）	清戴震撰	微波榭刻本	四十卷十冊	一	竹紙	拾貳

書名	著者	版本	卷册	部數	紙張・刊刻	價
關帝聖蹟圖誌全集	清芭楷林輯	湖北荆宜施道署藏版	十六卷 六册	一	道光丙申年重刊 綿連紙	拾貳
關帝全書	清黄啟曙彙輯	王家瑞重刊本	四十卷 十六册	一	綿連紙	拾貳
道古堂文集	清杭世駿撰	汪氏補刊本	四十八卷 十六册	二	毛邊紙 光緒十四年本	拾貳
海忠介公集	明海瑞撰	家藏版	六卷 二册	一	綿連紙	拾貳
瞿宗宣公集	明瞿式耜撰	光緒丁亥重刊 本	十卷 四册	一	綿連紙	拾貳
名賢手扎	清郭子靜輯	湘陰郭氏帖瞻堂摹刻本	四册	一	綿連紙 光緒甲申年刻	拾貳
忠宣公文集	元余闕著	清皖江泉署刊本	六卷 二册	一	綿連紙 同治丁卯年刊	拾貳
趙忠節公遺墨	趙景賢著	家藏版	一册	一	白紙 光緒八年刻	拾貳
李詩補注	唐李白著 明楊齊賢註	明版	二十六卷 十六册	二	青箱樓藏 毛邊紙	拾貳
東坡文選	宋蘇軾撰 明鍾惺定	明芭曆版	十卷 六册	一	毛邊紙	拾貳

一百零二

書名	大方萬文一統	張太岳集	唐陸宣公集	玉茗堂集	古文纂	纂輯武編	纂輯文編	曾文正公全集	天崇百篇	六朝文絜
著者	明李廷機編纂	明張居正著	唐陸贄著	明湯顯祖著	明張榜輯	明唐順之纂輯	明唐順之纂輯	清曾國藩撰	清吳關陵選輯	清許槤輯
版本	明刻板	明萬曆劉 唐氏廣慶堂刊	同立堂版	明刻版	明刻版	明刻版	明刻版	湖南傳忠書局刊本	經國書局刊	家藏版
卷冊	二十二卷 八冊	四十七卷 十二冊	二十四卷 八冊	四種共三十卷 九冊	五種共十二卷 六冊	前後計十二卷 十二冊	三十三卷 十三冊	一百二十八冊	四卷 四冊	一四卷冊
函	一	二	一	一	一	一	一	十二	一	一
紙	毛邊紙	竹紙	綿連紙	道光年刻 綿連紙	毛邊紙	毛邊紙 一夾板	毛邊紙 一夾板	光緒二年刊 南粉連紙	光緒年刻 毛太紙	光緒年刻 綿連紙
	拾貳	拾貳	拾貳	拾貳	拾貳	拾貳	拾貳	拾貳	拾叄	拾叄

書名	著者	版本	卷冊		刊年・用紙	價
欽定全唐文 附姓氏韻編一冊	清董誥等奉敕編輯	殿版	一千卷 二百四十一冊 一夾板	三十又	嘉慶二十三年刊 綿連紙	拾壹
鹿洲全集	清藍鼎元著	同文藏版 巾箱本	二十四卷 二十四冊	四	同治壬申年刊 毛邊紙	拾叄
經德堂全集	清龍啟瑞撰	家藏版	二十一卷 二十一冊	一	光緒四年刊 共計七種 綿連紙	拾叄
渠亭山人半部稿	清張貞撰	家藏版	四種共八冊	一	毛邊紙	拾叄
吾邱邊氏文集	清邊恩纘繕存	鈔印	四卷 四冊	一	綿連紙	拾叄
東里文集	清楊士琦著	楊敦本堂藏版	二十五卷 六冊	一	光緒二年刊 毛邊紙	拾叄
東里別集	清楊士琦輯錄	家藏版	三種 四冊	一	毛邊紙 夾板	拾叄
昌黎集	唐韓愈著	東雅堂本 江蘇書局重刊	四十卷 十冊	一	同治年刊 粉紙夾板	拾叄
初唐四傑集	唐王勃等著	星渚項氏校刊	共十二冊	一	白紙夾板	拾叄
雪橋詩話三集	清楊鍾羲選集	求恕齋刊	續集二十八卷 共二十冊	一	竹紙夾板	拾叄

集部

書名	著者	版本	卷冊	數	紙張・印行	價
薛文清公集	明薛瑄著	雍正年薛氏重刊	二十四卷 二十冊	一	白紙	拾參
國朝文匯	清沈粹芬輯行	國學扶輪社印 甲乙丙丁四集 共一百零一冊		十	宣統元年印 綿連紙	拾肆
皇朝經世文編	清賀長齡輯	原刻本	一百二十卷 六十四冊	八	綿連紙 道光丁亥年刊	拾肆
香樹齋全集	清錢陳羣撰	家藏版	八十七卷 二十四冊	一	夾板 綿連紙	拾肆
玉臺新詠	陳徐陵編定	明袁宏道批閱 明天啟壬戌年刻本	十卷 六冊 又續集四卷 二冊	一	竹紙	拾肆
結隣集	明周在浚等選	懷德堂藏版 賴古堂本 鈔	八冊	二	毛邊紙	拾肆
皇朝駢文類苑	清姚燮選	掃葉山房藏版	二十四卷 十四冊	二	南粉連紙 光緒年刊	拾肆
重編留青新集	清伊氏重編	銅鑄版 巾箱本	二十四卷 十二冊	一	洋粉連紙 光緒戊子年印	拾肆
柏堂遺書	清方宗誠撰	志學堂 家藏版	十六冊	四	竹紙	拾肆
俞曲園全集	清俞樾撰	家藏版	二百八十二卷 七十二冊	六	竹紙 共計二十一種	拾肆

一百零四　一

書名	著者	刊本	卷冊	部	紙／刊年	價
勸戒詩話	清黃坤元編輯	翼經堂藏版	八卷四冊	一	光緒癸未年刻 綿連紙	拾肆
漢魏六朝女子文選	清張維學選	海鹽朱氏刊本	二卷二冊	一	綿連紙	拾肆
諸家評點古文辭類纂	清姚鼐撰	都門印書局校印	十六冊	二	毛邊紙	拾伍
讀書堂全集	清趙士麟著	浙江書局刊本	四十六卷十二冊	一	光緒癸巳年刊 毛邊紙	拾伍
歸錢尺牘	明歸有光撰 錢謙益撰	虞山如月樓刊 顧氏藏本	五卷五冊	一	康熙己卯年刊 竹紙	拾伍
內簡尺牘	宋孫覿撰 李祖堯編注	寫刻本 家藏版	十卷八冊	一	乾隆十二年刻 毛邊紙	拾伍
古文辭類纂	清姚鼐選	堂校刊本 滁州李氏求要	七十五卷十二冊	一	光緒辛丑年刊 毛邊紙	拾伍
續古文辭類纂	清黎庶昌纂 初定本	金陵書局刊	二十八卷八冊	一	光緒庚寅年刊 綿連紙	拾伍
屈賈文合編	清夏獻雲校	夏氏刊于長沙	八冊	一	光緒丁丑年刊 綿連紙	拾伍
韓文	唐韓愈撰	日本版精刻本	五十卷六十冊	一	嘉永十年重刊本 東洋棉紙	拾伍

書名	著者	版本	卷冊	部	刷印紙張	價
笠澤叢書	唐陸龜蒙撰	家藏版	四冊	一	雍正年刊 粉紙夾板	拾柒
蟄菴日錄	明顧起元著	明天啟年刻	二卷 四冊	一	竹紙	拾柒
節盦先生遺詩	清梁鼎芬撰	家藏版	六卷 二冊	一	光緒年刻 綿連紙	拾柒
辭賦標義	明王皋如標義	明萬曆版	十二卷 八冊	一	竹紙	拾柒
歷代名賢手扎	清李江分輯	學古齋石印	八卷 八冊	一	光緒年印 粉紙	拾柒
龍泉師友遺稿合編	清王晉之分輯 家藏版	家藏版	八種計十二卷 共十二種計六十三冊	一	光緒年刻 竹紙	拾柒
避暑山莊詩	清康熙帝御製	石印	上下二冊	一	乾隆年印 粉紙	拾柒
古唐詩合解	清王堯衢註	致和堂刊	十二卷 八冊	一	毛太紙	拾柒
詩畸	清閩劉萼等著	家藏版	五卷 謎附拾二冊 外編二卷	一	光緒十九年刻 毛邊紙	拾柒
陽明先生集要三編	明王守仁著 施四明評輯	濟美堂藏版	共十五冊	二	乾隆年刻 竹紙 橫秋閣藏	拾柒

南陽集	古詩源	曲江集	趙文敏寫本兩漢策要	唐詩三百首註疏	淡勤室著述（孔庭學裔）	敬孚類稿	施注蘇詩	竹居小牘	文徵明甫田集
宋趙湘撰	清沈德潛選	唐張九齡著	元趙孟頫撰 張朝樂較閱	清衡塘退士手編 章燮註	清傅壽彤譔	清蕭穆撰	宋蘇軾撰 清施元之註	潑樓主人偶存	明文徵明撰
武英殿聚珍版	思賢書局刊	家藏版	同文書局石印	宋氏卷雨樓印	家藏版	家藏版	金閶步月樓藏版	竹居刊本	石印本
六卷 一冊	十四卷 四十冊	十二卷 八冊	十二卷 八冊	六卷 六冊	二五冊	十六卷 八冊	四十二卷 補遺二 選二 十二冊	二十二卷	三十六卷 六冊
一	一	一	一	一	一	一	一	一	一
竹紙 夾板	綿連紙 光緒年刻	綿連紙 光緒年刻	連史紙 光緒年刻	白竹紙	粉紙	毛邊紙 光緒年刻 夾板	乾隆年刻 夾板竹紙	綿連紙	粉紙 宣統三年印
拾柒	拾柒	拾柒	拾柒	拾柒	拾柒	拾柒	拾柒	拾柒	拾柒

一百零六

書名	著者	版本	卷冊	數	紙張年刻	價
溫飛卿詩集	唐溫庭筠撰 清曾益譔原註	萬軸山房刊 秀野草堂版	九卷 四冊	一	光緒年刻 白紙	拾柒
名賢手札墨蹟		岵瞻堂篆刻	四冊	一	連史紙	拾柒
百大家名賢手札		醉二室西法影印	六冊	一	連史紙 光緒年印	拾柒
同文文類聚	清桑世昌纂次	裕文堂藏版	十卷 四冊	一	白紙	拾柒
司馬長卿集	漢司馬相如著	明天啟板	一冊	一	竹紙	拾柒
校經堂初集	清曹鴻勛手訂	校經堂版	四卷 二冊	一	毛邊紙 夾板 光緒年刻	拾柒
雙魚偶存尺牘	清朱穎著	家藏版	二冊	一	竹紙 乾隆年刻	拾柒
惜抱軒遺書三種	清姚鼐撰	桐城徐氏集刊	共十一卷 四冊	一	綿連紙 光緒年刻	拾柒
太璞生文鈔	清傅以成著	金礦堂藏版	二卷 附古文撫拾卷 共六冊	一	竹紙 夾板 同治年刻	拾柒
楊忠愍公集	明楊繼盛著	思補堂版	四卷 四冊	一	竹紙 道光年刻	拾柒

575

書名	撰者	版本	卷冊	函	紙張	價
潛園友朋書問	存疁先生輯	家藏照原寫刊版	十二卷二冊	一	連史紙	拾捌
龍泉園集		家藏版	八種共十二卷十冊	二	光緒年刻 毛邊紙	拾捌
周文忠公尺牘	清周天爵著	蘇松太道署刊	十八冊	一	同治年刻 輸連紙	拾捌
古今振雅雲箋	明徐渭纂輯	明精刻本	附錄上下二冊	一	竹紙	拾捌
漢魏別解	明黃樹等選	香谷山房藏版 明寫刻本	十六冊	二	明崇禎戊寅年刊 竹紙	拾捌
西陂類稿	清宋犖撰	門人毛展等校 梓精刻本	五十卷二十冊	四	細毛邊紙	拾玖
王文成公全書	明王守仁撰	明萬曆丙申年刊本	三十八卷二十冊	四	廉沙紙	拾玖
黃忠端公全集	明黃道周撰	清乾隆年刻本	二十四冊	四	毛邊紙	拾玖
方望溪先生全集	清方苞撰	清戴鈞衡重刊本	三十二卷十四冊	一	官堆紙 夾板	拾玖
山谷內外集 附別集	宋黃庭堅撰	清楊守敬撫日本翻宋紹定本重刊	三十九卷二十冊	二	夾連紙 宣統二年刊	拾玖

書名	著者	版本	卷冊	部數	刊刻・用紙	價
唐詩三百首補註	清女史陳伯英輯	四藤吟社刊	八卷 四冊	一	光緒年刻 毛邊紙	拾玖
毘陵詩錄	清趙震輯	家藏版 鉛印	八冊 四卷	一	光緒年刻 毛邊紙	拾玖
夢窗甲乙丙丁稿	宋吳文英撰	王佑退仿宋刊版	一六卷 二冊	一	光緒年刻 絹連紙	拾玖
郭文簡公文集	董襄編次	思齊軒藏版	一六卷 一種	一	古鉥硯齋藏 粉雪齋紙	拾玖
安雅堂集	清宋琬著	家藏版	六種 計共十六冊	一	康熙年刻 夾板毛邊紙	拾玖
宮閨文選	清周壽昌輯	小蓬萊山館藏版	二十六卷 十二冊	一	道光年刻 夾白竹板紙	拾玖
二希堂緝齋文詩合編	清福敏撰 蔡世遠撰	閩漳多藝齋藏版	共十九卷附錄二卷詩稿二卷 計十四冊	一	光緒年刻 夾白竹板紙	拾玖
唐詩三百首注疏	清彌塘退士手編 章燮註	宋氏卷雨樓印行	六卷 六冊	一	道光年刻 雙白竹紙	拾玖
百宋一廛賦	清顧廣圻撰 吳縣黃丕烈註	楊文瑩寫 汪鳴鑾校刊	一卷 一冊	一	光緒三年刻 雙夾連紙	拾玖
陶樓文鈔	清黃彭年撰	家藏版	十四卷 六冊	一	光緒十四年刻 白紙	拾玖

一百零八

書名	著者・刊本	卷冊	部數	紙張・刊刻	價
王文敏公遺集	清 王懿榮著 求恕齋刊	八卷 二冊	一	竹紙 宣統年刻 此書共有四部	拾玖
籀高遺文	清 陳準輯刊 瑞安潁川書舍	二卷 二冊	一	平粉連紙 民國十五年印	拾玖
陳紫峰文集	明 陳紫峰著 湖南督學署刊	十三卷 五冊	一	白紙 夾板 乾隆年刻	拾玖
容城三賢文集	明 楊繼盛撰 孫奇逢撰 俞廷獻重修本	十二卷 十二冊	一	毛邊紙 夾板 光緒戊戌年刊	拾玖
二希堂文集	清 蔡世遠撰 家藏版	十一卷 六冊	一	白紙	拾玖
唐宋八大家文選	明 鍾惺選 金閶貽經堂藏版	二十二卷 十二冊	二	竹紙	拾玖
柏硯山房文集	清 梅曾亮撰 家藏版	三十一卷 八冊	一	綿連紙 咸豐六年刊	拾玖
柔橋文鈔	清 王棻撰 上海國光書局 鉛印	十六卷 八冊		有光洋紙	拾玖
郝文忠公全集	元 郝經撰 家藏精刻本	三十九卷 十三冊	一	綿連紙 嘉慶戊午年刊	拾玖
楊文弱集	明 楊嗣昌著 明刻本	五十七卷 三十二冊	四	竹紙	貳拾

書名	著者	版本	卷册	部數	紙	價
史院塡詞	清蔣士銓撰	紅雪樓藏版	十册	二	綿連	貳拾
去僞齋文集	明呂坤著	歸德府知府文焯重刊	十二册	一	夾板 光緒年刻	貳拾
鮎琦亭集	清全祖望撰	借樹山房藏版	三十八册	一	許翰藏 毛邊紙乾隆年刻	貳拾
歷代史論	明張溥論正孫執升砞批評點	蒼松山房刊	十六卷附明史左傳論六卷共六册	二	連史紙 光緒年刻	貳拾
聲調譜談龍錄	趙飴山著	雅雨堂版寫刻本	共三册一卷	一	粉紙 康熙年刻	貳拾
漁洋山人精華錄	清林佶編輯	家藏版	十卷四册	一	粉紙 同治年刻	貳拾
欽定雪山集	宋王質撰	白樂山房藏版	共十二卷十二册	一	連史紙 光緒年刻	貳拾
曾文正公家訓書	清曾國藩著	傳忠書局刊	六卷十二册	一	竹紙 光緒年刻	貳拾
小倉山房尺牘	清袁枚著	隨園藏版	六卷二册	一	粉紙 乾隆年刻	貳拾
陶樓文鈔	清黃彭年著	家藏版初印	十四卷六册	一	毛邊紙 民國癸亥年印	貳拾

集部

書名	著者	版本	卷冊	部	紙張	價
文略	明劉廣生選	明萬曆四十六年精刻本	二卷 一冊	一	精印 明開化紙	貳拾
唐宋八大家類選	清儲欣評	湖北官書處刊	十四卷 八冊	一	光緒年刻 竹紙	貳拾
問詩樓合選	天然主人著	抄寫本	一卷 一冊	一	乾隆年寫 毛邊紙	貳拾
滑疑集	清韓錫胙著	浙江處州府署藏版	八卷 四冊	一	同治年刻 連史紙	貳拾
求闕齋日記類鈔	清曾國藩隨筆 王啟原校編	傳忠書局刊	上下 二冊	一	光緒二年刻 毛邊紙	貳拾
怡情書室詩鈔	清和碩容恪親王撰	殿版	十卷 一冊	一	乾隆年刻 開花榜紙	貳拾
笛漁小稿	清朱昆田著	家藏版	七卷 一冊	一	道光年刻 竹紙	貳拾
文章軌範	宋謝疊山先生輯	三韓劉氏藏版	四卷 一冊	一	竹紙	貳拾
薛文介公文集	明薛三省著	明萬曆版	四卷 二冊	一	盧白軒藏	貳拾
蔣道林先生文粹	明姚世英等銓次	明萬曆版	五種共十三卷 五冊	一	毛邊紙	貳拾

一百二十一

書名	著者	版本・刻印	卷冊	部數	紙張・刻年	價
東萊先生古文關健	宋呂祖謙評	江蘇書局刊	上下二冊	一	竹紙 光緒年刻	貳拾
皇朝經世文新編	清麥仲華輯	上海大同譯書局石印	二十一卷 二十四冊	一	連史紙 夾板	貳拾
全史宮詞	清史夢蘭著	家藏版	二十卷 六冊	一	毛邊紙	貳拾
葆愚軒詩文集	清英啟撰	家藏版 寫刻本	二卷 二冊	一	連史紙 光緒年刻	貳拾
天壤遺文	明徐天池批選	家藏版	七卷 七冊	一	白紙	貳拾
治安文獻	清韓訥名輯	小萬柳堂撰	十一卷 十冊	二	毛邊紙	貳拾
御製全韻詩	清彭元瑞恭錢 重刊	殿版	五冊	一	綿連紙	貳拾
姚惜抱先生尺牘	清姚鼐著	海源閣本重撰 刊	八卷 四冊	一	毛邊紙 宣統年刻	貳拾
楊忠愍公集	明楊繼盛撰 楊遠修原校	家藏版	六卷 附表忠記二卷 五冊	一	夾板 毛邊紙 同治年刻	貳拾
劉孟塗集	清劉開著	姚氏樊山草堂刊	共四十四卷 八冊	一	綿連紙 道光六年刻	貳拾

書名	著者	版本	卷冊	紙・印	價
古今辭命達	明胡正心纂輯	明刻本	六卷一冊	竹紙	貳拾
古文苑	范文燕訂定	明萬曆仿朱刻本 十竹齋藏版	二十卷四冊	夾精板印 竹紙	貳拾
宋陳龍川先生文集	明王佐批閱	明崇禎年刻本	二十卷二集一卷四冊	白紙 熙春堂藏	貳拾
本朝文讀本	清馬俊良讀	小倉山房原本	四冊	白紙	貳拾
屈子楚詞章句	清劉夢鵬著	藜菁堂藏版	七卷一冊	白紙 嘉慶五年刻	貳拾
惜抱軒文集	清姚鼐著	桐城徐氏刊	十六卷後集六卷共六冊	白紙 光緒年刻	貳拾
國朝八家四六文鈔	清吳嘉鈔	紫文閣補刊	四冊	連史紙 光緒年刻	貳拾
黃忠端公集	明黃尊素著	姚江黃氏藏版 正氣堂刊	六卷附竹橋黃氏譜算數三冊	竹紙 嘉慶年刻	貳拾
黃梨洲先生年譜	清黃炳垕編輯	家藏版	一二卷附年譜二冊	竹紙 同治年刻	貳拾
黃氏世德傳贊	清黃炳垕輯著	留耕植閣藏版	一卷附竹橋黃氏譜算數五卷忠義測地記要四卷詩略二卷共四冊	竹紙 光緒年刻 以上三種共一夾板	貳拾

一百十一

項目	陶淵明集	康對山文集	秦漢人文選	岳忠武王文集	魯山木先生文集 附營晉之之文鈔	鬱華閣遺集	紀文達公遺集	讀雪山房唐詩鈔	寫禮廎遺著四種	蘇長公密語
著者	晉陶潛著	明康對山著 孫景烈選次	明王衡選	宋岳飛撰 清黃邦寧纂修	清魯九皐撰	清宗室盛昱撰	清紀昀撰	清管世銘鈔	清王頌蔚撰	明吳京纂輯
版本	陽子烈所編十卷本 莫友芝仿宋刻	武功縣藏版	明官版	清邠延年補修版 書林余泗泉梓	家藏版	精寫刻本 家藏版	紀樹馨編校 家藏版	湖北官書處刊	舒溪王氏刊	明天啟年刻版 硃批評點本 楮刻本
卷冊	十五卷 一冊	十六卷 一冊	六卷 一冊	四卷 一冊	八卷 共十六冊	四卷 一冊	三十二卷 十八冊	三十四卷 十二冊	四二冊	十六卷
數	一	一	一	一	一	一	一	二	一	二
紙/刊	咸豐年刻 精印	乾隆年刻 白紙	竹紙	土綿連紙 嘉慶二十一年刊	毛邊紙 道光十一年刊	宣紙 光緒三十一年刊	綿連紙 夾板	綿連紙 光緒十二年刊	竹紙	明綿紙
價	貳拾	貳拾	貳壹	貳壹	貳壹	貳壹	貳壹	貳壹	貳壹	貳壹

585

書名	著者	版本	卷冊		紙	價
文章軌範	宋謝枋得輯	蔣陽萬氏遽箋書屋藏版五色批點	七卷二冊	一	連史紙	貳壹
續古文辭類纂	清王先謙纂輯	長沙王氏家藏版	三十四卷十二冊	一	光緒年刻白服廠軒紙藏	貳壹
潛虛先生文集	清藏潛虛著	家藏版	十四卷八冊	一	康熙年刻毛邊紙	貳壹
古文辭類纂	清姚鼐纂輯	文章書局刊	七十四卷十一冊	一	光緒年刻綿連紙	貳壹
九水山房文存	清畢亨著	海源閣版	上下二冊	一	咸豐年刻竹紙	貳壹
禺山雜著	清李暘著	家藏版	三種四冊	一	竹紙	貳壹
新疆賦	清徐松撰	家藏版	一冊	一	綿連紙	貳壹
西藏賦	清和寧著	寫刻本	一冊	一	嘉慶年刻綿連紙	貳壹
聽園文存	清張學尹撰	師白山房刊	四卷八冊	一	同治年刻毛邊紙	貳壹
止止軒詩稿	清起鈞形著	石印本	六卷四冊	一	皮紙	貳壹

集部

書名	著者	版本	卷冊	函	紙張・刊年	等第
平園雜著內編	清林有席著	家塾版	十二卷六冊	壹	道光年刻 毛邊紙	貳
孟東野詩集	唐孟郊著	仿宋精刻本	十四卷四冊	壹	竹紙	貳
測海集	清彭紹升著	寶翰樓藏版	六卷四冊	壹	貴州綿紙	貳
震川先生全集	明歸有光撰	常熟歸氏重刻本	三十卷十二冊	貳	光緒元年刊 綿連紙	貳
唐賢三昧集箋註	清王士禎選本 吳煊等輯註	硃批評點翰墨園重刊聽雨齋本	三卷三冊	壹	康熙十一年刊 竹紙	貳
文選纂註	明張鳳翼纂註	清姚曾校刊本	十二卷二冊	貳	竹紙	貳
周文歸	明鍾惺選 陳渼子輯本	明崇禎年精刻本	二十卷十二冊	壹	毛太紙	貳
南山集	清戴潛虛著	家藏版	十四卷八冊	壹	綿連紙	貳
古文辭類纂（附續古文辭纂）	清姚鼐纂	王先謙重刊思賢講舍藏版	正集七十四卷十二冊續集三十四卷八冊	四	光緒癸巳年刊	貳
南宋雜事詩	清沈嘉轍輯	扶荔山房重鐫精寫刻本	八卷七冊	一	道光己丑年刊 毛邊紙	貳

一百十三

書名	撰者	版本	冊卷	部	紙・刊年	價
高子遺書	明 高攀龍撰	高芷生宜刊本	八卷 十三冊	二	綿連紙	貳貳
望溪集	清 方苞撰	程楚編次精刊本	八冊	一	乾隆十一年刊 毛邊紙	貳貳
絜齋集	宋 袁燮撰	舊精抄本	四冊	一	竹紙 本 卷一至卷四配補	貳貳
文苑英華辨證		精校刊本	十三冊	一	竹紙	貳貳
定盦文集	清 龔自珍撰	萬本書堂精校刊本	五冊	一	光緒丁酉年刊 毛邊紙	貳貳
楚辭燈	清 林雲銘論述	經國堂藏版	四卷 二冊	二	毛太紙	貳貳
六如居士全集 附畫亭新賦 花陣嘲吟	明 唐寅撰	果克山房藏版 清唐仲冕刊本	二十二卷 八冊	二	乾隆五十七年刊 竹紙	貳貳
張文貞集	清 張玉書撰	四庫全書本 松蔭堂藏版	六卷 十二冊	一	光緒辛丑年刊 土綿連紙	貳貳
文貞公集 附年譜	清 張玉書撰	張藻文等校刊本	共十三冊	一	光緒辛丑年刊 夾板 灰竹紙	貳貳
宋王忠文公集	宋 王卡朋撰 清 唐仲鈺重編	唐氏刊本	十卷 五十二冊	一	光緒二年重刊 竹紙	貳貳

588

集部

書名	撰著者	版本	卷數	冊數	部數	刊年・用紙	定價
楊文靖公集	宋楊時撰	清張夏補輯本 東林道南祠藏版	四十卷	十冊	一	康熙十六年刊 毛邊紙	貳貳
佈石齋記事稿 附遺稿	清錢儀吉撰	家藏版	共二十卷	十冊	一	光緒六年刊 毛邊紙	貳貳
寶繪堂集	清陳洪綬著	會稽董氏取斯堂重刊	八卷	八冊	一	光緒戊子年重刊 竹紙	貳貳
讀杜心解	清浦起龍講解	寧我齋版	六卷	八冊	一	毛邊紙	貳貳
惜抱軒集	清姚鼐撰	家藏版	八卷	八冊	一	綿連紙	貳貳
山曉閣重訂歷代史論 附東萊博議	清孫琮手評	寫刻 金閶龔晉梓行之本	共計二十卷	八冊	二	康熙癸丑年刊 竹紙	貳貳
藝苑名言	清蔣瀾纂輯	懷古軒藏版	四卷	四冊	一	乾隆乙未年刊 白紙	貳貳
詩說	清惠周惕著	真意堂刊本	三卷	三冊	一	嘉慶壬申年刊 竹紙	貳貳
楚辭		日本函碕文庫抄本		五冊	一	日本綿紙	貳貳
使黔集	清湯右曾撰	家藏版 精刻本	二卷	二冊	一	毛邊紙	貳貳

集部　一百十四册　一

書名	著者	版本	卷册		紙/年	
金忠節公文集	明金聲撰 清邵勳編次	嘉魚官署藏版	八卷 四册	一	道光丁亥年刻	貳貳
曝書亭詞拾遺	清朱彝尊撰 翁之潤輯錄	常熟翁氏校刊	三卷 一册	一	綿連紙	貳貳
小窗豔紀	明吳從先批選	明萬曆乙卯年寫刻本	八册	一	竹紙	貳
定盦文集	清龔自珍撰	成都官書局印行	六册	一	光緒戊申年刊 毛邊紙	貳貳
玉堂才調集	清于朋舉評	姑蘇原本	八册	一	竹紙	貳貳
古詩源	清沈德潛選	竹嘯軒藏版	十四卷 六册	一	竹紙	貳貳
復葊遺集	清詐玨撰	翁印本	二十四卷 八册	一	綿連紙 夾板	貳貳
清代名人書扎	資研社採輯	中華印刷局石印	二册	一	民國十六年印 綿連紙	貳貳
蓉湖草堂贈言錄	清麟慶輯	家藏版 精寫刻本	四册	一	道光十七年刊 毛邊紙	貳貳
蓉湖草堂贈言錄	清麟慶輯	家藏版 精寫刻本	二册	一	道光十七年刊 綿連紙	貳

書名	撰者	刊印	卷冊	部數	紙質・刊年	定價
陳氏遺書	清陳澄然著	家藏版	十二冊	一	共三種 綿連紙	貳貳
頻羅菴遺集	清梁同書撰 藏版	蛟川修綆山莊	十六卷 八冊	一	光緒十三年刊 竹紙	貳貳
籀膏述林	清孫詒讓撰	家藏版	十卷 四冊	一	毛太紙	貳貳
籀膏述林	清孫詒讓撰	家藏版	十卷 四冊	一	毛太紙 大開本 夾板	貳貳
古辭令學	清盧靖編	始基齋聚珍版印	二冊	一	民國十四年印	貳貳
一山文存	清章梫撰	嘉業堂劉承幹刊	十二卷 四冊	二	宜統戊午年刊 毛邊紙	貳貳
蛻私軒集	清姚永樸撰	周氏補刊本	一五卷 冊	二	毛邊紙	貳貳
宋李忠定公文集選	宋李綱傳 明左光先選 明本	清李榮芳宜刊	二十九卷 十六冊	二	康熙四十四年刊 毛邊紙	貳貳
古學彙纂	明周時雍輯 愛日齋版	明崇禎壬午年刊本	十四卷 十八冊	二	竹紙	貳貳
章氏遺書	清章學誠著	吳興劉氏嘉業堂刊	三十二冊	一	毛邊紙 夾版	貳貳

一百十五

古今小品	古文小品冰雪攜	徐文長四聲猿	存研樓文初集	王龍谿先生全集	龍川文集	湛然居士集	唐荊川文集	切問齋文鈔	古今濡削選章
陳天定評選	明衛泳箋	明徐渭撰 袁洪道評點	清儲大文著	明王畿撰	宋陳亮撰	元耶律楚材撰	明唐順之撰	清陸燿撰	明李國祥選
几水書院藏版	明崇禎年刊精刻本	明精刻本	靜遠堂藏版	明萬曆乙卯年刊本	明崇禎癸酉年刊本	漸西村舍版	明嘉靖己酉年刊本	家藏版精刻本	明萬曆辛丑年刊本
八卷 八冊 附鄉黨題目四卷	六冊	一冊	十六卷 八冊	二十二卷 十二冊	三十卷 六冊	十四卷 六冊	十二卷 十二冊	三十卷 十二冊	四十卷 三十冊
一	一	一	一	一	一	一	二	一	六
竹紙夾板	竹紙	清芬堂藏 竹紙	綿連紙	光緒元年刊 竹紙	毛邊紙夾版	綿連紙	竹紙	乾隆乙未年刊 綿連紙	竹紙托裱
貳叄	貳叄	貳叄	貳叄	貳叄	貳叄	貳叄	貳叄	貳叄	貳叄

集部

書名	撰著者	版本	卷冊	數	紙張	價
山谷尺牘 附題跋	宋黃庭堅撰	浦江紛欣閣校本袖珍本	共十四卷	一	竹紙	貳叁
五十名家書扎	清沈葆楨等	石印本	六冊	一	綿連紙	貳叁
桂林梁先生遺書	清梁濟撰	京華書局鉛印本	三冊	一	洋毛邊紙	貳叁
河嶽英靈	清衛濟世著	主一堂藏版	六卷四冊	一	咸豐辛亥年鐫 綿連紙	貳叁
俞曲園文牘	清俞樾撰	春在堂原本石印	一冊	一	連史紙	貳叁
羅鄂州小集	宋羅存齋撰	洪武本重刊	六卷二冊	一	光緒癸巳年刊 竹紙	貳叁
唐宋十大家全集錄	清儲欣錄	松鱗堂藏版	四十卷	四	毛邊紙	貳肆
文心雕龍	梁劉勰著	明刻本	四十卷	一	竹紙	貳肆
古詩歸	明鍾惺選	明萬曆丁巳年刻精刻本五色批點本	十六冊	二	夾連紙	貳肆
可儀堂一百二十名家製藝	清俞長城論次	家藏版	三十八冊	六	康熙己卯年刊 竹紙	貳肆

一百十六一

書名	著者	版本	卷／册	部	紙	刊年	價
笠翁一家言	清李漁撰	世德堂藏版	二十六卷 二十四册	二	竹紙		貳肆
楊忠愍公集（附表忠傳傳奇）	明楊繼盛撰	家藏版	九卷 五册	一	龍門紙	同治壬申年刊	貳肆
龍泉師友遺稿合編	清王晉之等撰	家藏版	十三卷 六册	一	竹紙	光緒二十二年刊	貳肆
潛廬先生文集	清宋澧廬著	舊精抄本	九卷 八册	一	龍門紙	雍正年刊	貳肆
關聖帝君寶訓像註		文采齋刊	四卷 四册	一	竹紙	太史連紙 貴文堂藏	貳肆
文心雕龍輯註	梁劉勰撰 黃敏崑輯註	養素堂藏版	十卷 一册	一	白毛邊紙	光緒年刊	貳肆
孫可之集	唐孫樵撰	讀有用書齋刊	十一卷 二册	一	毛邊紙	光緒戊子年刊	貳肆
諸葛忠武侯全集	漢諸葛亮撰 清胡升猷纂	岐山縣署刊本	二十一卷 十二册	一	毛邊紙	光緒辛未年刊	貳肆
楊園先生全集	明張履祥撰 門人姚璉輯	江蘇書局刊本	五十四卷 十六册	二	毛邊紙	同治辛未年刊	貳肆
漢魏六朝正史文選	明許清胤等輯 評	明崇禎八年刊本	八册	一	竹紙		貳肆

書名	著者	刊印	卷數	冊數	部	紙張	價目
蘭薰館遺稿	清陶玉珂著	上海聚珍仿宋印書局印	四卷	一冊	一	綿連紙	貳伍
陶元暉中丞遺集	明陶朗先著	陶元鏡重印　上海仿宋聚珍印書局印	四卷	四冊	一	綿連紙	貳伍
續玉臺文苑	明江元祚編輯	明崇禎壬申年刊本	四卷	五冊	一	竹紙	貳伍
宋王忠文公集	宋王十朋撰	清林培重刊本	五十卷	十冊	一	雍正己酉年刊　綿連紙	貳伍
南山集	清戴褤夫著	龍眠增訂本	十七卷	七冊	一	毛邊紙	貳伍
姚端恪公文集	清姚文然撰	盧直軒藏版	十九卷	九冊	一	竹紙	貳伍
李剛己先生遺集	李剛己撰	家藏版	五卷	四冊	一	中華民國六年刊　毛邊紙	貳伍
王文敏公遺集	清王懿榮著	南林劉氏求恕齋刊	八卷	二冊	一	毛邊紙	貳伍
蘇長公啟選	明鍾惺等選	明刻本	二卷	上下二冊	一	竹紙	貳伍
徐文長四聲猿	明徐渭撰　袁宏道評點	明刻本	一卷	一冊	一	毛邊紙	貳伍

書名	著者	版本	卷册	部數	刊年・用紙	價目
藝課古文匯選	清溫承惠評選	保陽督署藏版	八卷　八册	一	德化萬氏藏　嘉慶年刻　綿連紙	貳伍
四忠遺集	清朱薛原刻	楚體聚奎書閣藏板	共二十四卷　二十五册	二	同治十年刻　二夾板　連史紙	貳伍
唐文拾遺	清陸心源輯	進呈本　家藏版	七十二卷　續拾遺十六卷　共二十六册	四	光緒十四年刻　毛邊紙	貳伍
胡文忠公遺集	清胡林翼撰　曾國荃　鄭敦謹編輯	黃鶴樓藏版	八十六卷　二十四册	二	同治年刻　連史紙	貳伍
唐詩三百首	清蘅塘退士手編	文寶堂刊	八卷　八册　續選二卷	一	光緒十五年刊　竹紙	貳伍
王文成公集	明王幾選定	溪香館刊	二十六卷　四册	一	竹紙	貳伍
文粹·補遺	鍾惺評點	明刻本	三十二卷　十册	一	綿連紙刻　夾版　光緒年刻	貳陸
紀文達公遺集	清紀樹馨編校	家藏版	七十五卷　四十册	一	嘉慶年刻　竹紙	貳陸
東坡集	宋蘇軾撰	明刻本	四十卷　十五册	四	竹紙	貳陸
鹿忠節公集	清鹿善繼著	家藏版	二十一卷　六册	一	白紙　夾版	貳陸

599

書名	著者	刊本	卷冊	部	紙 / 刊年	編號
項城袁氏家集	清袁甲三等撰	清芬閣編刊本	五十六册	二	洋紙 宣統辛亥年刊	貳陸
岳忠武王文集	清黃邦寧纂修	活字版精印本	十四卷	一	綿連紙	貳柒
賁池二妙集	明吳應箕劉城撰	劉氏唐石簃鈔	五十一卷	一	白綿紙	貳柒
古謠諺	清杜文瀾輯	曼陀羅華閣精刊本	一百卷	二	竹紙 咸豐辛酉年刊	貳柒
元遺山全集	元元好問撰	清張穆宜刊本	四十六卷	二	綿連紙 光緒八年京都翰文齋印	貳柒
王文恪公集	明王鏊著	明嘉靖十五年刊字體仿趙松雪精寫刊本	三十六卷	二	白紙	貳柒
繡虎軒尺牘	清曹煜著	傅氏堂梓行	二十四卷	二	毛邊紙	貳柒
虞德園先生集	明虞淳熙著	明 見焚燬書目	八卷 四册	一	竹紙	貳柒
文苑英華	宋李昉等奉勅編	明隆慶元年御史途澤民等刊本	一千卷 一百五十册	二十	白紙 皖南張莜漁等藏	貳捌
廣文苑英華	明陳仁錫評選	明天啟甲子年副本	二十六册	二	竹紙	貳捌

601

書名	著者	版本	卷數	冊數	部數	紙	價
虞德園先生集	明虞淳熙作	明天啟癸亥年刊本	二十五卷	六冊	一	竹紙	貳玖
遜志齋集	明方孝儒著	清俞化鵬重輯劉本	二十四卷	十六冊	二	康熙戊寅年刻毛邊紙	貳玖
文苑英華辨証	宋彭叔夏撰	清武英殿聚珍版印	十卷	四冊	一	毛邊紙	貳玖
御製文初集	清嘉慶帝選	巾箱本	十卷	八冊	一	綿連紙	貳玖
御製圓明園圖詠	清乾隆帝選	天津石印書屋摹勒上石	二	冊	一	光緒十三年印綿連紙	貳玖
倭文端公遺書	清倭仁撰	六安求我齋刊	十卷	四冊	一	光緒元年刊綿連紙	貳玖
劉南豐文集	清劉孚京撰	上海聚珍仿宋印書局印	四卷遺一卷	四補一冊	一	綿連紙	貳玖
潛園友朋書問	存齋輯	家藏照剿本	上下二卷	冊	一	述史紙	貳玖
六朝文絜	清許槤評選	讀有用書齋刊硃批評點	四卷	二冊	一	光緒年刻綿連紙	貳玖
川書日記		抄寫本		二冊	一	開化紙	貳玖

集部

書名	著者	版本	卷冊	部數	紙張	編號
同文類聚	清桑世昌纂次	麟玉堂藏版	十四卷	一	連史紙	貳玖
汪穰卿遺著	清詁年編次	家藏版	八卷四冊	一	夾連史紙版	貳玖
江漢炳靈集	清張之洞輯	官版	四卷二冊	一	同治九年刻	貳玖
昱青堂詩集（附卦變解八宮說易象圖說）	吳脈邕著	吳佩孚刊 王芝祥校訂	共三種四冊零	一	民國十一年印 連史紙	貳玖
小題文府		上海點石齋縮印 袖珍本	二十冊	一	光緒十七年印 綿連紙 木夾板	叄拾
明文才調集	清許振禕編集	大梁東河行署刊本	四冊	一	竹紙	叄拾
廣理學備考	清范鄗鼎彙編	五經堂彙編本	六冊	一	白紙	叄拾
單縣周氏家集	清周鳴鑾著	仿宋精刊本	二冊	一	綿連紙	叄拾
熊耦頤先生集餘	清熊寶泰纂	家藏版 精刻本	一冊	一	綿連紙	叄拾
御製朋黨論	清雍正帝撰	殿版	二冊	一	滿文一冊開化紙 漢文一冊毛邊紙 夾版	叄拾

一百二十一

書名	著者	版本	卷冊	紙	價
樂道堂古近體詩	清恭親王著	家藏版	二卷二冊	綿連紙	叁拾
一山房集陶	清清素主人著	家藏版	二卷二冊	光緒年刻 綿連紙	叁拾
驪輪日記	清李厚滋著	家藏石印本	二卷二冊	連史紙	叁拾
震澤紀聞語	清王鏊著	家藏版	二卷二冊 共四	竹紙	叁拾
天崇讀本百篇	清吳懋政選輯	學庫山房刊	四卷四冊 一	光緒年刊 竹紙	叁拾
劉海峯制藝	清劉大櫆著	家藏版	上下二冊 一	光緒年刻 白紙	叁拾
歷科朝元卷		官刻本	二冊	綿連紙	叁拾
廣雅堂詩集	清張之洞著	石印本	二卷二冊	油光紙	叁拾
九家文鈔		明刻本	共二十冊	竹紙	叁拾
忍耐子詩鈔	清王從龍著	鉛印	一冊	竹紙	叁拾

鐵硯齋稿	也是集	榕村藏稿	墨井集	浪語集	夢仙詩稿 附畫	小學弦歌	許文肅公外集	奇觚廎詩集	辛巳簃詩讞	集部
清汪吟龍著	清英華著	清李光地撰	清吳漁山著	宋薛季宣撰	清孫雲著	清李元度輯	清許景澄著	清葉昌熾撰	欄柯叟撰	
鉛印 翰寶齋 印	鉛印本	敬忠堂本	土山灣印書館 印	兩淮馬裕家藏 本	珂羅版鉛印	文昌書局刊	鉛印本	家藏版	蘇州振新書社 印	
一 附續 冊 編	共 二 冊	三 冊	一五 冊卷	三 十 八 五 冊 卷 一冊	一 冊	八五 冊卷	四附五五 錄冊卷 一冊卷	共 五 五 冊 卷	三 一 冊 卷	一百二十一
油光紙	油光紙	竹紙	宣統元年印 油光紙	毛邊紙 火版	連史紙	光緒八年刻 毛太紙	連史紙	竹紙	竹紙	
叁拾	叁拾	叁拾	叁拾	小箱	小箱	小箱	小箱	小箱	小箱	

書名	著者	版本	卷冊	箱	紙/箱	等
奇觚廎文集	清葉昌熾撰	家藏版	共二卷 四冊		竹紙	小箱
文章指南	明歸震川選本	皖江節署刊	五集 四冊	一	光緒二年刻 竹紙	小箱
小窗豔紀	明吳從先批選	明精刻本	八冊	一箱	竹紙	叁壹
寒山子詩集	明寒山子著	明萬曆刻本	二十冊	一箱	樟木箱	叁壹
御製文第四集	清康熙帝撰	開化紙 殿版	三十六卷 二十冊	一箱	開化榜紙 樟木箱	叁壹
福堂寺人小草	明劉若愚纂	明精抄秘本	二十冊		毛邊紙	叁壹
李文忠公全集	渦李鴻章著	刊于金陵	一百六十五卷 一百冊	一箱	光緒乙巳年刻 竹紙	叁壹
御製擬白居易新樂府		精刻本 開化紙	四冊	一	鹽龍格印	叁壹
式古堂集	清張墨翼著	家藏版	四冊		王懿榮藏	叁壹
默盦集	清王舟瑤著	代印 上海國光書局	十卷 三冊		汕光紙	叁壹

606

抱潤軒文集	越台彙頌	鼓山集	涉江詩稿遺稿	水流雲在館集詩存	忍耐子詩鈔	大潛山房詩鈔	二黃先生集	印光法師文鈔
馬其昶著	清宗室耆英著	清張寅著	清唐晏著	清周天麟集	清王從龍著	清劉銘傳著	清黃紹箕著 家藏版 郭博古齋印	釋印光著
安徽官紙印刷局石印	寫刻本 紅格印	鉛印本	鉛印本	仿西法石印	鉛印本	鉛印	中國圖書公司 鉛印	
一九卷 冊	一冊	一三卷 冊	各一冊	二冊	一冊	一冊	一冊	二冊
粉紙 宣統元年印	綿連紙	毛邊紙	毛邊紙	粉紙 光緒十七年印	毛邊紙	油光紙	毛邊紙	竹紙 鉛印
叁拾	叁拾	叁拾	叁拾	叁拾	叁拾	叁拾	叁拾	叁拾

以上共計陸百叁拾捌種

書名	著者·註	版本（卷/冊）	冊數	函數	備考	編列號數
藏修堂叢書	清劉晚榮輯	藏修書屋版本	五十四冊	六	共六集計四十種	貳
晨風閣叢書	清沈宗畸校刻	家藏版	十六冊	二	宣統元年沈氏梓綿連紙共計二十二種	貳
嶺南遺書	清伍元微輯	文字歡娛室版	八十四冊	十二	道光辛卯南海伍氏刊毛太紙共五十九種白綿紙二百二十二種	貳
畿輔叢書	清王文泉彙刻	李順德印	一千五百四十五卷計訂四百二十五冊	五十	光緒己卯年刻白綿紙六集共五十九種	參
止園叢書	清尹昌衡著	中華書局鉛印	九十三種十三冊	二	民國七年印又通曹二册油光紙又首函重一部	參
古愚老人消夏錄	清汪汲著	古愚山房版	六十二卷二十四冊	四	共十五種毛邊紙	參
正誼堂全書	清張伯行輯	福州正誼書院藏版	五百零六卷共二百冊	五	同治五年刻板白紙五夾板	參
讀畫齋叢書	清顧修輯	家藏版	四百四十六卷六十四冊	八	綿連紙共四十八種	肆
稗海	清商濬輯	家藏版	八十冊	十	袁氏藏版竹紙共七十四種	肆

一百二十四

書名	編者	版本	冊/卷		紙/刊	
顔李·叢書	明 顔元撰 李塨	四存學會校刊本	三十二冊	一	連史紙 共三十九種	肆
寶顔堂秘笈		文明書局石印	四十八冊	六	綿連紙 共二百二十三種	肆
龍威秘書	清 馬俊良輯	大酉山房精刻本	八十冊	十	綿連紙 共一百八十種	肆
掌故叢編	清 蔣楅成等編	上海揣籥山房石印本	十四冊	二	洋粉連紙 共計八種	肆
唐代叢書	清 王文誥輯	家藏版	三十六冊	六	白毛太紙 共六集一百六十四種	肆
增訂集錄	清 于光華編輯	心簡齋本	十二卷	二	白毛太紙 共五十六種	肆
談藝珠叢	清 王啟原輯	長沙玉尺山房刊本	四十四卷	二	綿連紙	肆
味道腴軒叢書	清 徐桐軒輯	味道腴軒重刊	五卷	一	同治甲子年刊 綿連紙	肆
卹進齋叢書		歸安姚氏校刊本	二十四冊	一	光緒九年刊 綿連紙 共三十三種	伍
金陵瑣志三種	清 陳作霖編	金陵冶麓山房藏版	二十冊	四	光緒乙酉年刻 綿連紙	伍

書名	著者・輯者	版本	卷・冊數	函	備註	價
天蘇閣叢刊二集	清徐振飛輯	中華書局聚珍仿宋版	六冊	一	共十種　白竹紙　夾板本	陸
潛園二十四種	清魏元曠撰	本	四十八卷　十六冊	二	飲冰室藏　白紙	陸
漢魏叢書	萬曆壬辰年刻　明程榮校本	高麗	二百五十卷　五十冊	七	竹紙　商子配補本	陸
檀几叢書	清王晫輯　蕭泉堂版		五十冊	二	白毛太紙	柒
滂喜齋叢書	清胡祥麟等撰　潘氏八喜齋刊本		三十二冊	四	共五十四種　同治十一年刊　綿連紙	柒
蒙養函書三編（初編）	清張承燮纂　東聽雨堂刊本		十二冊	一	共四種　綿連紙	捌
連筠簃叢書	清靈石楊氏輯　靈石楊氏藏版		一百十卷　三十冊	六	共五十一種　道光戊申年刻　綿連紙	捌
玉函山房輯佚書	清馬竹吾輯　楙江李氏藏版		六百餘卷　八十冊	十	共計五百八十餘種　光緒十五年刻　毛邊紙	玖
功順堂叢書	家藏版		二十四冊	二	共計十八種　綿連紙	拾
呂子遺書	明呂坤著　家藏版		二十四冊	四	共六種　竹紙　康熙年刻	拾

一百二十五　一

叢書名	編者	版本	冊數	數	紙／備註	等級
士禮居黃氏叢書		印本　上海蜚英館影	三十冊	一	光緒丁亥年刻　綿連紙	拾壹
知不足齋叢書	清鮑廷博編	家藏版　巾箱本	二百四十冊	三十	綿連紙	拾壹
續知不足齋叢書	清高承勳刊	家藏版　巾箱本	十六冊	四	光緒丁未年印　共計九種　綿連紙	拾壹
麗廔叢書	清葉德輝輯	葉氏刊本	十七卷　八冊	一	共十七種　綿連紙	拾壹
梅瑞軒輯錄十種逸書	清茆泮林輯	梅瑞軒藏版	十冊	一	道光十四年刻　綿連紙	拾貳
章氏叢書	清章炳麟撰	上海右文社鉛印本	二十四冊	二	有光洋紙	拾叁
粵雅堂叢書	清伍崇曜輯	廣東版　小箱本	三百八十冊	二十	綿連紙　夾版	拾叁
津逮秘書種六		明毛氏汲古閣版	二冊	一	竹紙	拾叁
百川學海		上海博古齋影印本	四十冊	二	共計一百種　綿連紙	拾叁
藕香·零拾	清繆荃孫輯	繆氏精刻本	三十二冊	四	共計三十九種　毛邊紙	拾叁

叢部

書名	著者	版本	卷冊數	部數	附註	編號
昭代叢書丙集	清張潮等輯	原刻本	五十卷 八十冊	一	民國壬寅年刊 毛邊紙 共計五拾種	拾叁
觀古堂所著書 附叢刻書	清葉德輝著	長沙葉氏刊本	三十二冊	二	叢刻書十九六種 種刊 綿連紙 夾版	拾肆
廣快書	明何偉然纂	明刻版	二十六冊 又目錄一冊 十七卷	二	共計二十七種 竹紙	拾肆
徐氏三種		京師文成堂藏版	四冊	一	光緒辛卯年重刊 竹紙	拾肆
算經十書	魏劉徽等註	上海鴻寶齋石印本	二十四卷 八冊	一	光緒丙申年印 洋粉連紙	拾肆
藝海珠塵	清吳省闌輯	媚媆堂藏版	六十冊	一	光緒元年刻 綿連紙 夾版	拾肆
子書百家		湖北崇文書局刻本	一百十冊	六	竹紙 夾版	拾肆
閔士行快書五十種	明閔景賢纂	明刻版	十二冊	十	顧補過齋藏本 竹紙	拾肆
娛園叢刻十種	清許增輯 家藏版		四冊	一	綿連紙 夾版	拾肆
留坨叢刻	清博明等著	留坨重刻本	四冊	一	光緒庚子年刻 綿連紙	拾陸

一百二十六 　一

613

書名	編者	版本	冊數	函數	刊年・用紙	編號
區種五種	清趙夢齡輯	蓮花池刊	二冊	一	光緒戊寅年刊本 毛邊紙	拾陸
疊山先生評註四種	宋謝枋得評註	汪氏精刊本	四冊	一	同治辛未年刊 綿連紙	拾陸
陶廬叢刻	清王樹枏撰	家藏版	七十五冊	八	光緒乙酉年刊 綿連紙	拾陸
翠琅玕館叢書	清黃任恆重編	家藏版	八十冊	八	光緒癸卯年刊 共計四集七拾四種 綿連	拾陸
觀古堂書目叢刻	清葉德輝輯	葉氏觀古堂刊本	二十冊	二	共計十五種 毛邊紙夾版	拾陸
寫禮廎遺著四種	清王頌蔚著	野溪王氏刊	三十九卷		共四種 竹紙	拾柒
留餘草堂叢書	清吳承幹校本	吳興劉氏刊	十三冊	一	共七種 夾版	拾柒
後冶堂藏書五種	清三韓銘德輯	三韓劉氏藏版	十冊	一	道光癸未年刊 竹紙	拾捌
子書二十二種	清張氏輯	浙江書局據華亭張氏本校刊	八十三冊	八	光緒元年刊 毛邊紙	拾玖
道藏輯要	清賀龍驤初編	彭瀚然重刊本	二百四十五冊	五十	四川綿竹紙	拾玖

叢書名	編者	版本	冊數	函	附註	箱號
玲瓏山館叢書		文選樓輯刊 善成堂出版	四十八冊	八	共七十五種 太史連紙	拾柒
靈鶼閣叢書	清江建霞輯	元和江氏刊本	四十八冊	六	光緒乙未年刊 毛邊紙	拾玖
十萬卷樓叢書		歸安陸氏刊本	一百十二冊	十四	光緒五年刊 竹紙 共計五十種	拾玖
慎始基齋叢書	清潘世恩輯	汋陽盧氏刊	八冊	一	綿連紙 夾版	貳拾
潘刻五種		京都翰文齋藏版	六冊	一	綿連紙	貳拾
賴古堂藏書	清周在梁輯	賴古堂版	四冊	一	共十六種 竹紙	貳拾
古愚堂叢書	清汪汲輯	二銘草堂刊 古愚山房藏版	十六冊	二	共三十七種 嘉慶年刻 毛邊紙 二夾版	貳拾
惜陰軒叢書	清李錫齡輯	宏道書院藏版	八十四冊	十六	共計二十六種 道光年刻 白紙 毛邊紙	貳壹
郝氏遺書	清郝懿行撰	郝聯薇刊	八十四冊	十六	光緒八年刊 共計三十六種 毛邊紙	貳壹
惜陰軒叢書續編	清王治等輯	宏道書院藏版	九冊	一	共計五種 毛邊紙	貳壹

一百二十七 一

書名	著者	版本	冊／卷	部數	說明	架號
詩觸	清朱璟輯	家藏版五卷 小箱本十二冊	五卷／十二冊	一	共計十六種 士綿連紙	貳壹
屏廬叢刻		精家藏刻本	五冊	二	共計十二種 竹紙	貳貳
雅雨堂叢書	清盧見曾校刊	精寫刊本 雅雨堂藏版	二十冊	四	共計七種 綿連紙	貳貳
黃氏叢書	清黃以周等	兩菁講舍刊本 黃氏試館刊本	三十八冊	四	共計七種 竹紙 光緒癸巳年刊	貳參
一齋叢書	清邵一齋著	王容若校刊	四冊 五卷	一	共計四種 毛邊紙	貳參
涉喜齋叢書	清吳縣潘祖蔭輯	式古堂重編刊	四十八冊	五	共計五十一種 官統元年刻 五夾版 綿連紙	貳參
晨風閣叢書	清沈宗畸輯	番禺沈氏校 劉精刻本	十六冊	二	共計二十二種 綿連紙	貳肆
謝疊山先生評註四種合刻	宋謝枋得評註	清江樹昀校刊本	四十五卷	一	共計二種 光緒元年刻 綿連紙	貳肆
當歸草堂叢書		錢唐丁氏宜刊 木本	八冊	一	共計八種 同治二年刊 毛邊紙	貳肆
戴氏遺書	清戴震撰	微波謝刻本	二十二冊	四	共計十三種 毛邊紙	貳肆

617

叢書名	編者	版本	冊數	函	說明	編號
槐廬叢書	清朱記榮輯訂	吳氏家塾藏版	八十冊	十一	光緒丁亥年刊 共計五十二種 竹紙	貳柒
湘綺樓全書	清王闓運撰	東洲校刊本	八十三冊	十	共計十九種 毛邊紙	貳柒
快書五十種	明閔景賢纂	明天啟丙寅年刊本	二十四冊	四	共二十一種 夾竹版	貳捌
武林掌故叢編	清丁丙輯	嘉惠堂丁氏刊版	二百零八冊	二十	共計一百九十一種 光緒癸未年刊 毛邊紙	貳捌
三長物齋叢書	清黃本驥編輯	知敬學齋藏版	二百六十七卷	八	共計二十八種 道光二十七年重刊 毛邊紙	貳捌
巴山七種	清王侃撰	光裕堂刊	八冊	一	共七種 同治年刊 竹紙	貳玖
秘書二十一種	清汪士漢校	鴻文堂藏版	十二冊	一	共二十一種 夾竹版	貳玖
少石山房筆叢	明胡應麟著	明萬曆版	十七冊	四	共十三種 竹紙	貳玖
湖北書局叢書	湖北崇文書局輯	湖北崇文書局刊	八十冊	六	連史紙 光緒三年刻 六夾版 共三十三種	叁拾
嘉業堂叢書	劉承幹輯 吳興劉氏校刊		四十七冊	二	二夾邊版 毛邊紙 共十四種	叁拾

叢·部

書名	編撰者	版本	冊數	函／箱／櫃	刊年・用紙	定價
呂氏十七種叢書	明呂坤撰	明萬曆版	十九冊	一	粉連紙夾版共十七種	叁拾
呂氏十種叢書	明呂坤撰	明版	五冊	五	白紙共十種	叁拾
涵芬樓秘笈	涵芬樓輯	影印本	四十冊	五	連史紙共五集二十七種	叁拾
張氏叢書	清張澍輯	千頃堂藏版	共十二冊	一	道光元年刊綿連紙共八種	叁拾
翰苑分書臨文正宗	唐文治纂著	寫刻本	六冊	一	夾版共十三種	叁拾
茹經堂叢書	清蔣廷錫等奉敕校	湘鄂印刷公司印	三十四冊	一	光緒年印粉連紙	叁拾
圖書集成	商務印書館編印	圖書集成局版印	六彙編三十二典六千一百零九部計一萬卷共六千一百九十八冊	共一百六十四	民國壬戌年印毛邊紙	
四部叢刊	清張英等奉敕纂	涵芬樓初次影印本內真宜刊	共三百二十三部八千五百四十八冊	三大櫃	民國壬戌年印毛邊紙	
古香齋十種	清張英等奉敕纂	孔氏三十三萬卷堂藏版	四百五十卷共三百二十二冊	一箱	光緒六年刊綿連紙兩箱	
古逸叢書	清黎庶昌輯	影宋本　日本東京使署刊于	宋本二百卷一百二十九冊	一	光緒二十年刻六種綿連紙共二	

書名	編者／著者	版本	冊數／卷數	箱數	備註
湛文簡公遺書種三	明湛若水輯	資政堂藏版	四十冊	一箱	共三種 綿連紙
船山遺書	清王夫之著	湘鄉曾氏刊于金陵節署	一百冊	一箱	光緒乙丑年印 綿連紙
鄂刻叢書	清鍾謙鈞等輯	湖北書局刻版 巾箱本	三十六冊	一箱	共計二十九種 毛邊紙 同治四年刻 毛邊紙
古經解彙函 附小學彙函	清鍾謙鈞等輯	菊坡精舍藏版 粵東書局刊本	六十八冊	一箱	共計三十種 綿連紙
守山閣叢書	清錢熙祚輯	鴻文齋局石印	六百五十二卷	一箱	共二十八種 綿連紙 光緒丁酉年刻 叁壹
別下齋叢書	清蔣生沐輯	印武林竹簡齋藏 別下齋校本	二十四冊	一	共二十五種 綿連紙 叁壹
涉聞梓舊	清蔣生沐輯	別下齋校本	二十四冊	二	共二十種 綿連紙 叁壹
南宋羣賢小集	南宋陳起編輯	讀書畫齋重刊	四十冊	八	附江湖後集共八十一種 太史連紙 叁壹
崔東壁叢書	清崔述著	古書流通處影印	二十冊	二	共十九種 油光紙印 叁壹
漢魏六朝百三家集	明張溥輯	信述堂重刊	一百冊	一箱	光緒乙卯年刻 綿連紙

書名	編輯者	版本	卷・册	箱	用紙・備註
學津討源	清張海鵬輯	涵芬樓影印照曠閣本	一千零四十三卷　二百册	二箱	毛邊紙　共計一百七十三種
皇清經解	清阮元㟍輯	番禺黎永椿校刊本	一千四百零八卷　三百六十册	二箱	毛邊紙　共計一百八十八　補刊咸豐十一年毛邊紙
皇清經解續編	清王先謙編輯	江陰南菁書院書局刊本	一千四百三十卷　三百二十册	二箱	毛邊紙　光緒十五年刻　共計二百零九種
涵海叢書	清李調元輯	廣漢萬宏樓原本　仿萬宏樓原本	一百六十册	一箱	綿連紙　光緒七年刻
眞文忠公文集	宋眞德秀著	拱極堂刊本祠藏版	一百册	一箱	官堆紙　共五種
小石山房叢書	清顧湘編	虞山顧氏刊	五十八卷　十六册	一箱	竹紙　同治己巳年刻　共四十一種　叄壹
古今說部叢書	清王文濡輯	國學扶輪社鉛印	六十册	一箱	油光紙　民國四年印　共十集

以上共計壹百貳拾陸種

一百三十一

621

書名	著者 註	版本	卷冊 數	函數	備考	編列號數
宗人府選冊		抄本	四冊	壹	夾連紙	壹
上海租界問題	王揖唐撰	聚珍仿宋印書局印	三卷 一冊	壹	民國四年印 連史紙	壹
二樹紫籐花館印選	顧鰲選	法輪印字局銅印	四冊	壹	嘉慶八年出版 連史紙	壹
續集漢印分韻	清謝景仰纂	漱芳堂藏版	二卷 二冊	壹	宣統三年版 油光紙	壹
普通百科新大辭典	清黃摩西編輯	中國詞典公司鉛印	十五冊	貳	光緒丁未年刻 毛邊紙連史紙各一部	貳
讀律一得歌	清魯棨增撰	治心養氣軒刊本	四卷 四冊	叁	光緒年刻 連史紙	叁
紀慎先生求雨全書	清紀大奎著	剝鵠齋版	上下二冊 一卷	叁	無套 連史紙	叁
宦鄉要則	清張鑑瀛著	經香閣石印	七卷 四冊	肆	光緒己亥年印 洋毛太紙	肆
歷代史略鼓詞	買鬼溪撰	家藏版	上下二冊	肆	同治九年刻 毛邊紙 又抄本一本	肆
雜 部			一百三十一			

書名	著者	版本	卷冊		紙張刊印	價
百美圖新詠	清袁枚鑑定	集腋軒藏版	四冊	一	綿連紙	柒
鸞宮敬事錄	清桂良輯	本學藏版	四冊	一	同治年刻 連史紙	叁拾
居仁日覽	阮忠樞進呈	石印本	一冊	一	宣紙	叁拾
清語摘鈔	聚珍堂錄	聚珍堂刊	四冊	一	光緒年刻 竹紙	叁拾
西國近事彙編	美國林樂知口譯 清蔡錫齡筆述	鉛印本	戊寅編四卷 四冊	一	毛邊紙	叁拾
西國近事彙編	美國林樂知口譯 清蔡錫齡筆述	鉛印本	己卯編四卷 四冊	一	毛邊紙	叁拾
軍樂稿	消李映庚訂	石印本	四卷 四冊	一	報紙 宣統元年印	叁拾
巴拿馬賽會直隸觀會叢編	直隸實業廳編	鉛印本	二十四卷 十六冊	一	夾版毛邊紙 民國十年印	叁拾
世界海軍現狀	清丁士源著	鉛印本	一冊	一	開化紙 油光紙 宣統元年印	叁拾
新編繙譯清語		精寫本 滿漢字	二冊	一	夾硃欄版	叁拾

書名	編著者	刊印	卷冊		年印	紙	價
蘇聯陰謀文証彙編	張國忱編纂	鉛印本	十一冊	二	民國十六年印	粉連紙	叁拾
社會學	呂復著	北京中國印刷局印	四卷四冊		民國十六年印	連史紙	叁拾

以上共計貳拾壹種

經史子集叢雜陸部統計貳阡伍百伍拾壹種

書名拼音索引

632

633

638

641

648

656

659

S

664

670

678

679

684

690